TWICE AS FAR

The True Story of SwissAir Flight 111 Airplane Crash Investigation

by: Thomas C. Juby

TWICE AS FAR

The True Story of SwissAir Flight 111 Airplane Crash Investigation

BY: THOMAS C. JUBY

SERGEANT - RETIRED
ROYAL CANADIAN MOUNTED POLICE
FORENSIC CRIME SCENE INVESTIGATOR
&
FORENSIC PHYSICAL EVIDENCE EXAMINER
SWISSAIR 111 TASK FORCE
HALIFAX, N.S.

ISBN-13: 9781540879592
ISBN-10: 1540879593

Copyright and Published (01.2017)
by
RJ PARKER PUBLISHING

http://RJParkerPublishing.com/

Published in Canada

Copyrights

This book is licensed for your personal enjoyment only. All rights reserved. No part of this publication can be reproduced or transmitted in any form or by any means without prior written authorization from RJ Parker Publishing, Inc. The unauthorized reproduction or distribution of a copyrighted work is illegal. Criminal copyright infringement, including infringement without monetary gain, is investigated by the FBI and is punishable by fines and federal imprisonment.

> "A MAN WHO IS A MAN
> WILL GO ON UNTIL HE CAN DO NO MORE
> THEN HE WILL GO
> TWICE AS FAR"

An Old Norwegian Saying

IN APPRECIATION

To my parents – they taught me right from wrong

&

To Sherry and our children – they are the reason why

PHOTOS, DOCUMENTS, AND VIDEO
RELATING TO MATTERS DESCRIBED IN THIS BOOK
CAN BE VIEWED AT THE WEBSITE
www.twiceasfar.ca

Table of Contents

Prologue..6
Forward...8
SOME OF THOSE MENTIONED IN THIS BOOK...............10
CHAPTER 1 - VICTIM IDENTIFICATION..........................12
CHAPTER 2 - THE INITIAL INVESTIGATION......................33
CHAPTER 3 - FRICTION..87
CHAPTER 4 - THE RESPONSE..96
CHAPTER 5 - CHANGE THE NOTES..................................116
CHAPTER 6 - STILL MORE BAD APPLES..........................136
CHAPTER 7 - MERE SPECULATION...................................156
CHAPTER 8 - CONLIN'S REPORT..165
CHAPTER 9 - GOING OUTSIDE..198
CHAPTER 10 - MAKE IT SO..216
CHAPTER 11 - HOW FAR DOES IT GO?..............................255
About the Author...285

Prologue

This book and the accompanying website
are written without prejudice to those persons mentioned herein.
These matters have not yet been adjudged in a
Criminal Court of Law in Canada.

A major disaster occurred at 10:31:18 pm on the evening of the 2nd of September, 1998, seven kilometres off the coast of Nova Scotia, Canada near the small fishing village of Peggy's Cove. A Swissair passenger jet with two hundred and twenty-nine people crashed into the ocean with the complete loss of life of all those on-board.

The events that occurred over the next few hours forever scar the lives of many of those who attempted a futile rescue. Others involved in the recovery and identification of those killed in the crash have even more intense scars, and many have their haunting memories.

For the relatives and friends, their tragic loss creates a degree of pain and suffering that can never be forgotten. However, the loss of human life is a time of grief sometimes consoled by believing everything possible will be done to correct whatever went wrong. People expect the investigation will be conducted professionally and objectively without hesitation or restrictions.

However, once that investigation is complete, the public must be allowed to judge the success and truth of its result. It must be done not by viewing only limited and carefully selected evidence, but by knowing all the contributing issues with unrestricted witness accounts and investigators' testimony. As in any Court case, to judge the truth the public must know all the relevant facts. In such matters, even determining what becomes admissible is decided upon by an independent and qualified Judge of proven legal capability.

Has that been the case with this investigation? The public, as well as concerned parties, have all been asked to trust that truth and honesty are the yardsticks employed to discover and correct the cause of this crash. When the Transportation Safety Board disclosed the results of their investigation with their final report, the readers can judge how truthful that report was and whether the relevant facts were presented.

This book is the true story of the Swissair flight 111 investigation as told from the experiences of a forensic physical evidence investigator of the Royal Canadian Mounted Police who searched for that truth in the remains of the human flesh and aircraft debris. For more than four years, I took part in the investigation to discover the cause of the crash and to aid in the effort to make air travel safer. After some of the most advanced scientific techniques in the world revealed credible evidence of a criminal involvement, politics and intrigue prevailed to suppress that evidence, silence what had become a one-man criminal investigation, and ruin the career of this police investigator.

Many sources have been used to provide the true and basic facts for this story. It shows how two federal government agencies failed to follow the evidence trail. Instead, they chose a path made of pseudo-science and deceit that in the end provided nothing to the relatives and the people of this country except deception and lies. Whether they acted legally and in a manner morally acceptable to a democratic Canadian society is now up to the reader to judge.

Forward

Some people may be critical of this book by suggesting that if this story is accurate, then why was it not disclosed years ago. That criticism is likely a natural reaction to the shocking facts revealed in these pages, or in some instances it may be to suit various agendas. Whatever the reason or purpose, the problems encountered in disclosing the facts of the story are all shown to the reader in this book. Not until 2015 did access to information requests provide key material, while other information remains hidden. The reader must also realize there continues to be a feeling of guilt and futility for not being able to do what was right by those who perished in this incident. Add then the failure to prevent the 9-11 terrorist attacks that followed three years after this crash. There are reasons to believe this crash was linked to those attacks.

Efforts were made to handle this matter legally through an internal complaint system while living my private life after having retired. When those efforts failed, it was shown that a form of corruption existed in the upper bureaucratic levels of the RCMP. Attempts to inform the public were then started. The one person who immediately grasped the significance of this story went on to try to write his book. Claims were made that it was a conspiracy theory and the publishers knew the agencies involved would never stoop so low to do what he asserted. Only when the CBC's The Fifth Estate ran their documentary on television in 2011 did the public learn some of the truth behind the faulty investigation. Many in the audience wanted more information.

As for the credibility of the notes used for this true story, this book shows how my management reviewed those notes on two different occasions. Each time they offered no argument against their accuracy and genuineness, only that they contained too many incriminating details.

Revealed in these pages is material that should be shocking to many Canadians. Unfortunately, some of the managerial methods detailed here have become the way of the RCMP over the past decades. Abuse of authority and harassment of personnel, incompetent and inept management, and nepotism are methods disclosed in these pages. Despite legislation and written policies, these management styles are too often the practice of supervisors at all levels of management. Those actions have victimized too many of us. What's more, the incident described in this book was not the first time senior management has interfered in a criminal investigation.

The actions revealed in this book should make it obvious that something is seriously wrong with the RCMP's management system. While the Canadian public often hears similar complaints, this time it comes from a knowledgeable inside source with the documentation to prove it.

You are asked to read this story and then consider two questions. Do you believe all of this occurred within the scope of the Transportation Safety Board of Canada and the Royal Canadian Mounted Police? More importantly, can and will it happen again if the proper action is not now taken to deter similar instances both now and in the future?

SOME OF THOSE MENTIONED IN THIS BOOK

RCMP

Phil Murray	Commissioner of the RCMP at the time of the crash
Giuliano Zaccardelli	D/Commissioner of HQ Div., overall in charge of initial investigation, replaced Murray in September 2001 as Commissioner
Robert Elliott	Replaced Zaccardelli as a civilian Commissioner
Steve Duncan	Criminal operations officer in Halifax, responsible for file locally
Lee Fraser	Ident Inspector overseeing morgue, then promoted as Superintendent, Director of RCMP Forensic Identification Services in Ottawa
Andy Lathem	Inspector in Charge of Halifax Major Crime Unit and Swissair Task Force
Vic Gorman	Ident Staff Sergeant second in command of morgue & Swissair Task Force
Neil Fraser	Ident Staff Sergeant for morgue DNA, commissioned as an Inspector
Karl Christiansen	Corporal plain clothes investigator for Swissair Task Force
Peter Purchase	Corporal plain clothes investigator for Swissair Task Force
Brian London	Corporal plain clothes investigator for Swissair Task Force
Keith Stothart	Constable plain clothes investigator for Swissair Task Force
Andy Kerr	Constable investigator for Swissair Task Force
Duane Cooper	Constable investigator for Swissair Task Force
Wendy Norman	Crime Lab chemist & physical evidence examiner
Dave Ballantyne	Crime Lab chemist & physical evidence examiner
Brian Yamashita	HQ Ident scientist/advisor

TSB

Vic Gerden	Investigator in Charge for TSB's investigation
Larry Vance	Assistant Investigator in Charge for TSB's investigation
John Garstang	Main TSB investigator, oversaw the physical evidence safety examination
Don Enns	TSB investigator, assisted Garstang in the physical evidence examination
Jim Foot	TSB's electrical inspector responsible for electrical systems analysis
Gus Sidla	TSB's metallurgist

Canadian & US Agencies & Other Civilians

Dr. Jim Brown	Government scientist, CANMET, Natural Resources Canada
Dr. R.N. Anderson	University Professor, created theory for timeline of short-circuits in a fire
Dr. Quintiere	Considered one of the two most knowledgeable in aircraft fires
Dr. Lyon	Head of the FAA Burn Center & one of the two experts in aircraft fires
Dr. John Butt	Chief Medical Examiner, Province of Nova Scotia
Irwin Sproule	Government scientist, Natural Research Council of Canada
Pat Cahill	FAA employee conducting insulation burn tests
Larry Fogg	Boeing representative/investigator for the crash investigation
Paul Palango	Author of several books about the RCMP
Linden MacIntyre	Investigative journalist for the CBC's The Fifth Estate
Rob Gordon	Producer for the CBC's The Fifth Estate
Morris Karp	Producer for the CBC's The Fifth Estate
Fritz Muri	Producer for Swiss TV

CHAPTER 1 – VICTIM IDENTIFICATION

"Ambulances from across the Province are headed to Peggy's Cove, Nova Scotia. A passenger jet has crashed into the ocean near Halifax and so far, no survivors have been brought to shore."

    Those were the icy words that froze my attention after pausing at CNN while channel-surfing. My wife Sherry and I had just returned home from watching Bruce Willis blow up an asteroid somewhere in deep space. Now I learned that a real Armageddon of a more horrific nature had occurred just one hundred kilometres away. If the news report of the location was correct, the crash site was in my work area, and it would mean a major effort by many to recover any survivors. By morning it would be known all two hundred and twenty-nine of those on board had perished. It would then be a painstaking and intensive effort to recover both the bodies of the deceased and the plane's wreckage. At that moment, there was no way of knowing this event would dominate my life for the next four years. What's more, its haunting effects would consume my waking days and sleepless nights for endless years thereafter.

    This was to be my first night off after a week of ten-hour shifts and being on call, so another Ident member, Bob Gaudet, had received the first call-out. A check of the answering machine revealed there were no messages. There was no sense calling the RCMP's Telecoms Centre as they would be busy enough without having me bother them. After a quick assessment, I decided it was best to get a good night's sleep because beginning tomorrow, I would probably get little of it in the next couple of weeks.

    The next morning, I was assigned to work in the temporary morgue in Hangar B on the Shearwater Naval Airbase in Halifax. I arrived there about ten o'clock with Inspector Lee Fraser in his van loaded down with fingerprint and other supplies. A heavyset bear of a man just under six feet tall and with a dominating presence, Lee was the Regional Forensic Ident Supervisor for the Atlantic Provinces. We had been good friends since our survey and transit course back in 1977 at Carlton University. While he had more time in Forensic Identification than me, his time in the field was less because he had performed administrative duties in Ottawa for several years by running the RCMP's fingerprint bureau. Lee had gone to Ottawa when he realized Headquarters was the place for personal advancement in Forensic Identification Services.

As for the base, Shearwater had been part of the naval establishment in Halifax for many years, and it was the home of the Sea King helicopters. Everyone in the area knew of the Sea King because they had been around since the late sixties. That made them older than most of the pilots who flew them. The Shearwater base consisted of half a dozen aircraft hangars, each large enough to hold more than a dozen of these aircraft. This day Hangar B was assigned a new duty.

Walking into the big open aircraft hangar, it was obvious the Air Force personnel had been busy. It seemed like the entire floor, about fifty metres wide by one hundred and fifty metres deep, was covered in yellow duct tape outlining two hundred and twenty-nine rectangles. Each was just big enough for a body bag. Looking at all those floor positions made it sink home just how many people had been on that plane. Over it all was a double layer of clear plastic sheeting placed there to keep the hangar floor clean. However, it was impossible to walk on because it was two layers thick, something I quickly learned after taking my first step.

An Air Force Sergeant came striding up to me to comment on the work they had done. I noticed he had come around the perimeter of the plastic so he did not slip and fall. Just as I was about to say something about their setup, a truck loaded with plywood and lumber rolled through the wide open main hangar doors. A Department of Public Works supervisor that I knew got out and immediately asked me where I wanted this load. I must have given him a questioning look as his arrival was unexpected, so he quickly explained he had lumber and a construction crew who were ready to put nails to wood. Where did I want him to set up the rooms? Now we were talking on the same wavelength. Pointing to the front right corner of the hangar next to the main doors, I said "Over there, start the rooms over on that side." I looked at the Sergeant as I grabbed the corner of the plastic and said perhaps they might want to salvage some of this sheeting since it will not now be needed. We were going to have a real morgue, not just a display of black and green body bags.

After laying out the floor design for two rows of rooms with a wide walkway between, the public works people put together about a dozen plywood-lined rooms twelve feet by twelve feet each. The rooms were wide open to the walkway at their front, and each of the three walls was eight feet high. Six rooms were to be used for post-mortem examinations. Each had a stainless-steel morgue table in the centre with makeshift but acceptable lighting, running water and a temporary sink with a drain. A fresh air filtration system followed once the Division's Health and Safety Nurse arrived. The other rooms would have different purposes including a dedicated room for rolling the victims' fingerprints. For the next few days, the sounds of saws cutting wood and of hammers driving nails were the music of the hangar. Added to this was the long, heavy reverberating roar of turbine engines as Sea King helicopters taxied by the hangar just metres from the open front doors. They were a reminder this work had a purpose, and it was sobering to imagine what was headed our way.

Lee had given me three tasks in the morgue. My main job was to look after the fingerprint identification of the deceased. In addition, I was to maintain the logistics for the Identification members as they would need a variety of supplies. Then, once the body examinations began, I was to oversee the quality control of the forensic procedures in each of the autopsy rooms. An Ident member and a pathologist, each with a note-taker, were assigned to each room. The Ident member was to be in control and set the pace. Using 35 mm film, everything had to be recorded in a precise manner. Due to potential Court, no Polaroids were to be used. Since we were dealing with victims from many countries, international standards had to be met. This was not a problem because our country matched those for the USA and the Western European Countries. However, there was a need to ensure it was all done correctly and consistently.

Supplies needed a little time to put in place. Just three months previously I had increased the Halifax Ident Section's stock of safety supplies and materials needed by members when attending crime scenes. Several hundred safety suits, five thousand plastic surgical-type gloves, and a multitude of other supplies were brought into the hangar. However, all of this was not going to last a week. A Kodak order was completed for a thousand rolls of 35 mm film, and another purchase of ten thousand pairs of gloves was made. A limited supply of exhibit bags was brought in from our Division stores. By Monday morning, requests had gone out to every Division as far West as Manitoba to send us every exhibit and body bag they could muster. That was just a start. These purchases of supplies would be repeated several times before we were finished with the morgue. More than twenty-five thousand Tyvek type white safety suits were ordered and provided by the end of the fifth day. Everyone had to wear hospital greens with a safety suit over the top once the changing rooms and lockers were set up. Doing that used up at least two suits a day for each of the nearly two hundred people in the hangar. Many double gloved for added safety with most of the staff going through several dozen pairs each day.

My supplies were not the only expenses incurred as preparations progressed. As an example of other costs, the Division Health and Safety Nurse spent more than a million dollars on safety clothing and equipment for the body and debris recovery teams. Thousands of dollars were spent on plastic storage tubs with lids, all of various sizes and colours. Many were used to store human remains in the freezers. The dental and hospital staff utilized X-ray films by the thousands, and DNA sampling supplies were used by the thousands of units.

Putting my part of this together was exciting and gratifying. Because it was a disaster effort, that alone set the bar at a high level. If I estimated I would need a thousand batteries, two thousand were ordered. I did not second-guess the orders because I knew the supplies would eventually be used. All anyone needed to do was to look around the hangar to realize this effort was a major undertaking. What I did do was to have every order go through my secretary, Gail Jay, at the Halifax Ident Section where she recorded all the details. By the end of the first week, she had become popular with those who filled her orders for supplies. Six video and a half-dozen digital cameras were purchased. By the end of the file, at least fifty thousand floppy disks had been bought for digital cameras. Digital photography could not provide the exacting detail that was needed. Instead the cameras provided an instant photo of personal effects or identifying marks. This new form of photography using digital cameras with floppy disks instead of film was a first major step towards an entirely new system for recording evidence.

The Department of National Defence Dental Team parked two equipment vans inside the hangar during the morning. Their team consisted of nearly a dozen dentists and technicians with Lt. Colonel Reid in charge. He would prove to be knowledgeable not only in his Forensic Dental profession, but in a process we would use over the next two months to preserve decayed and damaged victim fingerprints. I had read about this method of casting years earlier, but it required cadavers on which to work. My fingerprint team soon became experts in the process.

Soon after lunch DND pathologists arrived led by Captain Trevor Jain. Originally from the Annapolis Valley area where I lived, I knew him from a previous Canadian Army Explosives Demolition Course we had both attended. Slight and of average height but full of confidence in his Army greens, he immediately approached me with a big smile. He soon told me whatever I needed for the morgue, if he could get it, it was mine to have. It turned out he could get many of the items we needed to make the place run smoothly, and he had a knack of overcoming almost any obstacle.

The Army would eventually present him with the highest Military award a Reserve Soldier can receive in a non-battlefield environment for his work during the first thirty days of the morgue. Several other military personnel would receive other conduct medals. The RCMP decided to handle the matter differently. With so many members involved in Operation Homage, senior management felt they would present a commendation to the whole division. It consisted of a plaque that would go on a wall of Halifax Headquarters. There would be a ceremony for the presentation about thirty days into the file, but it turned out to be a heavy day at the morgue. That is my excuse for not attending. The Force was celebrating a job well done, yet there was still an enormous amount of work left for those of us still in the morgue and the reconstruction hangar. As well, there were those out on the recovery barge in the rough open seas. What's more, Fingerprint and Photo Section people in Ottawa were providing a tremendous effort in identifying the deceased, some even taking fingerprint copies home with them to search during the evening on their own time. Crime Lab people across the country were working long hours perfecting the DNA process that would soon identify all who had been on board. Forensic Ident members had come in from Newfoundland, New Brunswick, PEI, Quebec, and Ontario, and there were other members, too many to mention, who did other jobs elsewhere than in this Province. Not being part of 'H' Division, they were not included in this award. Yet they were working long hours on this crash. If I had attended the ceremony, I might have said something unwelcomed by the haughty commissioned officers who stood around eating finger food and smiling. Their pressed uniforms with their white shirts and polished brown shoes would have seemed ostentatious by those of us still involved in the file. Many of us were working amid the putrid, nasal-burning stench of the rotting flesh and the nauseous stink of the fuel oil-soaked debris brought up from the ocean floor.

That would all come later, but the first day in the hangar was just a blur for me. There was so much to be done and to organize, and everyone was so eager to do their part and more. By 2 o'clock there must have been two hundred people in the hangar, everyone putting together their equipment or setting up their work areas. The X-ray staff from the local hospital took over the washrooms as darkrooms because of their running water and drains. X-ray equipment was positioned as far away as possible from the other work areas so as not to endanger anyone. The dental trucks were parked, and the military dentists set up a room at the side of the hangar as their dental x-ray comparison room. Refrigerator trailers were arranged outside the hangar doors. One side of the hangar's front apron was designated for incoming remains, and the temperature in those trailers was set at just above freezing. The other side was for examined remains, and those trailers were set at minus twenty degrees Celsius. Because the X-ray staff had taken over the washrooms, Johnny-on-the-spot porta-potty units were positioned outside the hangar.

The Army provided young stretcher bearers who were to move the bodies from the helicopters to the refrigerators, to each morgue room, and back to the freezers, all under the control of several RCMP members. One day while watching them, I had to ask one young girl how old she was. She assured me she was eighteen, but she looked no older than my daughter who was just fifteen. Most of them were mere teenagers or not much older, but what they saw and did every day without ever complaining would make even hardened civilians on the street break down.

At times, I forgot my real reason for being there. I began to think it was an exciting place to be, especially with all the noises and the hubbub. People were going in every direction, some carrying equipment, others returning for more from their vehicles parked outside. However, each time a helicopter taxied by the hangar, reality would abruptly return.

Cell phones were not a common personal item. Someone showed up with a cardboard box containing dozens of them, and I was told to take one and keep it. A short time later a Maritime Tel & Tel operator called to enquire who I was and what I did. She told me I would have priority on any call to or from my phone. She explained there was a shortage of mobile channels, so they had to watch their use, and any phone such as mine would receive priority clearance. I thought that was great especially since I had always had a line attached to my phone. Over the next few weeks, many news people and others had their phone call suddenly cut for some reason unknown to them.

Dr. Butt was the Chief Medical Examiner for the Province. He looked very much the part of a competent and confident British doctor. A few years earlier, he had come to Halifax to replace one of the most obnoxious and incapable people I have ever worked with in a morgue. Dr. Butt, with his British accent, gave an air of a gruff and no-nonsense professional, someone with whom I should not argue. "Don't get in his way" were the words of caution I had received before meeting him the first time over a stainless-steel morgue table. Since then we had worked together on dozens of bodies and each time I marvelled at his professionalism and willingness to explain his work. I only needed to ask. Having experienced many hundreds of post-mortem examinations, I knew the questions to ask and what answers to expect. We worked together easily even if we did have our disagreements over some of the files. During the next two months, we would mesh well even though his work would prove to be extremely difficult for him. Dr. Butt's real problem was that he failed to remain detached and separate from the everyday work of the morgue. Instead, he would contend with the horrendous carnage in the hangar to then leave and meet with the next of kin. There he would have to deal with the emotions involved with the victims' families. I do not know how anyone could do that just once, let alone do it for weeks. That is why he finally had to take a break from it all. No one could stand that mental strain for the full duration of the morgue. There was only just so much 'keeping a stiff upper lip' anyone could do under those conditions.

During the late afternoon of that first day, Dr. Butt came into the hangar wearing an orange hardhat and carrying a megaphone. He found a crate on which to stand and called everyone over for an announcement. Dr. Butt said he had just returned from flying over the crash site. In an emotional tone he said there were trails of debris floating on the ocean surface that were being swept away by the currents. He paused, and then went on to say he had no idea how many bodies might have already been lost. On hearing these words, everyone's enthusiasm suddenly came to an abrupt halt. The question we thought, but no one dared to ask, was what could be done about it. Dr. Butt was obviously upset and distraught over this obvious loss. When he finally said there was nothing that could be done about it, there was a sense of shock and frustration among those present. He assured everyone the recovery was underway and bodies had already been retrieved. The Navy's supply ship, HMCS Preserver, was on site, and the Navy was holding everything onboard until the morgue was completed. It was a significant relief to know we had some breathing space to finish many of the preparations.

Dr. Butt went on to say if anyone needed anything, no matter how small or trivial, to find his orange hardhat as he held it up for all to see. He would ensure every need was fulfilled. I turned to Lee Fraser when I heard this. He had come in with Dr. Butt and was standing beside me. More as a command than as a request, I immediately told him to get Dr. Butt out of the hangar and into his office. I said Trevor and I had been working all day to have people come to us with their problems, and it was finally coming together. The last thing we both needed was someone else getting involved who had no idea what was being done. Lee agreed and went over to speak with the Doctor when he finished his announcement. Obviously, Dr. Butt agreed and threw the hardhat and the megaphone into a cupboard because they were never seen again.

The end of my first day came about eleven o'clock. It was an hour's drive as I commuted the one hundred kilometres between Halifax and home. There was a lot to keep my mind busy as I drove. Perhaps day two would prove the worth of what we had done today.

Day two saw more work in preparing the hangar and it was anticipated that bodies would be coming ashore soon, perhaps by the afternoon. The crash site was about seven kilometres offshore from Peggy's Cove in about two hundred feet of wide open Atlantic Ocean. The Canadian Navy's HMCS Preserver with several Canadian Coastguard ships were on site. The RCMP had several small boats to patrol the area and beaches, and the Sea Sorceress with its crane and barge would arrive in a day or two. For now, the Canadian Navy divers, soon joined by US Navy divers from the USS Grapple, would descend with cages to the wreckage to look for bodies and key items. Debris had floated away from the site, and some of it had come ashore along the hundreds of kilometres of coastline. This needed a concerted effort by the RCMP, DND and volunteer search and rescue personnel to recover every piece. This was a gruelling task for many because the Nova Scotia coastline was rocky and treacherous along much of its length.

The day was filled with expectation, but for many there was boredom because the human remains were being held at sea. What I first expected was that bodies would arrive to be dealt with in an organized routine, each taking one to two hours. The morgue would last no more than two to three weeks. My experience with plane crashes was that the victims would be mangled after receiving massive injuries, but most would be intact. I thought our biggest problem would be handling the sudden influx of dozens of corpses all at once.

What I did not know and would never have expected was that at the moment of impact everyone on board the MD-11 aircraft except for one person almost instantly became fragmented pieces of flesh. They were bits and pieces because the plane, like a cigar tube, smashed nose first and possibly upside-down into the solid granite-like ocean surface at nearly four-hundred miles an hour. As the cold quarter-inch thick alloy skin of the plane met the water, it shattered into small metal shards, each with sharp, jagged edges. As more of the aircraft with its contents moved forward to the water, more bladelike metal pieces were continuously created. Finally, the tail met the nose in less than a quarter of a second. Those sharp alloy blades served to cut and shred the contents, all except the one body that somehow was ejected through a crack in the fuselage.

What I would later learn was the impact itself likely was not the cause of their deaths. As the investigation progressed, there developed enough evidence to believe all were dead before the impact. They would have been overcome by the poisonous fumes from the burning plastics and materials that fed a massive onboard fire. That fire would have caused a lowering of the oxygen level in the cabin's atmosphere. However, that knowledge would only come later.

By the afternoon of day three, the first of the human remains started to come in. The helicopters taxied up to the unloading zone on the hangar's apron to stop fewer than fifty metres from the now-closed hangar doors. The noise was deafening and the buffeting of the huge rolling hangar doors at first threatened to blow them off their tracks. Soon, a few body bags were brought in by the young stretcher bearers. The first bag was light. I knew there had been children on board so perhaps it was the body of a small child. The remains from the first bag were placed carefully on the stainless-steel morgue table. The sight surprised and shocked all who had gathered around. It was not a child's body. It was a piece of an adult's body at most weighing ten to fifteen pounds. As the pathologist worked, those of us watching had no idea what was headed our way.

Soon enough the smell in the air was of jet fuel, but not from the helicopters. The remains reeked of it. The smell spread throughout the hangar even though it had come from only a few pieces of human flesh. I already had an idea what it would soon be like. In Hangar A next door where all the floating and shore debris had been laid out on the floor, the smell of fuel oil from the plane was toxic and overwhelming. I had been in to view the small pieces of aircraft and collect film. The smell had been so intense it was at times difficult to breathe. Their hangar doors were wide open and they had large industrial fans blowing, but the smell, much heavier than mere gasoline and more intense and smothering like diesel or furnace oil, just hung on everything.

My thoughts were that perhaps the next helicopter would bring in complete bodies. Instead, they brought in more pieces, then more, and still more. Looking at all this, I thought maybe they were keeping the heavier body bags for delivery by ship. After all, weight was a serious consideration for a helicopter. "We will receive complete bodies tomorrow when the ship comes in from the crash site" was what I said to others around me.

At first, we only received small numbers of body bags. The good news was there were whole sections of the aircraft with bodies still in their seats. This information was the latest passed up from the divers as they worked the seafloor. It had come to us from the helicopter crews. As it echoed around the hangar, everyone believed or perhaps they hoped it was true. I remember Dr. Butt saying the Navy divers had to be careful to record the seat number for each body during its recovery. Doing that would aid in identifying the victims.

The next day we learned the horrible truth. A quiet came over the morgue even though there were more than two hundred people present. Everyone stood silently as Dr. Butt told us the news. Suddenly there was this overwhelming realization that every body was in dozens if not hundreds of pieces. Even the children. He told us the debris field was extensive, deep, and extremely dangerous for the divers. The wreckage with everything else at the site was in small pieces. They had found only one intact body, and the divers now believed there would be no more.

It was overwhelming, insurmountable. How were we to deal with all of this? That was the question everyone thought but no one dared to ask. A numbness set in with the realization there would be a seemingly never-ending stream of bits and pieces of human remains. No more was there an air of enthusiasm, no eagerness to get the job done. There was no end in sight. For all of us, it soon became a matter of coming to work each day to handle what we could in that day. Every day I did my job for the next sixty days. Five days in, two days out. Somebody had to do it!

Some of the first x-rayed material provided a few tense moments. The films showed small spots throughout the fleshy portions of some of the body parts. Those spots suggested small metal balls or pellets, and the first response was they were shotgun pellets. Now that presented a problem because there should not have been a shotgun on board, and if there had been, just what had happened? On closer examination, it was realized the pellet size was too small for a normal shotgun shell. Remembering that some .38 special calibre shells contained pellets instead of a slug, I wondered if that might have been the reason. After someone checked the cargo list, the answer became clear. There had been a shipment of many tiny ballpoint pen tips, those round tungsten balls that fit inside the end of the ink cartridge to contact the surface when writing. While it had never been a major nagging question of how the ink made its way to the paper, now I knew tiny tungsten balls were the answer. After all, they were called ballpoint pens.

There had been many thousands of them on board and eventually we found they had infiltrated everything, including most of the body parts. Later throughout the investigation, they would continually appear in insulation and plastic materials.

Another item appearing in large quantities in nearly everything was the twelve-volt receiver unit housed in a vehicle's dash in which the cigarette lighter or cell phone is plugged. When we finished, there were enough to fill at least two large 1.5 cubic metre tri-wall boxes.

By nightfall, everyone in the morgue knew the only way to handle this mentally was to become numb to the working conditions. A person could not think of the remains as human flesh, but merely material to meet some legal need. There was an effort to keep anything human related, such as names and addresses, separate from the morgue workers. We just could not think of what came through the door as being some person's father or son, mother or daughter, and above all, a child. As a form of psychological protection, everyone used the term "material" instead of bodies to refer to what came across the morgue tables. Only one complete body was ever brought in, and of the rest, perhaps the largest piece of material weighed about twenty-five pounds.

When the day's end came, I decided to stay overnight at the base barracks. It had been a tough day, and there was still more to do during the evening. Fingerprints were coming in from the FBI, and they now needed organizing. Other supplies had arrived, so they needed sorting and storing. There was much to do, plus there were a few issues I had to settle in my mind even though I still had hope conditions would improve.

I had set up a supply station at the end of one of the rows of three examination rooms. It was central to the work area and provided the various small items needed by many. Coming in the next morning, I noticed someone had written on the plywood wall above the shelving the large letters in black spelling out "Tom's Place." By doing that, someone had seemingly cemented into one solid unit all the various agency and department personnel who worked in the hangar. Given what we faced, we knew our new close-knit community could now count on one another to do his or her part.

Lee Fraser advised there was a Rabbi in the hangar who had asked for and offered his help. According to Jewish religious demands, any Jewish person must be buried before the sun sets three times. We knew by then this was an impossible requirement. As Lee thanked him for his presence, the Rabbi explained he could be of great help to us. All he had to do was to view the human remains to identify those who were Jewish. Lee was more than a bit callous in doing it this way, but when he showed him the first bits of remains, the Rabbi was noticeably shaken. He demanded to know how he could say these remains were of a person of the Jewish faith. Lee told him this was precisely our problem but he had claimed to be able to help. An obvious impasse. Lee suggested the best we could do was to ensure that as each piece of material was identified, it would be returned to the next of kin before the three-day deadline. He accepted this because he had no choice. We followed this routine for every bit of material that was identified.

During the next two months, one family would bury their next of kin and reopen the casket twice more to add additional parts of the body. They would then ask that we store any more material identified as their loved one until the closure of the morgue. Still another family at first refused to supply any DNA samples and simply said that their relative was to remain undisturbed on the ocean floor. Every jurisdiction has laws dealing with identifying human remains, so it was in their interests to help in the matter. Using tact to overcome the problem, the member dealing with the family simply stated that to comply with their wishes, we first had to determine which body was that of their relative. Once identified by DNA, they could do as they wished. They complied.

After five days in the hangar, I was scheduled for two days off. I had spent three of the five nights in barracks on the base because of the late nights. Now this would be my first day off in over two weeks because of my shifts before the crash. Just before leaving, Lee Fraser came to me to say he wanted me to attend a non-denominational religious service that was to be held the next afternoon in the hangar. Especially since I was senior to most of the people in the hangar, I should set the example. I asked Lee if he thought it to be a good idea. His puzzled look quickly changed to a snarl as he called me a 'God-damned atheist'. I did not care what he thought about me or my religious beliefs as they were none of his business. I had no intention of driving more than one hundred kilometres each way to spend one of my two days off in the hangar away from my family. My feeling was we already had a chapel on the base for anyone to attend. Also ministers and assistance people were readily available for those who needed support. What we were doing here in the hangar was unhuman and abnormal. Handling bits and pieces of human flesh was not a normal human activity. It was better to disassociate it from anything ordinary and natural. However, Lee was the officer, and he was right, so he thought. After all, he and his second in charge, S/Sgt. Vic Gorman, spent little time in the morgue throughout the sixty days and never got their hands dirty. They did not have the same experiences as did the many of us who were there all day long every working day. Lee held the religious service while I stayed home with my family.

When I came back to work on day eight, there were two FBI agents in the hangar whom Lee Fraser asked me to look after. "Get them out of my hair!" were his words. He had some important matters to attend to, and he could not deal with them. My thoughts were that I had matters at least equally important to deal with, identifying human remains.

I showed the two agents around the morgue setup including the fingerprinting arrangement. Then I took them across town to see the Halifax Ident Section. Wearing the expected standard dark business suits, these two agents were experienced in sudden death investigations. They were from the FBI's National Fingerprint Bureau in Washington, D.C. Their everyday role was to verify fingerprints that were fewer than ten points of identification. Our methods were different. Technically, we do not count points. If an Ident member made such an identification, any other Ident member is trained to verify that identification. When asked, the two agents revealed their experiences with mass disasters. They had both been at Jonestown in Northwest Guyana twenty years earlier. They had to identify the bodies from the mass suicide by cyanide of nine hundred and nine American citizens. After that, they had been at nearly every major mass disaster in the US. So their expertise in these matters was great.

Over the next several days I lost track of their whereabouts until the two agents showed up in the hangar early Monday morning. I had just made a fingerprint identification of a US citizen, so I asked if they would like to verify it for me. Instead of just standing around to watch them, I took my second fingerprint collection book and searched the next fingerprint from my stack of victim forms. Within a minute, I had a second identification of another American citizen. When the two agents were finished, I handed them the second comparison saying they might as well check this one too. I told them I had just made it while waiting for them to finish. However, I did not dare press my luck to try for a third as they examined the second comparison. They soon verified that it too was a match. They asked a couple of questions to confirm that I had just made the two identifications, especially the second while they had verified the first. They seemed satisfied with my answers. One agent then looked at the other and said they might as well go home. He said they were not needed here, and they could tell Washington the fingerprint desk was in good hands. The other nodded agreement, and they both said their goodbyes as they left. As quickly as that! Later, Lee showed up to ask where they were as they had gone without saying anything to him. I told him about the fingerprint verifications, but he would not believe I had made them as cold hits, that instead I had set the whole thing up. I do not know if Lee ever came to believe me.

I ran into a Canadian Navy diver at supper in the mess a few days later. I did not know him, but by his t-shirt insignia and appearance, it was obvious what he did. Sitting across from him, I commented about the great job he and his diving buddies were performing every day. They went down among all the sharps and shards of cutting metal to recover bits and pieces of human flesh and key debris. One of their numbers would soon become entangled in the sharp pieces and pierce his suit, something that could have cost him his life if it had been his air hose. I never asked this guy's name, but when I finished offering my appreciation, he just looked at me and, pointing up the hill, asked if I worked up there in the morgue. I nodded yes, and as he looked straight at me, he said he would not trade places with me for anything. I replied that he worked in extremely dangerous conditions, I did not, and that he walked on ground with two hundred feet of water over his head. That put him in a league second to none. He said he did that for a living, day in and day out, but only for an hour or so a day. He and his buddies expected that, and for them it was normal. He went on to say this morgue was not normal, not something that was done daily and never could be part of everyday work. When he was in the water, he was in his suit with clean, fresh air pumped to him. He said that in the morgue, I worked in and had to breathe and smell that putrid air all day long. He did not!

After he left, I pondered what he had said. Long ago I had gone into the raging and frigid Bella Coola River in winter to save an eleven-year-old native child and his grandfather from drowning. Their disabled boat was precariously pinned by the rushing waters to a stump above a dead tree snagged across the river. However, what he did was different. It was his daily job. I hated the water and could never have walked in his boots. Those guys were special.

The morgue had come together in just a few days because of the combined work of several hundred people from various groups and organizations. Dozens of RCMP members oversaw and worked in different areas of the hangar. Local hospital staff handled the X-ray equipment and various other areas. DND doctors, nurses, technicians, and the young stretcher bearers all had a major role to play. The Medical Examiner staff looked after the legal paperwork for each identified victim. More RCMP personnel assisted them and looked after next of kin contacts. Throughout there were the member assistance people who helped others through some of their worst moments. Then there were hangar security and maintenance people. Recovered personal effects and valuables had to be sorted and kept secure by RCMP members. Something as simple as the coffee wagon behind the hangar was a place of refuge for many to spend a few moments away from it all. Those ladies put up with a great deal from all of us. There was an overwhelming amount of work. While the morgue was open, everyone came together as a team that worked well with most problems solved soon after they came to light.

What we saw in the morgue was something ideally no one should ever have to see. The material coming in by helicopter and by boat at times was overwhelming. During the first three weeks, it was soaked in fuel oil with a smell that was chemical and toxic. Later it came in rotten with a cutting sulphurous smell that by 8 am gave me an all-day headache.

Several Ident members helped me with the fingerprinting. After rolling each digit, we compared it to the books of the known fingerprints that had been received from the FBI and elsewhere. I became so familiar with those fingerprints and names that on several occasions while rolling the print, I knew whose finger it was. The only way to handle it mentally was to realize I did not know the person. The name was merely an identifier. Cold as it may seem, I did not need to know anything more about him or her. This approach worked for the adults.

There had been several young children and babies on board. They too had suffered the same impact effects. About ten days into the crash I received a set of baby footprints in a letter. Later I was told I should never have received that letter. It had been a mistake for it to go into the morgue, and it should have gone to the RCMP's administrative team who looked after such things. They had already received several similar letters. It was a plea from an obviously distraught grandmother to identify her grandbaby who had been on board with both parents. She had included a poor quality copy of the baby's footprints on hospital letterhead paper.

For hours, I examined the footprints we had taken in the morgue. It was futile. Comparing finger or footprints usually needed complete concentration for extended periods of time, and that was not possible under these conditions. My fingerprint desk was within a few feet of the front hangar doors and right behind the second row of examination rooms. Every few minutes I was interrupted by an incoming Sea King helicopter stopping not fifty metres from me through the hangar doors. By now I had come to realize the doors were not going to fall off their tracks, but they rattled and shook each time. If not a helicopter, it was someone who wanted information or supplies, or it was some other distraction.

Even though the quality of the hospital photocopy was poor, I continued to try to make the comparison. Finally, as a last hope, I gave the hospital administrator a call to get the original prints. After explaining everything, she steadfastly refused to turn the original prints over to the grandparents or the FBI for fear of being sued. She said only the parents could make the request. My reply was they were now dead. Their remains were somewhere among the fragmented material coming through the hangar door. She would not budge. She had her set of rules to obey.

I have seen too many death and assault files involving children of all ages during my service. Like many people, I have always had a problem in dealing with the afterthoughts of it all. This was far worse. Suddenly it all became just too much, too futile, and I had to leave. I do not remember getting up or leaving the hangar, or even walking the distance. The first I do remember was standing out on the grass beside the end of the runway nearly a mile from the hangar. I could still hear the refrigerator and freezer trucks and the helicopters, and I could still smell the stench clinging to my clothes. I just could not go far enough to get away from it. I sat down on the grass and tried to put all the thoughts and feelings in proper order even though it all seemed overwhelming and hopeless. This woman had asked me to do something that should have been simple. However, I could not do it because some fool administrator had her insane bureaucratic red tape controlling her actions. Remembering the cell phone, I called home to my wife because that was the only sane thing I could think of. After rambling on that I could not make the match, I realized she had no idea of what I was saying. I managed to calm down and finally say something sensible to her. After I hung up, I stayed out there for nearly an hour until I finally came to my senses. I had to go back in because if I left, someone else would have to do the work. I could not put this onto someone else. I was being counted on to do this job and I had to do it. Besides, there were far worse places to be, and I had it easy compared with those people.

I had a saying that I had come across when I was a young boy. I had found it in a book about the British and Norwegian soldiers who destroyed Hitler's heavy water plant in Norway. Those few who barely survived their ordeal had been helped by this old Norwegian saying. It had been with me through all my toughest times. "A man who is a man will go on until he can do no more, then he will go twice as far." These words always came to me when I needed them most. I made my way back to my fingerprint desk and got back to work having passed that first hurdle all the member assistance people said was bound to occur. Most made it while some didn't. Over the next four years, this would prove to be the first of many times this saying would help.

At the end of the thirty days, the military and other morgue staff were moved out of the hangar. For psychological reasons, thirty days was the limit. They were replaced by other RCMP members, new hospital staff, civilian dentists, pathologists, and mortuary people. When approached by Lee Fraser, I asked where I would be going next. I suspected that management would not return me to regular Ident duties while bringing in others from elsewhere. Management had been planning a new recovery method. Lee told me I was to be in charge of a team who would spend twelve hours each day on a barge positioned over the wreckage site seven kilometres from shore. A crane with a clamshell grapple bucket would lift the material from two hundred feet below and deposit it on the barge. We would then sort it for human remains and aircraft debris. Working out there was to be my new job because the morgue was too much of a mental strain.

Lee's plan did not appeal to me. I had flown over the recovery site on day four in the Coastguard helicopter to take photos and video, so I knew what was out there. I simply said to Lee that I was not going. I said I had put too much effort into the fingerprint process to leave it now and have someone else start over. Besides, the quality control needed a continuity of process. Lee was not pleased, but there was little he could do. I told him if he thought this change of scenery was going to improve my mental health, then he had been in the job too long himself.

I remained in the morgue. Throughout the sixty days, we were exposed to the horrible sights of fragmented body parts in various states of devastation and decay. While the conditions during the first half were terrible, the second half became worse. My daily headaches increased in intensity due to the sour, sharp sulphurous-like smells of organic decay. The Halifax Ident Section had two part-time public servant positions, and Linda Gray had spent the first month in the offices beside the morgue. She now moved to the hangar floor to do her work. Each morning she began her day by lighting more than a dozen scented candles on her makeshift desk. It was an attempt to try to reduce the horrendous stench, but they did not help much. We put up with it and continued to work. We knew that each of us in the morgue was going to show up to do the job required of us. No one was going to let anyone else down.

Of course, by the second half of the morgue, the beach workers and the Admin people at Headquarters had returned to their regular duties. Only those in the Headquarters building paid much attention to the plaque on the wall that, of course, everyone deserved. RCMP members were still working on the barge when the weather allowed. Both the morgue and reconstruction hangars were in full operation. I happened to run into a member whom I knew well. He had worked during the first weeks of the file with others in DEOC, or the Division Emergency Operational Centre at Halifax Headquarters as one of the media relations people. I knew they had worked in a soundproof, air-conditioned and climate controlled environment at the Headquarters building. The loudest noise was from a computer keyboard or a phone ringing. The smells would have been of Tim Horton's coffee and doughnuts. He happened to say he had suggested the idea of the Division commendation plaque to the Commanding Officer. Then his boasting comment was that he felt good about his part in the effort and that he had his finger on the pulse of the file during his time in DEOC. I just looked at him, shook my head, and made a comment he seemed not to appreciate. I simply said, "That is nice, but unfortunately what my guys and I still have our fingers on no longer has a pulse." I say what I think without covering it with niceties.

During the sixty days of the morgue, the fingerprint team identified forty victims. The dental teams identified one hundred and two, and X-rays identified several. Of course, identifications of some victims were made by both dental comparisons and fingerprints. However, the DNA method identified everyone.

The closure of the morgue created a controversy about the identification of the rest of the human remains. Many of the next of kin expected the return of every piece of flesh. The Chief Medical Examiner decided this was not practical. There had already been two thousand, four hundred and ninety-nine body parts identified by DNA comparisons. So, a political decision was made. There would be a mass grave at the Bayswater Memorial Site. Actually, an unknown quantity of the human remains had already been lost because of natural forces. Seagulls and aquatic life of all types had taken their share. This was something natural and expected. Then came normal decomposition. Even so, good quality fingerprints were rolled from the recovered digits even on the last day. However, few known fingerprints were available for comparison. This same material that on day sixty was suitable for fingerprints was unsuitable for DNA due to decomposition. The material went to the mass grave because of that main reason. Some may have suggested that cost was the reason for the decision. It had nothing to do with the closure. Legally, a death certificate only needed proof of death. Nothing said that all of a person's remains must be put together in the same casket. The real reason was the human remains were unsuitable for a DNA sample, and no other method could provide a means of identity.

Perhaps there should have been an effort to use DNA. However, there were not enough Lab facilities to carry out all the added tests. Crime labs across the country were only just beginning to establish their DNA sections. This file had severely stretched the resources of the RCMP's Crime Lab system. As an example, one body bag of human remains came in weighing one hundred pounds. From it seventy DNA samples were taken, each of a separate piece of material. They were identified as twenty-nine individuals. Since the average piece of material was well under ten pounds, the lab system would not have been able to test all the extra samples.

Now, consider the next of kin of a homicide victim or an innocent suspect sitting in jail. What would their feelings be if first on the waiting list were all the thousands of other DNA examinations for the Swissair file, all of them now legally unnecessary?

During December of 1999, I attended a meeting with Doctors from the Transportation Safety Board (TSB) and Federal Aviation Administration (FAA). They had processed the records of the morgue examinations and provided their results. Before the meeting, some of the latest remains were examined including two five-pound clear plastic bags full of teeth. They had come from the final recovery that had vacuumed the sea floor. A few had gold fillings, others were bright white, while others were stained and tainted with bridges and other fixtures. These remains were unidentified, so this material went to the mass grave for the victims.

After everything else I had seen so far in my long career as a crime scene investigator, these were more terrible sights to be added to all the other thousands of horrific images in my memory's collection. In the years to come, they would all be repeatedly viewed by my mind's eye.

CHAPTER 2 – THE INITIAL INVESTIGATION

Four days after the morgue shut down, Ken Almey called me at home from Hangar A. He was the Ident member working there that week. Many Ident members had rotated through the reconstruction hangar and the morgue, but Ken had spent the longest of any of them. Ken was an old hand at Forensic Identification, and he normally worked out of Port Hawkesbury Ident. Very knowledgeable, he could always be counted on to do his job, and I completely trusted his judgment. Because I was now in charge of the Halifax Identification Section, he thought I should know what was happening in the hangar. My promotion to Sergeant had occurred two weeks after the crash and was based on my work that I had performed before Swissair.

The Identification function was vaguely similar to what a person might see in any of the Crime Scene Investigation programs on TV. However, there were many differences. Time and distances were greatly expanded. Women with long cascading blond hair did not enter crime scenes, let alone stoop over dead bodies without being clad in a hooded white safety suit. Masses of police did not occupy the crime scene while it was still being examined. Fancy Hummers had never been in the Ident vehicle inventory. The list goes on.

Ken found he was too busy to complete all the Identification tasks in the hangar. This created a problem. Some TSB members were not following the requirements of the Memorandum of Understanding while conducting their investigation. The MOU had been agreed upon in 1993. The RCMP was to assist in the areas of lab analysis, photography, physical evidence, and exhibit control. The TSB was to fully investigate the matter. If they found evidence of a crime, they were to immediately notify the RCMP. Of importance in the MOU, the TSB agreed to abide by the rules of evidence provided by the Force. The purpose of this was to ensure evidence could be entered into Court if the need ever arose. In contrast, the American NTSB and the US police agencies cooperated so the police maintained their investigation until the incident was judged to be an accident instead of a crime.

A week earlier, Lee Fraser and I had attended a meeting to discuss these issues with John Garstang of the TSB. He had warned these problems were occurring. John wanted at least one Ident member working directly and full time in the investigation. He would then be positioned to overcome these problems. He could also maintain a knowledge base of the process and the information as it became available in case it resulted in Court. Lee ignored his request.

Sunday afternoon, I entered the hangar with an assortment of gear. Cameras, a microscope, and other equipment and materials were set up in the TSB's lab area. John had recommended that location for a very practical reason. My equipment went onto a table between Jim Foot, the TSB's electrical and systems investigator, and Gus Sidla, their metallurgist. I would come to know them very well. It was mid-week before I met with Fraser. After explaining my actions, he told me to work with the TSB as Garstang had requested.

I had never met John Garstang before the crash. When first meeting him, I immediately felt I had known him for a lifetime. It was his friendliness and his way of conversing. John was a mechanical engineer and ran the TSB's engineering lab at the Ottawa airport. Besides aircraft, the TSB was also responsible for the safety investigations of ships, trains, and pipelines. So, it would not be uncommon for him to be climbing through a train wreck somewhere in the country, a pipeline blowout, or a plane crash. He had been in the HMCS Okanagan, the Canadian Navy Submarine that went looking for this aircraft's crash site. Until the sub homed in on the pingers in the aircraft's black boxes, no one knew the exact location of the debris field.

I would work with John on a continuous basis over the next four years as he was the main TSB physical evidence investigator for the TSB. Every time I asked about some piece of equipment or how something on the aircraft worked, he had an answer that was technical but easy to understand. If he did pose a question to a technician from Boeing or Swissair, it was to confirm something he already suspected about a special piece of equipment. To know the aircraft and every piece of equipment as he did, John had spent many hours of his own time researching and reading the manuals.

John later told me he had grown up in Saskatchewan as the son of an RCMP Corporal. He joined the Air Cadets at the age of twelve where he thoroughly enjoyed learning about aircraft and flying, but he loved camping. Unfortunately, the troop did little of it. So, while still an Air Cadet, he joined the Army Cadets. Not only did they camp and target shoot, they had their meetings on different evenings. He said as far as he knew, there were no rules against it. His problems occurred when both troops were at the same ceremony such as Remembrance Day. Which troop would he parade with while keeping out of sight of the other?

Louis Landriault worked closely with John as the TSB's computer expert. There was nothing Louis did not know about computers or how to apply them to this investigation in a practical manner. Louis dealt with the masses of photos, drawings, and data to create a computer program for the investigators. They used it to see important parts or areas of the aircraft in a panorama view, both in its normal and burnt conditions. Louis knew the aircraft, and it allowed him to instruct other co-workers on the correct manner to complete certain tasks.

Both Louis and John were practical jokers. An example was when Louis took time away from the investigation to go into hospital for surgery. When John visited him one evening, unknown to Louis he left something to keep Louis's spirits high. On leaving, John complained to the nurse about the bag of garbage under Louis' bed, that perhaps he was hiding something. What the nurse found was a half-eaten Big Mac. That was bad because Louis was on a strict diet. However, what riled her and caused her to scold Louis was the empty beer bottle in the bag with it. John and eventually Louis had a good laugh over that one.

Beginning on my first day in Hangar A, I started working closely with John, and over the four years of this file, we would become good friends. I must say he would be a far better friend than some of those whom I had mistakenly called by that term before this crash occurred.

Like all the TSB members in the hangar, John was casual in his dress. They all wore jeans and a blue golf shirt with the TSB emblem on it that was the Canadian Coat of Arms. Within another month, the RCMP members would adopt a similar uniform. It would be a golf shirt or a T-shirt over issue blue cargo pants with no yellow leg stripe. The shirts had the Force's crest with RCMP through it and 'Operation Homage' below it as the file's name. It was a practical solution to the dust and grime that covered and invaded everything in the hangar.

From the first day in the reconstruction hangar there was a steep learning curve. The hangar, identical in size to Hangar B at fifty metres wide by one hundred and fifty metres long, was divided into specific areas to support various activities. Next to the dozen or so main roller doors that went across the front width of the hangar was the initial debris examination table with its sorting line. The incoming debris was examined at this location. TSB, Boeing, and Swissair personnel with two RCMP members staffed the sorting line. One was from the Explosives Demolition Unit and the other was a Crime Lab Chemistry member from Ottawa. Both had an extensive background in explosives. Burnt items and other specific pieces were selected from the broken remains of the aircraft to be sent to a nearby table where RCMP members exhibited and photographed them. They then went to their proper area of the hangar floor or were stored in tri-wall boxes for later work. The rest went into storage at the nearby Hangar J, built for that purpose.

Along each of the long sides of the hangar were office and utility spaces. Entering by the main doors, the TSB had set themselves up on the right side and the RCMP on the left. By my second day, I had arranged my camera equipment and microscope in the centre of the hangar floor. Months later, an office on the RCMP side became vacant when the explosives members left, so I moved in there to create the RCMP's smallest Ident office.

Initially, being in the centre of the hangar placed me with everything going on around me, so I could easily see and learn what the TSB and others were doing. A walkway with a plywood wall had been erected along the TSB side of the hangar, and on it and elsewhere on stands were several dozen very large photographs of key areas of the aircraft's interior. They were to help the investigators identify some of the many thousands of pieces of debris.

I was now in the middle of the hangar's reconstruction work, but how did I come to be there? My Dad had managed a two-thousand-acre collection of what were smaller adjoining farms near Magog, Quebec, all owned by a family from Montreal. The family's father had been the senior surviving Canadian Prisoner of War in Hong Kong during the Second World War, and he had later retired from the Canadian Army as a Brigadier General. His five sons and a daughter had their businesses in the Province and their hands in politics. Occasionally they came out to the farm to enjoy the country life for a weekend, or in the winter to ski at nearby Mount Orford. The farm had great potential, and if they had wanted to, it could have produced enough beef and lamb to feed half of Stanstead County, and maple syrup for all their pancakes.

My two brothers and I grew up on the farm and looked on it as our home. Having learned to drive a tractor at the age of nine, I could operate all the farm equipment by the age of thirteen, or fix it if it broke. After all, by the age of seven I had preferred assembling my Meccano set over watching Gordie Howe and Bobby Hull on Hockey Night in Canada. The farm machinery included a ten-ton bulldozer and equipment to bring in over five hundred tons of hay, that much silage, several thousand bushels of grain, and then take it out the other way once processed by the more than three hundred head of livestock. By the time I turned nineteen, I could determine the quality of a cow, sheep, or horse and had raised some prize-winning lambs.

I remember at the age of about seven or eight changing my aunt's flat tire on her Pontiac while it was in our roadway. I had never changed a tire before but had seen Dad do it once or twice on our car. I knew there was a jack in the trunk that fit in the massive chrome bumper, and the wheel nuts had to come off once the tire was off the ground. They went back on after the spare was installed, and when checked, they were tight enough for the garage mechanic who tried later but could not tighten them further. All the while she kept saying perhaps I should find my Dad to change the tire. I simply told her I could do it, that he was too busy baling hay.

My older brother joined the Force in 1964, spent years in the Musical Ride training riders and horses alike, and even had a horse he trained presented to the Queen. It turned out to be her favourite mount for the Changing of the Guard parades. He became an Inspector and retired in Whitehorse. My younger brother also joined the Force a few years after I did and ended up in the Lower Mainland as one of British Columbia's top arson investigators.

I had done well in school even though I had been at least a year younger than everyone else in my class. My Dad always said they enrolled me a year early at the age of five because if they had waited another year and I decided not to go, I would have been too big for them to make me go. We went to an English Protestant school in Magog with about five hundred other students. It covered grades one through eleven which at that time was as far as anyone needed to go to graduate and have their junior matriculation in Quebec. Everyone knew everyone else by their first name. I played soccer along with track and field, and set school records for distance in shot put and discus. Maths and science were my subjects in high school, and I didn't have to take the books home to study. With little interest in literature or languages, I had a slide-ruler and knew how to use it. Physics was a breeze because it involved what I thought were practical matters. When I wrote the Provincial physics exam to graduate high school, I finished the two-hour paper in under twenty minutes and was upset I only received a 97%.

When I graduated high school two months after turning sixteen, I was offered a scholarship to an American University if I would play football. I had all the qualifications except I had never played on an organized team. This route was an attractive way to earn a mechanical engineering degree since I had no money for university. However, my parents intervened to say I would not be going. My mother, being a former British Territorial Army Sergeant and a war-bride, would have nothing to do with North American style football. English football, or soccer as we called it 'over here', was the game of choice, and I had played much of that. So, I went to grade twelve in Montreal, the equivalent to first-year of university. After that, I worked on the farm until I turned nineteen. I had considered joining the Canadian Air Force and then the Canadian Coastguard, but it was the time of Paul Hellyer's unification of the Canadian Military, so I had little chance of getting into the Air Force, and the Coastguard was full. I even considered going South and joining the US Air Force. I wanted to fly big jets, and the B-52 was the aircraft of my choice. However, the Vietnam War was raging, and my parents were afraid I would end up there.

Dad had joined the Canadian Army in 1940 and was on a troop transport in mid-Atlantic during the sinking of the Bismarck. He had joined the Canadian Forestry Corps and had gone to fight the Hitler peril and defend the British Isles, his ancestors' homeland. Later, in the British Columbia Regiment, he fought in and repaired Sherman tanks across most of Belgium, Holland, and into Germany. I wondered if perhaps Vietnam was to be my war. However, things changed, and the sound of distant drums faded for a while. When I turned eighteen, I applied for the Force and was accepted a year later. On the first of September, 1970, I headed out to Depot by train and was one of the two youngest in my troop of thirty-two.

    Depot training was very tough, but in some ways it was easier than the farm work I had been doing. The pay was much better, the food was good, and there was plenty of it. What's more, I had Saturday afternoons and Sundays off to go into town without returning for chores. At least, I went out on those few days we were not confined to barracks because of some foolishness or other. That was all part of the game. I was a non-swimmer, so I had to learn to swim. I developed blood poisoning in my feet because I scuffed the bottom of the pool so much, the dye from my issue blue socks infected the cuts. I then cracked a finger in self-defence, but that did not slow me up either. The hardest was trying to stay awake in law classes. The rest was easy, even having a Corporal yell and curse at me just nose to nose. He could not begin to match a barn full of cattle or two hundred and fifty sheep at feeding time. At six-foot-one and just over two hundred pounds, he could not do anything to harm me. In the first physical fitness test, I finished first in the troop and set the Depot record for that test. In another, the clean and jerk record for the 125-pound bar was eighteen lifts in thirty seconds. If I had been a quarter of a second faster, I would have made nineteen. Then there was running. By the time a troop was finished training, a marathon would have been easy.

    Four-and-a-half years of detachment work in three very violent locations made me realize I needed to do something else. I had more than my share of fights where some fool wanted to kill me. One night I nearly shot a guy high on drugs when he came at me with a large club, intent on only one of us leaving alive. Assaulting an old woman was his ruse to force the confrontation. In his drug-induced state, he was immune to pain while his strength was enhanced. We fought, and when he broke free, he picked up the four-foot club and came at me saying he was going to end this fight by killing me. He suddenly changed his mind and ran when he saw I had cocked my revolver after aiming it at his chest. Luckily, I had found it in the sand at my feet. He had managed to remove it from my holster during the fight. Because of sand in the cylinder, I had to force back the gun's hammer. However, I knew I couldn't fire or the gun might explode in my face due to damp sand blocking the barrel.

There had to be more to this job than dealing with drunks, druggies, and misfits. My hobby was photography, and my interests were in Forensic Identification. When I had been interviewed for my first posting, I had told the Depot Staffing Officer that I would eventually apply for Ident. He just laughed, but he had no way of knowing I would be one of the most junior members ever to become a Forensic Crime Scene Investigator. However, becoming an Ident member did not mean I was free from violence and personal danger. What's more, I would see the aftermath of many acts of savagery and enough needless death to last many lifetimes.

After two years in Prince Rupert Ident, my wife and I moved to Bathurst Ident for five years. We then went north with our son to Frobisher Bay, or what soon would be called Iqaluit. After three years and a new daughter, we moved west to Yellowknife Ident. Three years later when the Division Staffing Sergeant asked me about my move out of Yellowknife, I told him New Minas, Nova Scotia was open and I wanted to go there. He quickly told me I could not tell them where I would be going and I had to submit five locations. He would not accept New Minas in all five positions on his piece of paper. I told him to fill in anything he wanted in the other four locations, but either I was going to New Minas or I was staying in Yellowknife. I then got up and walked out of the meeting as I had finished with him. I had more important things to do than argue, something he seemed intent on doing for some reason. Two weeks later, the Staffing Inspector called me into his office. As I entered, he shook my hand while saying I was going to be the newest member of the New Minas Ident Section. That was in 1988, and it was the first location I had moved to in eighteen years that another member wanted. I had done my time in the less desirable locations. After eight years, I was transferred to Halifax Ident, but I refused to move. Instead I commuted the one hundred kilometres each way.

Besides all of this, I had a background with aircraft. I had flown in nearly every type of bush plane and helicopter available during six years in the North Coast region of British Columbia and five years in Northeast New Brunswick. With six more years in the Eastern and Central Arctic, I had well over a thousand hours in twin otters and nearly as much in other small aircraft. Many of those hours had been in the right seat beside the pilot. I had even been in what the pilot called a very hard landing of a Grumman Goose in

Telegraph Creek, B.C. Many, though, might have considered it a crash landing. The aircraft had skidded on its nose along a logging road for several hundred yards before the tail finally banged down onto the ground. I had been in every community North of Sixty and East of the Yukon border, as well as many of those just South of Sixty. I had experiences where we had circled the runway for hours until there was a lull in the snowstorm. On one occasion, we landed with less than fifteen minutes of fuel left. It had been a blinding snowstorm in midsummer. There was not a community in the North where a pilot and anyone with him would have survived a missed airstrip landing if he had to 'put-down' blindly. I had more aircraft experience than anyone else in Forensic Ident. Other than the Force's pilots, few in the Force had more time flying in small aircraft than I.

I also had an extensive background in fire investigations, an area in which most Ident members had no training or experience. This knowledge included a short DND course on explosives demolition. Simple enough, I had been given a brick of C-4 explosive, detonation cord, a detonator, a length of fuse, and an ignitor. After correctly assembling the device, the fuse was struck and a minute later it blew up. It was the experience of working with the materials and knowing what they were that counted, and what the result was. The bonus for this file was I had met Trevor Jain on that course. That provided dividends for our work in the morgue.

It was also necessary to learn about this aircraft. The MD-11 was almost the size of a Boeing 747, so there was much to know. What's more, we were conducting the first computerized investigation. There was a need to learn the software while keeping old handwritten systems. Even the software was continually changed.

It was a continuous and steep learning curve. At first, it was formidable, as the hangar was like a foreign country. The aircraft was Swiss owned, so we had employees of Swissair as well as the company that conducted all their aircraft maintenance, SR Technics. The Boeing Company from the USA supplied many people from various US locations. The plane had been made in Long Beach, California, having been designed by the McDonnell Douglas Company. Boeing had taken over that company several years earlier, so they supplied the various technicians and resource people. The NTSB or the National Transportation Safety Board, the US version of the TSB, were present with several of their members because the plane had left from the JFK Airport in New York. Members of the FAA, or the Federal Aviation Administration, were present as well as the Air Accident Investigations Branch for Great Britain and the Swiss Accident Investigation Board. Many other companies were represented because of the many thousands of parts in the aircraft.

Besides the people involved, there was another language to be learned. It was the vocabulary of the industry, both from Boeing and from McDonnell Douglas. As an example, Boeing used the term 'stringers' for the ribs forming the circumference of the aircraft hull, while McDonnell Douglas and Swissair called them 'longeron.' 1R, 1L, 2R, 2L, were examples of the Boeing hull door numbers while McDonnell Douglas and Swissair called them 1.1, 2.1, 1.2, 2.2. Add in that every piece of equipment and every point on the aircraft had a coordinate in the x, y, and z, their original drafting table coordinates. The 'x' coordinate was either left or right of aircraft centre with negative on the left side or Captain's side. The 'y' coordinate was from the nose to the tail with any key point called a 'station' along with its distance number. The 'z' coordinate was the elevation with above centre being positive while below centre was negative. Each piece of equipment, made up of many broken debris pieces, had a name and a specific location referenced by the coordinate system. When finished, I knew the location details and the purpose of many pieces of equipment and thousands of broken exhibits from the aircraft.

First, though, it was a matter of setting up my equipment in the centre of the hangar to start the photographic process of the various debris pieces as directed by John. At different times during the day, I would tour the hangar to speak with others and see what they were doing. Initially, I sensed that since I was the police, they had to be careful around me. To overcome this, I wore blue coveralls with no shoulder flashes, practical since the hangar was cold and drafty. When the weather warmed up, I wore a lab coat over our new hangar T-shirt and blue cargo pants.

While it was daunting, there never was a feeling that I had no business being there. I was an experienced RCMP Forensic Ident investigator. It was routine to be called to an address and take control of the physical scene no matter what it was or who was there. There was always a common theme with most scenes. Go carefully in an organized and purposeful manner, tread very carefully as if in a minefield, examine, photograph and record everything, and destroy nothing. My experience was that few, if any, of those working on the file either knew or could do my job. Still fewer wanted my job. It was my scene, and until I left no one came in unless I let them. I had been criticized for it by some, but my thoughts were they obviously knew nothing about crime scenes and physical evidence. It was minute, fragile, elusive, obscure and above all, easily destroyed. If destroyed, it might never have been there as no one would know. It could never be restored. As for doing the work, no one told me what to do in a scene or what they thought I should be doing. The less I knew about a suspect or what the investigators thought the story was, the better. My intention was to be an impartial Court witness who presented all the physical evidence in the best possible manner and not just another witness for the prosecution. If they did not like it or my results, the next time they should call someone else. I usually got results, just not always what the main investigators wanted. I was not there to please them or to merely convict the suspect. I was there to find the evidence of what had happened and present it to the Court. Let a jury convict the suspect if the evidence warranted it. That was not my job. In Court, I was once asked by a defence counsel if I was a professional witness. It was an intended derogatory comment alluding to the fact that I received a salary while giving evidence. My response was that I tried to be as professional a Court witness as possible, beginning with the initial crime scene and ending with my presentation of all the evidence to the Court.

This file was different, though, in that I could not take over the debris processing. There was a need to let the individual specialists put their pieces together to see what had contributed to the crash. It was a matter of ensuring the debris was handled correctly so it could go to Court if the need ever arose. Besides, it made common sense to address things in a meticulous and organized manner. Most of the TSB members had never worked on anything this big, so everyone would have to come together as a team to ensure the work was done correctly.

As time progressed and with constant work and determination, I became familiar with the debris and the people. While doing that, this file would slowly begin to fit the same mould as a normal investigation, but with one exception. John Garstang was knowledgeable in forensic work and photography, so he was a resource person for me. His problem was he was limited by the TSB. The same would happen to me, but it would be the RCMP who handcuffed me.

Besides the investigators, there was the aircraft. It was huge. The diameter of the plane's hull would not allow its reconstruction inside the hangar. Plus, the wing span far exceeded the hangar's width. The problem was overcome by limiting the reconstruction to the area of the fire. That proved to be the forward overhead or attic area with the forward cabin floor and flight deck area. Nothing occurred below the cabin floor or after the second set of first-class seats. However, in that burnt area, there were many thousands of pieces. All of them had to be pieced together, some after having to be reformed by aircraft technicians from the Air Force. These we fondly called our 'tin knockers.' The local Department of Transportation built a frame representing the upper forward section of the hull to which the debris pieces were fastened. As for the wings, they were reformed in the outside storage area at Hangar J, the storage hangar.

On a daily basis, I worked directly with the TSB members and the representatives from the various foreign agencies and companies. They were working together to find out what had happened to the aircraft, and I was learning first-hand from them all.

At first, I had no interference from my RCMP managers. I was given complete freedom to work with my TSB co-worker and supervisor, John Garstang. In 1999, three trips were made to Zurich to examine MD-11 aircraft in the Swissair hangar. I travelled during the first two trips with John and examined two of the Swissair aircraft under a complete refit or what was called a D-check. The aircraft interior was stripped out to the bare metal and base components. We then examined more than a dozen other Swissair MD-11 aircraft to view various areas and parts. The main effort was the forward overhead or attic area of each plane.

These aircraft were all found in Swissair's main hangar at the Zurich Airport. To say it was a large building would be like saying the Pacific Ocean was just a large body of water. A 747 passenger plane was parked to one side of the hangar. Two MD-11 aircraft were next to it with space for dozens of vehicles and ramps, stairs, and other equipment. Two more MD-11 aircraft were positioned at the other side of the hangar with room for still more. It was all under one suspended roof about twelve stories high. This was a huge building by anyone's standards, especially since the tail of the MD-11 rose to over sixty feet above the ground with a wing span of more than one hundred and seventy feet. The aircraft was more than two hundred feet long, and the hull was nearly twenty feet in diameter.

There was a high skywalk opposite the hangar doors where I could look down into the hangar and take photos. The aircraft were a vista to see. Then I noticed the vehicles. Full-sized passenger vans were tiny tinker toys beside the gigantic planes. After watching all the little people move about, I noticed a small hole open in one of the large hangar doors. In drove a tiny toy vehicle that was a full-sized truck and trailer. The doorway inside the great twelve stories high rolling door was barely noticeable until it lifted and the truck drove through. So, it was little wonder the Swissair employees were shocked at the piles of small pieces their plane had become.

As for the SR Technics personnel, they treated me well. I wore my blue coveralls with the RCMP shoulder flashes while in their hangar. I did not know how they would take the idea of a Canadian police officer in their midst, but in fairness, I did not want to pass myself off as a TSB member. The first morning, two of the technicians approached to speak with John and me. Seeing my RCMP shoulder flashes, they had some questions about why I was there. I explained I was helping the TSB, and if anything criminal was found, we would investigate it. Their response was unexpected. After looking at each other, there seemed to be a sense of relief and approval from them. One turned to me and said thank you, they were worried Canada would not take the crash seriously and would brush it off. However, with the RCMP present, they knew it would be investigated fully. Thereafter, whatever I did on those planes, I always had people willing to help.

The news of the crash and destruction of Vaud, the name of the aircraft, and all the passengers and crew had hit the SR Technics and Swissair people hard. The company brought in counsellors for them because not only had they lost people, they had lost an aircraft that was part of their family. Technicians who had last worked on Vaud questioned themselves about what they might have done during the last maintenance that possibly could have caused the fire. What did they miss that they should have seen? No one had an answer. That did not help because they had lost Vaud and all those people. I spent seven weeks in the hangar during the three trips, and I came to see that these workers strove for perfection. Nothing less was acceptable.

My third trip to Zurich was made alone. I was to work with the SR Technics people to recover insulation blankets and specific aircraft parts from another MD-11 during its D-check. John, as the TSB member responsible for this area of the investigation, told me he had no one else in the TSB who knew the plane, the materials, and the Swiss technicians as well as I did. I had his confidence. That was especially important since I was the main RCMP physical evidence investigator for the file. Soon I would be the only one. My arrival met with a degree of disapproval from the Swiss. The SR Technics supervisor's comment on learning that I was alone was "You God-damned Canadians. You send one person to do the work of ten!" We had a good laugh, then we worked together and successfully completed the task.

During the four years of the investigation, I worked with all the various investigators to take more than a hundred and fifty thousand photos. Many were of the broken aircraft, registered as HB-IWF and given the name Vaud. Fifteen other Swissair MD-11 aircraft were examined and photographed. I examined wreckage in the many hundreds of thousands of pieces and made thousands of physical matches. I came to appreciate the professionalism of the SR Technics people in Zurich and the Boeing technicians in Seattle. Their electrical shop made hundreds of short-circuited wires under various controlled conditions. Later I attended at Long Beach, California, to fly on an eight-hour test flight of a sister MD-11 aircraft. With TSB members and some of Boeing's top engineers, we conducted airflow tests to understand the air currents in the overhead area where the fire took place. Then there was a need to determine the fire-related properties of the flammable materials in the aircraft. To accomplish this, three separate sessions of burn tests were held at the FAA Burn Center in Atlantic City. I attended each to help create, photograph, videotape, and above all to observe the results.

I came to value my working relationship with the on-site Boeing representative, Larry Fogg, who had an extensive knowledge of the aircraft. Larry, who lived in Los Angeles, was originally from the mid-West. He had worked his way through Boeing and had become one of their top aircraft accident investigators. His scruffy beard and graying hair reflected his years of experience that included nearly every type of Boeing commercial aircraft. Boeing had bought McDonnell Douglas years ago, so even their aircraft were included in his knowledge bank.

One of Larry's earlier accident scenes had been in the Florida Everglades. He said they had waded through water waist deep to find aircraft debris. I suggested it was likely a dangerous undertaking because of the natural wildlife. He just looked at me and matter-of-factly said no, they never saw a single 'gator or snake'. They had all left as the fuel from the crash spread out over the waters. Larry was very much a professional, and I never saw him upset. Even when someone made serious mistakes in putting together debris pieces, he merely took it in his stride. After muttering a few choice words, he just started again. Larry knew from experience the investigation would be a long-term and massive undertaking. Therefore, it was necessary to take the time to do it correctly. Larry's work in the hangar was instrumental in reconstructing the aircraft, as it had to pass his final inspection. Larry was a source of information for me that was honest and unwavering throughout my time in the hangar.

The only other person to rate with Larry's expertise was John Garstang. John's experience included the Air India flight 182 bombing. He had worked on the wreckage recovery and cause determination in Ireland in 1985. That Boeing 747 aircraft was blown out of the sky over the Atlantic killing all on board including several hundred Canadians. It was his work that first determined and then confirmed a bomb had brought down the plane. His further work identified the correct location of the device within the aircraft. In doing so, he contradicted the Indian investigators who misidentified the bomb's placement, some think on purpose. Many of the documentaries on the Internet today still do not have the correct story.

I learned about the MD-11 aircraft from John and Larry, and with them I took part in nearly every important test. This experience allowed me to become more informed of the events leading up to the crash than any other member of the RCMP. What's more, I was as up-to-date as many of the key members of the TSB.

I had a broad experience in forensic physical evidence processing, and I was one of the most qualified in the Force to do the job that I was doing. Besides attending many thousands of crime scenes of all types, I had investigated more than a dozen light aircraft crashes. One was a Twin Otter twelve-passenger fatal near Terrace, B.C. I had many advanced courses in arson and fire investigation to my credit. In addition, I had taught students of fire courses some of the many aspects of forensic photography and physical evidence handling during fire scene investigations. With the added knowledge and experience gained from investigating several hundred fire scenes, I had been allowed to provide expert opinion fire evidence in Court. Judges in New Brunswick, North West Territories, and Nova Scotia had qualified me in both Criminal and Civil Court for fire cause determination and propagation. As for death investigations, I had seen just about every way a person can die. It included more than a hundred murder scenes and well over a thousand sudden death scenes. When I retired, I was the most experienced air crash physical evidence investigator in any police force in this country.

On entering the hangar, I had no preconceived ideas about the file except to believe it would be handled professionally by competent people with the proper skills. However, during the first fifteen months, signals to the contrary surfaced that became increasingly more frustrating to work with and impossible to ignore. As an example, by about two weeks into the file, it was ruled as an accident even though only a few body parts and hardly any wreckage had been recovered. The TSB based their decision solely on the limited information on the cockpit voice recorder (CVR) and the flight data recorder (FDR). No bomb had exploded so the TSB automatically believed the cause of the crash was accidental, and senior RCMP management agreed.

One of the senior managers was the Officer in Charge of the RCMP's Swissair Task Force, Inspector Andy Lathem. At over six-and-a-half feet tall, Andy towered above most people. Plus, he was athletic. He kept himself in excellent shape by running and exercising daily. Andy always wore a dark business suit with a white shirt and a very conservative tie. I always wondered if his shirts were starched as much as was his stiff personality. Only after working for him for several years did I learn about his previous background. As a Constable, he had no investigative background at all, and as a Corporal and Sergeant, he had only limited detachment experience. After obtaining his Officer's Commission, he became the Inspector in Charge of the Halifax Major Crime Unit. Luckily, he had some excellent investigators who worked for him. Unlucky for me, he was now the RCMP's onsite commander. He worked out of the hangar's back office with several dozen plain-clothes investigators that soon dwindled down to five.

After my experiences with him on this file, my firm opinion was he lacked the competence and ability to perform the needed tasks of proper leadership and file management. Even my opinion about his integrity and honesty as a police officer changed. That meant that soon I would be out in the cold and working on my own to do what I had been trained to do over the years - follow the evidence trail wherever it may lead.

There were dozens of other members of the RCMP who worked on the hangar floor during the first two years, sometimes under very adverse circumstances. They were skilled investigators and did excellent work. I worked with several Identification members whom I knew through previous experiences, and they all did good and important work. It also included two Constables, Duane Cooper and Andy Kerr, who worked in the hangar until December of 2000.

Duane Cooper was a tall and solidly built young Constable, good-looking, easy to talk to, and always friendly while businesslike. He was a knowledgeable police officer with considerable municipal detachment experience for his service. His advantage was he was fluent in the new use of computers, especially the way the Force made use of them. We had a saying that there was a right way, a wrong way, and an RCMP way of doing things. Duane knew the RCMP way of computers. I was no slouch with them either. I had bought my first, a TI-99, back in 1982 and then taught myself 'TI BASIC' computer language. However, the Force had to have something different and unique, so it took a special person to follow their path. Duane could do that.

The Force's way was to adapt an investigation to a computer instead of the other way around. That was why I stopped using the Force's program called Evidence and Reports for my notes. It could not handle the technical data I recorded, and I refused to adapt my notes to the limitations of the computer database.

Andy Kerr was the opposite of Duane only as far as height. Short and slight, he made up for it in his work habits and abilities. I had worked with him on several files while he had been on one of the local detachments. He never shirked his duties and could always be counted on to do more than his part. He too was junior in service, but he had considerable municipal detachment experience. Municipal detachment members handled much more work than did rural detachment members merely because they had less distances to travel while covering a larger population. Kerr ran the exhibit desk in the hangar and taught his people to handle efficiently and effectively the debris pieces coming across their table. He oversaw the storage hangar and its database. Because of his work, I would easily find the thousands of pieces of debris the TSB would soon need. The TSB said there were two million pieces in that hangar. The problem was they had lost count part-way through. There were more than twice that many, as several of the tri-wall boxes held more pieces than anyone could count in a month. Andy taught many of the TSB members the rights and wrongs of exhibit handling, and if they did not do it right, he quickly corrected them.

Both Cooper and Kerr would be taken advantage of by Lathem during the latter part of their time in the hangar. They eventually saw through Lathem for what he was and had become. Lathem appeared to me to have a self-image problem. He seemed intimidated by anyone who learned how incompetent he was and how corrupt he had become. He eventually resorted to intimidation and punishment to overcome and compensate for it.

As for the Transportation Safety Board, many of their floor people proved to be highly capable and professional safety investigators. However, some others were not. I soon learned the TSB would never perform a criminal investigation of the crash. Their job was to undertake only a safety investigation in what they called an attempt to create a safer travelling environment. Thus the word 'Safety' in their name. Their legislation did not allow anything else. Even though there was a Memorandum of Understanding between the two agencies, I was told their management would never fulfil it. The truth of this would become evident by the end of the investigation.

Quickly I learned that some of the TSB investigators worked by a policy that came about due to their legislation. Except for exceptional circumstances, TSB members would never give evidence in a Court of Law, either criminal or civil. They were accountable only to their own Board of Inquiry. Being non-accountable to an independent judicial system allowed some of them to feel they did not have to follow the strict rules of evidence or correct investigative procedures. In fact, more than one of their members said 'TSB' stood for 'The Speculation Board', and their motto was 'why investigate when we can speculate'. It meant there was opportunity for some to control and manipulate evidence examinations and results. I witnessed the actions of several key TSB investigators who thought close enough was good enough. In many meetings with Vic Gerden, the TSB's Investigator in Charge, he boldly stated that indeed they could be wrong in their findings, but it did not matter. Their purpose was safety, not prosecution.

Very soon, aspects of the crash became known. A serious fire had taken place in the forward area of the aircraft due to an unknown cause. It had resulted in the loss of power to many of the automated systems including the autopilot. Six minutes before the plane flew into the ocean, the cockpit voice recorder and flight data recorder failed. The exact moment of impact was known because it registered on local seismic recorders. There had been no explosion. The first smoke had been smelled by the captain and first officer while on the flight deck. A flight attendant then confirmed there was no sign of smoke in the galley area behind the cockpit. When the flight attendants were told to prepare for a landing, there was no urgency in their preparations. So it was likely the passengers and flight attendants were unaware of the fire during its first stages. Injury analysis showed that first-class passengers had been moved to the plane's rear.

It was also known that some of the onboard materials were flammable. Some thermal insulation blankets had already been ordered to be removed from all Boeing aircraft. The FAA had ordered a five-year replacement plan in the amount of eight billion in 1998 US dollars.

The pilots had prepared for an emergency landing at Halifax. Being too high and having to dump fuel, they turned away from the airport to head out over St Margarets Bay. Confirmation of the fuel-dump took three years. It occurred in the fall of 2001 when I attended the flight path area in Blandford to investigate a complaint of possible aircraft debris on the beach. While retrieving pieces of cabin carpet, I noticed a male on an all-terrain vehicle leaving the beach with a trailer load of seaweed. So I went over to their nearby house to make inquiries. Speaking with the man's wife, I learned she had lost part of her garden during the week following the crash. It could only have been due to fuel contamination. By the quality of the rose and vegetable gardens she had when I spoke with her, there was no other reason for her plants to wither and die as she described. This was a task that should have been completed by investigators during the first weeks of the file. Instead they went door to door during the first days, long before any of the plants showed any signs of fuel contamination, and never returned to complete a follow-up.

Keep in mind the shore area reeked of jet fuel due to the quantity that had been on board. No fire occurred on the water because the burning area inside the aircraft was driven underwater by the force of the impact. Normally this plane would jettison its fuel at an altitude above ten thousand feet with the fuel then dissipating into the air with nothing reaching the ground. However, Vaud had been well below that altitude and flying much slower than normal. While crossing the Aspotogan Peninsula at a height below two thousand feet above sea level, much of the fuel would have reached the ground to contaminate its flight path. Yet even a complete jettison of fuel meant seven thousand pounds remained in the tanks. Because of that, the contamination along the nearby shores that had come from the actual crash was extensive.

Within days of my interview with this resident, other witnesses corroborated the fuel dumping by describing damages to their own properties. Confirmation of the dumping removed one important potential source for the fire. It accounted for a certain valve found to be in one position when otherwise it should have been in the opposite position. In total, it took twenty-seven valves and pumps to operate in exact sequence to allow the fuel dump. Fuel dumping was something that should never have been overlooked.

One of the problems encountered in the initial confirmation of the fuel dumping was the TSB lost the fuel sample that had been taken at the JFK airport immediately after the crash. The container turned up on someone's desk about a year later, but by then continuity for legal purposes was no longer possible.

Other facts were known about fires in this type of aircraft. Being a high-altitude jetliner, its hull was an enclosed and sealed environment except for an air intake system allowing the addition of fresh air to the recirculation system. Prior to the crash, the settings allowed the addition of thirty per cent replacement air during each cycle. While its filters were of the high-quality HEPA type, they did not remove the poisonous and lethal carbon monoxide and cyanide by-products of burning plastics. While never proven through blood toxicology because no blood samples were ever obtained, it was believed everyone succumbed to those gases before impact. Also, the fire would have reduced the oxygen content in the plane to a level that likely could not have sustained life. It was nearly certain it lowered enough to cause the first stages of unconsciousness due to a lack of oxygen. All the passengers and flight attendants would have simply passed out. Toxic air was a common cause of death for fire victims.

The plane's routing called for an altitude of thirty-three thousand feet. Flying at that height for nearly an hour before the fire had caused the skin and frame of the aircraft to reach a temperature of nearly minus 60 degrees Celsius. Being an aluminum alloy, there was a high rate of heat transfer from the inner to the outer surface with cold air passing over it at more than six hundred miles an hour. That was why the interior surface of the skin was lined with two layers of insulation. Each layer was a sealed shiny plastic-like envelope called Metallized Mylar or MPET that enclosed a fibreglass blanket. The sealed envelope was present to keep the insulation not only in place, but dry. The average Swissair flight carried as much as five hundred kilograms or over half a ton of water due to the condensation of the water vapour exhaled by each passenger. This liquid water formed on all the cool surfaces in the overhead area including the Metallized Mylar. So when the fire started, likely many of the above-ceiling surfaces were damp. This would reduce the chance of a mere spark igniting the MPET material. Also, during the fire, the aircraft skin acted as a heat sink to absorb enormous amounts of heat energy before parts attached to it could melt. Even so, reconstruction of the forward overhead area provided evidence of extensive molten sections of the aluminum alloy frames.

During the initial investigation, engineers from various agencies and companies including Swissair, Boeing, as well as members of the TSB and other agencies offered their experienced opinions. They said the extensive melting of the frame was unusual, never seen before, and possibly it could not have been caused solely by flammable material in the area of the fire. That flammable material was called the fire load. Knowing this, during my third

Zurich trip I met with the TSB's main electrical investigator, Jim Foot. He had flown over for meetings and to view the aircraft's electrical systems. Over supper, he stated that at first he had believed the cause of the fire was an incendiary device. This was an astounding revelation, but he never gave any reason why he had changed his mind. Perhaps it was his lack of fire investigative skills. When the first short-circuited wire was found, Jim immediately went to his boss, Vic Gerden, to proclaim he had found the cause of the fire. Another knowledgeable TSB investigator who was present told him he could expect to find dozens of shorted wires. They had been part of a normal electrically charged system during the fire, so a short-circuit was not indicative of a fire cause. In fact, many more were yet to be found. This was basic knowledge for any fire investigator. The question was, did the short-circuit cause the fire or did the fire cause the short-circuit?

Also, two pieces of tile from two small sections of the ceiling at the forward doors were found to have burnt for ten minutes at a temperature of 1100 degrees Fahrenheit. The first finding was they had burnt for five minutes at 1700 degrees Fahrenheit, an extremely high temperature unacceptable to the TSB. The two pieces were identified due to their thickness. Yet neither area had anything above it that would have burnt at that temperature, and certainly not for that long at that temperature. The same area on the plane's right side showed massive heat damage to the forward lift-door track. It was twisted and molten metal was present on it. However, during its handling by TSB members, this molten material was somehow destroyed before it could be properly recorded and analysed. Nevertheless, something at that point burnt for a long time at a high temperature. The location was close to the aircraft skin that was a heat sink to suck away huge amounts of heat, and official burn tests of the materials in the area revealed they did not burn at such excessively high temperatures. This was never properly addressed by the TSB.

During the four years of the investigation, several dozen TSB members worked in the hangar. Many were there for only short periods, but I worked with most of them.

Elaine Summers was one, and she performed a professional investigation of the three engines. Her mannerisms and the way she literally read them impressed me. The engines had a story to tell, and Elaine was the person able to hear that story and coax even more from them. It was no small task considering their size and complexity.

Each engine was controlled by a system called FADEC, or Full Authority Digital Electronic Controls. Attached to each engine, it contacted the plane's Flight Control Computer twenty-five times a second. After receiving directions from the computer, each FADEC adjusted and maintained the settings for its engine. When the electronic connections to the Flight Control Computer burnt off between 1:25:05 hours and 1:25:18 hours GMT, each FADEC maintained the last setting it had received. The crash occurred at 1:35:18 GMT, so the aircraft flew for ten minutes with the engines at settings the pilots could not alter.

No suitable controls were recovered for the #1 engine on the left wing. As for the #2 engine, FADEC showed it had its fuel shut down. It was the engine in the vertical stabilizer at the rear of the aircraft, and this matched its damage as the blades were turning only slowly at the moment of impact. The proper term was 'windmilling' and it was due to the air flowing through the engine as the plane moved forward. The #3 engine was on the right wing. Both #1 and #3 engines may have been at different power settings, but the settings were sufficient to maintain flight. This was evident from the different amounts of damage to the internal fan blades in each engine. What was unusual was that the #3 engine had a bend in its central shaft that was most certainly due to the impact with the ocean. Of interest, neither engine could have been shut down without engaging the engines' manual fire extinguishers if the aircraft had successfully landed.

Randy Vitt worked on various projects including the hydraulic systems. He proved to be very knowledgeable and professional in his work. Both he and Elaine provided me with information about their work and often asked that specific items be photographed or videotaped.

One of the main investigators for the TSB who worked closely with John Garstang and me was Don Enns. Don found key evidence to help in the fire investigation, and he continuously provided advice and help in my investigation. During the file, he too would be divided between offering me support and following the directions of his TSB managers.

While I worked and spoke frequently with all the TSB members to view and understand their parts in the investigation, my main effort was with the four TSB members who actively worked on the file from start to finish. With them, I attended the major tests that gave the most information about the fire and why it should have been investigated as a fire of a criminal cause or arson. The two most important test series were purposely mishandled by the TSB and the RCMP. The first was discredited by underhanded and illegal means. The second was marred by a dishonest test that was then followed by the fraudulent display of a contrived piece of fire evidence.

Auger Electron Spectroscopy was the first test series. AES is the acronym for a specialized analytical method that uses an energetic electron beam to probe the surface and near-surface of a solid specimen (the short-circuited copper beads in this case) while positioned in an ultra-high vacuum. Electrons are emitted that the equipment analyzes to determine their element of origin. At the time of this investigation, it had been in use for more than twenty years. AES is broadly used in industry, university and government laboratories today. It is a major tool for materials research such as thin films, coatings, corrosion, adhesion, and other similar applications. It is used in the Nuclear industry to characterize defective components, in Catalysis R&D and in the computer and microelectronics industry for quality control and development of solid state devices to name just a few fields. AES was instrumental in the investigation of the Challenger space shuttle explosion. At the time of this crash, AES was a proven and accurate scientific method, and above all, it was very expensive. In 1999 it cost approximately one million dollars for a dedicated AES instrument and about the same amount each year to operate it.

AES was used in this investigation because a US university professor named Dr. R.N. Anderson had taken a long-established rule of physics called Sieverts' law and adapted it to fire investigations. He theorized that when an electrical wire, more accurately called a cable, short-circuited during an ongoing fire, the area of the copper wire molten for a small fraction of a second absorbed in its outer layer the smoke surrounding it. However, if the fire started due to a short-circuited wire, at that instant the molten area of the shorted wire absorbed normal clean air because the fire had not yet begun. AES was the method to determine the difference.

Just to clarify, a short-circuit on a wire occurs where an electrically charged bare wire contacts a grounded surface or another bare wire. The result is a spark, extreme heat, and the melting of the metals at the point of contact to solidify usually as a bead-like structure. Anyone who has seen lightning in the sky has witnessed nature's short-circuiting event in action. Being a sound scientific method, AES was the best technique to find the contents of the bead's outer layer. Dr. Anderson, whom I met in Seattle, interpreted that data to create a timeline for the absorption of those elements, but his method was merely a theory. One important factor that Dr. Anderson stated in Seattle was the short-circuited bead of copper keeps no memory of how it was made. Variations in the type of current, the voltage, or the amperage played no part in the results. That the metal liquefied and again solidified in an instant was all that mattered. Sieverts' law, the basis for Anderson's theory, was a long-proven rule of physics, and in common language, it stated a liquid absorbs the gasses surrounding it in direct proportion to its temperature and pressure.

Typical of fires involving an active electrical system, when all the aircraft debris was recovered and examined, more than thirty short-circuited locations were found on some of the two hundred and fifty miles of wiring. Due to the nature of the fire, it was worth the effort to use the AES process and see if Dr. Anderson's theory would work. Anderson had done the work over a period of years, but his results were never verified and documented in a proper scientific manner. His theory was relatively unproven even though he had successfully provided Court evidence in the US on at least one occasion. While the idea behind the Anderson theory and Sieverts' law seemed obvious, throughout the AES testing for this file, numerous problems would arise to put unnecessary confusion into the outcome.

The TSB had located an AES unit in Ottawa at CANMET, the Canada Centre for Mineral and Energy Technology of Natural Resources Canada. Dr. James Brown operated the system, having used the AES equipment for more than twenty years. Jim, who had a Ph.D. in Geology from the University of Western Ontario, held several patents for inventions resulting from his research activities, had lectured across North America, in Europe and Japan, and had written articles, too many to state here. He was recognized as the best AES operator in Canada and likely all of North America. AES was not a simple system to use or they would not need a Ph.D. It required a complete knowledge and understanding of chemistry, geology, and other advanced sciences to interpret the results. What's more, it required experience and patience. Jim Brown had these qualifications. When first asked about Dr. Brown, the TSB member, Gus Sidla, said Dr. James Brown was the best and we were lucky to have him.

On meeting him, Jim immediately impressed me with his ease and confidence with the equipment and the process, along with his vast knowledge of chemistry and the other sciences needed to be the best in his profession. Jim was a big man, but his actions were gentle and with much finesse. When operating equipment dealing in depths of mere angstrom units, there was no room for harsh and abrupt actions. One inch is 254 million angstrom units. An average human hair is about 800,000 angstrom units thick. The depths we were examining ranged from about 10 to 5,000 angstrom units deep. To help me understand it all, Jim had the ability to communicate science in such a manner that he could just as easily have taught a high school class of chemistry or physics one day and then gone to teach an advanced university course on geology the next. He equalled John Garstang in his ability to describe a highly complicated and intricate system in such a manner that someone like me with no prior knowledge of the procedure and with only a basic background in chemistry and physics could understand.

Beginning in September of 1999, five trips were made to CANMET to have Dr. Brown analyze three separate sets of short-circuited wires, technically called cables. The main set, of course, consisted of the debris wires from the aircraft. The second set were those made at the Boeing Electrical Lab in Seattle under controlled conditions. Because of what Dr. Brown found during the debris wire examinations, a third controlled series of cables was created in the hangar and subjected to the special conditions he determined as necessary.

This third series was divided into three identical groups of various types of cables, each about 45 cm or 18 inches long and bare at both ends. Each group was fixed to its own specially prepared pallet. One group consisted of wires attached to the pallet with their bare ends free. A second identical group had one end of each wire fastened through individual holes in an aluminum alloy frame piece fixed to the pallet while the other end of each wire was in direct contact with a secured piece of pure magnesium rudder pedal from the aircraft. The remaining third group had one end of each wire fixed to another piece of aluminum alloy in the same manner while the other end was free. The three pallets were submerged separately in fifty feet of ocean for thirty days.

The AES tests conducted during the first trip revealed the presence of varying amounts of magnesium, aluminum, iron, and traces of zinc in some of the aircraft debris beads. The twisted strands of wires were pure copper with a thin coating of nickel or tin on each of the eighteen strands making up the insulated cable. Some of the beads revealed these four elements while others showed only the basic original elements. Mere traces of other elements also appeared periodically. As might be expected when it is understood that smoke is a variable and inconsistent physical mixture of the many compounds found in the burning materials, none of the AES test sites on the debris wire beads provided data that was the exact duplicate of other locations. This was true even when two or three test sites were on the same wire bead but positioned on different sides. That same trend was found in all the examined aircraft and test wires. One test site provided a magnesium reading of forty-five percent without any aluminum at all, and another of forty percent. Other sites provided aluminum and magnesium in nearly equal amounts or aluminum with no magnesium. In some sites, the amount of oxygen nearly equaled the combined amounts of aluminum and magnesium, while it was much less at other locations. Other beads showed nothing but copper and either tin or nickel plus the expected atmospheric elements. While an unbiased expert would consider these results to be a natural occurrence when formed under certain conditions, unfortunately, that was not the attitude of some of the TSB members and those Force supervisors who oversaw the RCMP's file. That they had no knowledge or expertise in the matter made no difference to their belief they could carry out the correct interpretations of the AES test results.

As in any arson investigation, legitimate onboard sources were sought. Over the next two years, exhaustive examinations of aircraft samples and the specially designed exemplar wires failed to locate a legitimate source for these unexpected elements.

One of the problems for the AES data interpretation was that both the aircraft skin and the frame materials were made of an aluminum alloy containing small amounts of magnesium. It was less than five percent with minute amounts of other specific elements added for strength. As the investigation progressed, I came to see that pieces of the frame material and other internal structures had melted due to the intense heat of the fire. However, those high temperatures came nowhere near what was required to burn the aircraft's alloy material containing the magnesium and aluminum. The flame front temperature for the MPET was just too low. While some areas of the frame material had melted, in adjacent areas there was no damage to the inside surface of the skin alloy and even the paint was untouched as the blankets of insulation had provided protection from the heat and flames. After extensive testing, Dr. Brown determined with confidence that the magnesium and aluminum in the short-circuited beads could not have come from the aircraft skin and frame or any other legitimate onboard source. Long before that happened, at the end of the initial test session at CANMET, Dr. Brown provided three possible scenarios as a preliminary attempt to explain the presence of these questioned elements.

The first scenario was that there had been an exceptionally high-temperature fire in which the aircraft skin, frame, and other objects were already burning. The molten wire bead then absorbed the magnesium that was already released from the burning structural aluminum. However, this would require what he called selective absorption of the mere five percent of magnesium in far greater quantities than the aluminum. That just did not happen in nature. Where did the iron come from as there was none in the fire zone? Where did the other alloyed elements go? He thought zinc might have been present in the paint but to what quantities he did not know. Tests would later prove it was not the source. There was no zinc in the aircraft paint.

Besides the points against this scenario offered by Dr. Brown, what would have caused the extremely high temperatures required to enable the solid aluminum alloy frame to burn? Undoubtedly an enormous amount of accelerant was needed to acquire such temperatures.

The second possible scenario was that the wires absorbed magnesium, iron, zinc and aluminum while on the seafloor. Because of the activity of seawater or the presence of minute fissures or cracks in the wires, there may have been a movement of those elements into the wires. However, Dr. Brown felt this was highly unlikely because he had not found the other elements that were present in seawater. Saltwater contained an abundance of various elements, the majority of which were missing from these beads. He suggested clean, new sample wires should be submerged in the immediate area for a month to see what would happen and, as described already, this was eventually done. The resulting tests showed there was no transfer of the suspect elements.

The third scenario was an incendiary device high in magnesium and the other elements that he was finding. The nature of the device was open to one's imagination.

Consider this. John Garstang explained that the solid alloy skin and frame were impossible to ignite except with exceptionally high heat, well above the range of this fire. However, magnesium ribbon or powder was easily ignited and was commonly used to ignite aluminum powder. A thermite device along with many criminal incendiary devices utilized these ingredients. They burnt hot enough to melt aluminum, and considerable amounts of molten aluminum were found in the debris. Such devices were frequently used to weld rails during railroad track repairs.

BURNING MATERIALS TEMPERATURE CHART

	Ignition Temp C° / F°	Melt Temp C° / F°	Flame Temp C° / F°
ALUMINUM BLOCK	3826/6920	659/1218	
MAGNESIUM BLOCK	3099/5610	650/1202	
METALLIZED MYLAR			1203/2200
ALUMINUM POWDER	760/1400	659/1218	3173-3273/ 5743-5923
MAGNESIUM RIBBON	473/883		2482/ 500
CHARCOAL FIRE	349/660		750-1200/ 1382-2192
CANDLE	650/1202		1100-1400/ 2012-2552
GASOLINE	400/752		1026/1879
WOOD	300/572		1027/1881

THE LAST FOUR ITEMS IN THE LIST ARE PROVIDED TO ALLOW A COMPARISON OF MORE COMMONLY KNOWN FIRE MATERIALS

During the AES testing, Larry Fogg was present throughout and recorded all the readings that he then forwarded nightly to the Boeing engineers. Because of this, he and his Boeing contacts were completely aware of the AES findings and their implications. Throughout the testing, these issues were frequently discussed with him. When Dr. Brown provided these three scenarios, it did not come as a surprise to either of us.

Once Dr. Brown told me of his preliminary opinion based on his initial findings, I needed to act on it immediately. Dr. Brown was a highly credible and reliable information source and his preliminary findings and explanations had to be forwarded to my supervisors as soon as possible. Indeed, this was the most important information we had yet received regarding the cause of the fire, and for me, it contributed additional grounds to suspect a criminal cause for the fire.

My immediate RCMP supervisor in the hangar was Staff/Sergeant Vic Gorman. Vic was one rank above me but had been in Ident Services a few years less than me. About seven or eight years before this crash, he had moved into the blood spatter interpretation unit in Halifax after several years of training in Ottawa. His position was classified as a S/Sgt due to the special work the unit did, so he completely bypassed the Sergeant's rank. Vic had been second in charge in the morgue as an administrator, and we had worked well together even though there had been some friction over the purchase of supplies. However, there was nothing that had not been ironed out when the morgue was finished. Vic, with his bushy mustache and graying hair, appeared as easy going and was well-liked by everyone. I had known him since my time in Yellowknife when he was on the south side of the Great Slave Lake in Hay River Ident, N.W.T.

Vic's new boss on the file was the Officer in Charge of the Swissair Task Force, Inspector Andy Lathem. An Inspector was the first rank of the commissioned officers of the RCMP. Like the Canadian Armed Forces, officers in the RCMP obtained a Queen's Commission, and with it came certain legal powers and privileges. While I had worked with many of Lathem's investigators from the Major Crime Unit, I had met him only once before this file and had only minimal contact with him so far in this investigation.

His task force had an office in the back corner of the hangar from which they came and went. Most of the members of the group

I knew well, while others I was meeting for the first time. In the first days of the investigation, the unit had been quite large with several dozen members, but it slowly dwindled down until, by September of 1999, it only had two Constables and three Corporals along with Vic and Andy doing the administration supported by a public servant position. Of the group, only Vic and one of the Corporals had any background in fire investigations. Because of that, part of Vic's work entailed specialized photography to record the fire damage on some of the skin and frame pieces. The time he spent doing this was curtailed due to his Court commitments around the Maritimes for his previous blood spatter job as well as his role as the acting Identification Supervisor for the Maritime region. Lee Fraser had been promoted due to the success of the morgue and had gone back to Ottawa as a Superintendent with the title of Director of the RCMP's Forensic Identification Services for the country.

Once Dr. Brown provided me with his preliminary opinions, I put together a memo for Vic and Andy. I had been speaking with Gus Sidla and Jim Foot of the TSB and knew they did not consider the results to be at all important. They were simply looking for a 'clean' wire, one with only copper, either tin or nickel, and normal atmospheric elements. Nothing else seemed to be of importance to them. What's more, the Swissair representative had already complained the process was taking too long, and it should either be sped up or stopped. Foot's reaction to this was that Dr. Brown would be conducting the testing at his pace, thus making it a slow process. This statement left me confused. There was a strong possibility Dr. Brown had found evidence of a criminal cause for the fire. That was something I understood the TSB did not handle. Why was he so adamant the present test methods would continue? Before too long I would learn the truth of Foot's statement and what his actual desire was for the AES tests.

As strange as it may seem, my actual fear was the Force would overreact and demand to take over the testing. The TSB's floor investigators had warned if this ever happened, they would be out of the hangar so fast there would be just a cloud of dust left behind. Knowing the limited resources we had for investigations of this sort, we needed John Garstang's abilities and experience to guide the way. Other knowledgeable TSB floor investigators would be very difficult to replace, including Don Enns. John had already told me that as far as the TSB's legislation was concerned, Air India was his only criminal investigation. He and others had warned that none of the TSB members could ever conduct any criminal investigation on the Swissair file. I was also worried about Lathem's capabilities and decisions so far in this file. It had taken a concerted effort to have him and Gorman agree to my attendance in Seattle for the creation of the short-circuited test wires, and only after stressing the special handling and processing of the actual wire exhibits did they realize I had to attend. Even then, I had to overcome the protests of Jim Foot while they both stood silently by.

What I hoped for was a continuation of things as they were, except we would have more input and control of the AES testing, and especially more of a two-way flow of information. Most of the work was being performed by the RCMP solely for the TSB's safety file. There were already areas of the debris damage that were suspicious, and I felt there was a need to know certain details and facts. Too often I had asked for test results or official information only to be told I would have to submit a memo through Gorman to Lathem outlining my reasons for obtaining it. Only if they both agreed would it be sent off to the TSB where Gerden would make the final decision. Usually, I received a negative response along with the explanation that since I was not a pilot or connected to aviation, I would not understand the implications of the information. Some of the time, that denial came from Gorman or Lathem when they refused to forward the requests. A negative response never deterred me because I had other sources. Their actions were at the very least a nuisance and aggravation as I was not accustomed to being denied anything in an investigation certainly not by a civilian agency with no knowledge whatsoever of how to conduct a criminal investigation, and that lacked the proper resources to do their own.

So, a memo was written to show the importance of the findings while trying to keep my management from overreacting. This was overly successful. When I returned from Ottawa, I found everything still the same. No one knew of the results as Vic had issued a strong warning to me not to discuss any of this with anyone, even in the hangar. Andy had decided it was now classed as secret even though outside civilian agencies and foreign companies had that data.

On Sunday, I received a phone call from the Officer in Charge of Criminal Operations for Nova Scotia's 'H' Division, Chief Superintendent Duncan. He had read the memo and understood my intentions. As the Criminal Operations Officer, his statement to me was I must be present for every test and maintain an active involvement in all aspects of the physical evidence file in case it proves to be of a criminal origin. His directions covered only part of what I had wanted, but there was going to be nothing else. What's more, these instructions would be short-lived.

Several weeks later during an RCMP investigators' meeting, Lathem again made a statement that he had made soon after my return from AES. He said it would be "folly and reckless" to change the course of the investigation. The Force would maintain its present position of support to the TSB and nothing else until there was "irrefutable evidence of a criminal act." Lathem said that C/Supt. Duncan was aware of this as was the Division Commanding Officer, Assistant Commissioner Bishop. Supported by Gorman, Lathem went on to describe the initial AES findings as "merely opinion evidence and not as reliable as first-hand eye-witness evidence." When I heard this, I quickly wrote it down because I would never have believed a senior police officer had said it. Once I finished pondering what I thought was the sheer stupidity of his statement, I asked about demanding a better information flow between the two agencies. Three of Lathem's investigators quickly told me Gerden would only supply what he wanted us to know and nothing else. They went on to make comments about Dr. Brown having a cottage bought and paid for by Boeing, and they belittled the AES tests. Neither Lathem nor Gorman objected. Their statements offended me. I wanted to tell them that had they experienced what I saw and did in the morgue, perhaps they would have had a more professional outlook. However, such an experience should not be required for proper police procedures to be followed. These guys were amateurs, and they had insulted both Dr. Brown and me. I was disgusted, and these statements started me to doubt not only my RCMP supervisors' abilities, but even their integrity.

This meeting was a turning point in my relationship with Lathem and Gorman. Until now I had been part of the investigative team. I knew what my role was and what they were to do. I was to handle the physical evidence and to follow the trail it created. This had been confirmed by Lathem back on the 26th of November, 1998, when in a meeting, he stated the physical evidence had to be processed in accordance with court requirements. As for the role of

Lathem and Gorman and those above them, they were to provide administrative support and guidance and, above all, not to hinder or interfere. That was certainly in line with what Duncan had said to me over the phone. Now everything had suddenly changed, and I had a problem with what they had expressed in this meeting. However, any attempt at a protest on my part was met with a brick wall. The file would be handled as Lathem had stated.

Immediately upon making my first comment, Lathem would have known what I was thinking. My face always gave me away because I was never good at hiding my feelings. Lathem and the others would have been able to read me like a book and know I did not agree, that I felt it was completely wrong to handle the file in this manner, and that I was disgusted with their attitude. Because of his lack of experience with both physical evidence and serious investigations, Lathem probably felt intimidated by me and considered me to be a major threat to whatever had been planned for the file. His way of overcoming that, for now, was to set himself apart from me by ensuring Gorman was the go-between and that I had no direct contact with him. Later, after Gorman left, I would see the use of intimidation and punishment tactics.

As for the TSB, when Foot and Sidla, actively involved in the AES process, realized the implications of the magnesium, aluminum, and iron issue, they began a continuous and active move to shut down the tests. I could not allow this even though it became more and more difficult to counter. During a much later meeting with Duncan, Lathem condescendingly described me as the conscience of the TSB because of my stand on this testing.

Opposition continued from the two TSB members. What I realized were false contaminated wires were supplied in what could only be described as a concerted effort to sabotage the overall AES test results. When Dr. Brown officially asked for specific test cables, I put together a plan to create a series of short-circuited wires that were exposed to somewhat similar conditions as were those from the aircraft. Continuous opposition was encountered from the TSB against the creation of these seawater test wires with various excuses being given. However, after extensive efforts and persuasion, suitable test wires were created with some being exposed to a pure magnesium rudder pedal from the aircraft. Only four such pedals were on the plane and the only other pure magnesium parts on the MD-11 consisted of small pieces in the door locking mechanisms. Nothing else on the aircraft was made of pure magnesium, so no such source was in the fire zone. Nor was there any pure aluminum source since all the materials were an aluminum alloy with various other elements added for strength.

Around this time, I had a conversation with the TSB member who investigated the In-Flight Entertainment Network, or IFEN. Andre was tall and athletic, well educated, and gave the appearance of a cool, calm professional. In his time off, he sailed and had plans to travel along the East Coast waters during the upcoming summer. He stated he felt it unlikely the IFEN had been the cause of the fire. He had searched the history of the system in the Swissair aircraft and found they never had a fault in any unit in their fleet. The Swissair system was different to those installed in other airlines around the world. Those systems suffered problems that had branded all entertainment systems alike. He admitted there had been something wrong with the wiring installation, but that had been because, after viewing the setup, the TSB did not like how it had been put together. Therefore, they had labeled it as faulty, something that was their opinion and contrary to that of the company's. As for turning off the system, all wires had been properly fused. It was simply a matter of not routing them through the normal bus system switch. The pilots had never been alerted that they needed to go to the fuse panel to shut down the system. While it was more of a Swissair managerial fault than an installer's, that lack of knowledge on the part of the pilots proved they had never had a previous fault in the system, certainly not while in the air, or every pilot would have been told how to shut it down.

In a much later conversation with the same investigator, he continued to say that nothing had ever occurred in one aircraft of the fleet that had shown a system fault that might then happen in several planes. Unlike the many car companies' recalls for repairs of brakes or ignition problems due to faulty parts, nothing like that had ever occurred in the Swissair fleet.

During the conversation, Andre was astounded when I told him of the AES findings, and he stated there was nothing on board to account for those readings. What was even more important was that his reaction had shed light on how the TSB worked. He did not know of the AES results because the TSB compartmentalized its information on a 'need to know' basis even though they had weekly information meetings to discuss their progress and important factors. As for Swissair, one of their managers later revealed he had been told the magnesium issue was solved. At the time, there was still an ongoing but failing attempt to find a legitimate source.

Meanwhile, one of Lathem's back room investigators, Karl Christiansen, had identified possible subjects of interest including bin Laden and his jihadist group, Al Qaeda, if the file ever became a criminal matter. Besides his other tasks, Karl had been asked by Lathem to consider an Internet reference that Swissair 111 had crashed on the anniversary date of the destruction of Pan Am 103 over Lockerbie, depending, of course, on what calendar system was used. That was a proven act of murder and terrorism that had killed two hundred and fifty-nine passengers and crew onboard a 747 aircraft as well as eleven people in their homes in the Scottish town of Lockerbie when much of the debris fell on the town. Karl's extensive examination involved research of recent world events, open-source information and further expansion of the limited passenger information available to investigators. It must be noted this was taking place in 1999, more than two years before bin Laden and his group became common household knowledge because of his cold-blooded and cowardly terrorist attacks of 9/11.

Like many others, Karl had come into Hangar A immediately following the crash to help organize the initial stages of the reconstruction process. Once finished, he returned to his regular duties in Halifax Headquarters only to be brought back shortly after I started in Hangar A. He was now on indefinite secondment to the Swissair Task Force as there was a need to examine all the burnt pieces of debris. They had to be categorized as to the amount of burning they had undergone. Karl's team viewed the discolouration of the item's paint, or if no paint, then the discolouration of the metal. Sample pieces of the various metals had been specially baked at specific times versus temperatures, and they were used as a guide for comparison purposes. Since Karl had training and experience in fire investigations, besides his other responsibilities he was assigned to work with Gus Sidla of the TSB as a member of the burn team.

Vic Gorman was to be their photographer. Because of his other commitments, Tim Walker soon replaced him. Tim had completed his training as a firearms examiner for the Forensic Crime Lab, so his qualifications to examine metal were extensive.

He would soon become a valued member of the Halifax Ident Section.

During this period, I worked with Clyde Cantelope, another Ident member, to physically match and photograph all the debris pieces hung on the airframe reconstruction jig. He had been a great Sergeant to work for in Bathurst, N.B., and in this file we worked equally well together.

As for Karl, he had previously been in the Criminal Intelligence Branch as the Corporal in Charge of the Casino Intelligence Section. He oversaw investigations into the involvement of organized crime and corruption in the casino industry in Nova Scotia. Karl had an extensive background in the investigation of major crimes and knew what should be done by a police investigator when working a file like this, especially when doing the work tasked of him. Karl thought more than he talked, and when he listened to others, he was taking mental notes of what they said. The transfer of that information to computer notes, especially in areas concerning the cause of the fire, created an issue between Karl and some of his backroom co-investigators. Karl, like me, believed the notes needed to reflect the tone and rationale of the investigation if it ever became a criminal matter. Some lawyer would surely ask why something was or was not done, and there was a need to include those details for credibility and clarity of testimony in Court. The TSB had already suggested a three-year investigation would not be uncommon for an incident such as this, so there would be many details to remember. What can only be called interference by Karl's co-investigators was passed up the chain of command to Lathem who then handled the matter his way. However, considering what Karl knew and suspected at the time, and everything that came after that stage of the investigation, I would call Lathem's methods criminal obstruction.

Karl had successfully lobbied for a meeting with the FBI investigators from New York, specifically those involved in the TWA 800 crash investigation. That 747 passenger jet had taken off from JFK airport on July 17th, 1996, and twelve minutes later, it blew up over Long Island, New York, killing all two hundred and thirty people. It fell into the Atlantic Ocean eight miles off shore. Initially, Karl wanted the FBI investigators to visit the Shearwater Hangar to view the partial aircraft reconstruction and to offer their experience and expertise developed during the TWA investigation.

This original plan soon changed when Lathem indicated the venue had to move. Specific backroom investigators would travel to New York to undertake the meeting there. Lathem never explained his reasons for wanting the change, but it effectively prevented the FBI's crash investigators from viewing the Swissair 111 physical evidence. Lathem, Stothart, London and Karl met with several US government agencies in New York to discuss various aspects of the investigation. Included in the array of topics were discussions about the burnt areas of the MD-11 aircraft and the AES testing. While only I had proper firsthand knowledge of these specific physical evidence topics, they were presented by other RCMP investigators who knew nothing about the aircraft or the scientific process. The reason given by Lathem for my non-attendance was that I had already travelled enough, so I had to remain in the hangar. On returning, Lathem provided me with false information about the FBI's failed experience with AES and short-circuited wires on the TWA investigation. Soon after, a report was submitted to senior Force management that I thought was amateurish. That report, none of which was authored by Karl, was prepared to summarize the points of discussion with the various government agencies during the meeting. However, its contents and conclusions were far from being unanimous amongst the investigators who had attended in New York.

Among other things, it contained statements attributing the high heat and fire damage to dust balls and aluminum filings within the overhead system. However, no such thing existed in the attic area on any of the examined aircraft. Even if it had existed, it would have contributed only a minuscule amount to the fire load, a mere moment's flick of a Bic lighter. While London wrote of dust balls, he failed to mention the lack of a fire load. Later discussions with him revealed that his opinions had been based on my written observations in my Zurich trip notes. However, the more he argued his point, the more his recollection of my notes and observations seemed to have been misconstrued. London told me he had no fire investigative skills whatsoever; therefore, he should never have attended the meeting, let alone go on to write the report.

It was eight pages with many sections faulty to the point I had to wonder if it had been written so on purpose. London did recommend passenger profiling should be continued, but with it being more than a year and a half into the file, it was evident that was never going to happen. This report went forward to senior Force management with a cover memo from Lathem, parts of which were written by London and Purchase, the third backroom Corporal. Lathem recommended the closure of the investigation because there was no evidence of a criminal act as the cause of the crash even though he had the AES results staring him in the face. Soon after, the RCMP's investigative file was shut down, and Lathem's investigators left the hangar.

Before they left, several meetings took place in the hangar between the TSB and the RCMP investigators including the TSB's Vic Gerden. He was small of stature, very quiet and focused. As a retired Canadian Air Force Colonel, he purportedly had flown fighter aircraft. Gerden proved to be very capable of gliding around issues while refusing to make the decisions I thought should have been a normal progression of events.

My supervisors, Andy Lathem backed by Gorman, failed to provide support for what I believed should have been a parallel criminal investigation. In one of the many meetings with the TSB dealing with AES and the magnesium issue, Gorman assured Gerden that no criminal investigation was being carried out by the RCMP. In several of those meetings, the TSB's electrical investigator, Jim Foot, made statements that AES was undertaken only to locate the initiating short-circuit and not to find some other fire cause or magnesium source. What appeared to be a bias that the fire cause could only have been due to an accidental electrical short-circuit was so blatant I felt it was interfering with a fair and objective investigation. My supervisors failed to take heed that any investigation must follow the trail of evidence and not go only in the direction as plotted by a safety investigator and his management team.

To reinforce their stand, in several closed-door encounters, both Lathem and Gorman met with me in my small Ident office to forcefully demand I cease my activities and not conduct a criminal investigation of any kind. They said the Force was in an 'evidence gathering mode' and once everything was examined, if the TSB deemed it necessary, only then would we conduct a criminal investigation. On several occasions, I was accused by Gorman and Lathem of trying to lead the evidence examination into a criminal investigation when there was no reason or authority to do so. I assured them I was merely following the evidence trail. Their response in no uncertain terms was to tell me to cease. Their tone was sufficiently threatening that I knew I could not openly fight their demands, and instead I had to work as quietly as possible. However, I did not need to lead anything into a criminal investigation because the evidence was going there on its own, and I was following along right behind it whether or not they wanted or liked it. I was conducting a criminal investigation, and I did not need their blessing to do it. They could only stop me by removing me from the hangar. Even though that would be illegal, I knew Lathem would do it if ever he felt he had adequate reason to make that decision. So, I had to work as secretively as possible while maintaining an involvement in as many areas of the investigation as I could.

The die had been set in the very first of these meetings when Gorman, without Lathem present, told me he agreed with my position regarding the need for a criminal investigation. However, he then continued to add that Lathem had ruled against it and he must support his officer. My thoughts were that Gorman had reneged on his duties. This file was a sudden death investigation, and there was an evidence trail to follow. Since Lathem seemed to be in the dark in knowing how to follow that trail, he needed to be given a flashlight and a road map with directions on how to use both. While my memos and reports were providing the information and direction, Gorman, as an experienced Ident member and the second in charge, should have provided him with the guidance whether or not Lathem wanted it.

These meetings at times became quite intense. The Ident office was two rooms. The back room, about ten by ten feet, was used for storage only. The front office area, a bit larger at about ten by twelve feet, had two desks in it, several file drawers and an upright storage cabinet. The free space in the centre of the room amounted to about four by five feet. When two people were there, it was close. When it was three, it was tight. As I had only two chairs, we stood or sat on the edge of the desks. Moreover, it was noisy. Even closing the door did not keep out the noise from the hangar floor. Our military tin-knockers pounded and drilled all day long, and others were always moving something about to create loud noises. The high pitch of the air drill was similar to the sounds of whales calling, only even more shrill and much louder. Add in a forklift along with the helicopters travelling by the hangar. Voices were naturally raised during any meeting merely to overcome the external sounds. Those loud voices certainly did not help keep the atmosphere calm considering some of the things being said.

One favourite complaint from Lathem was that I had not put my latest memo or report through the proper channels before he received it. It was supposed to go through Gorman who first was to review and add his comments. Sometimes it ended up on Lathem's desk first. Considering there were about ten feet and three inches between Lathem's and Gorman's desk and both were in the same office facing each other, I did not think he had a complaint. Several memos and many verbal communications were expended telling me they had to go through Gorman first. Rather trivial considering I was trying to investigate the possible murder of two hundred and twenty-nine people and Gorman was often out of the hangar for weeks on end.

As for the other meetings, they were all a continuous attempt to control what I was doing in the hangar. In any investigation, what the physical evidence indicated and what was done about it was not a decision to be made by a file administrator. After removing the rank and ceremony, Latham was only a paper pusher who appeared to know nothing about physical evidence or fire investigations. What's more, his effort in this actual investigation was minimal. I don't think he spent more than a quarter of his time in the hangar, and seldom was he ever on the hangar floor to see what work was being done. As time progressed, he spent even less time on this file. He had a Major Crime Unit to run as well as other duties, and he travelled across Canada giving lectures with a variety of prepared Power Point presentations of the Swissair file. Gorman paralleled Lathem's activities with his duties outside of the hangar. When they were in the hangar, each made sure they took their allotted daily breaks along with their extra half-hour exercise time. So as the onsite physical evidence investigator with more than sufficient qualifications and experience, it was my call. I was the person who would be accountable to a Judge to tell him I now had reasonable and probable grounds to suspect a criminal incendiary device may have caused the fire resulting in the deaths of two hundred and twenty-nine people.

These things were not said to Gorman because I knew Lathem would react adversely and remove me from the hangar. I had continuously gone against his expressed orders. By doing that, I faced not only his temper, but his authority to do as he wanted. He had the ability to intimidate merely by his presence and presentation, let alone by the power of his position that would provide him the means to punish me for the rest of my career.

These were not my first discussions with Gorman as we had spoken about various aspects of the file much earlier. Each time it had become more and more evident his position was to support Lathem in whatever he said. My suspicions were later confirmed that everything I said and did was reported back to Lathem. What's more, Gorman was not the only one reporting to him. To say the walls had many eyes and an equal number of ears was an understatement.

I soon learned Gorman was seeking his commission as an officer, and for him to go against Lathem would end any chance he might have had for that promotion. By the time of the AES initial testing, Gorman had taken a largely administrative role in this file, and soon enough he only rarely ventured onto the hangar floor to take photos. He occasionally spoke with the TSB investigators, but only sporadically, and certainly not often enough to know the dynamics of the physical evidence investigation as each facet progressed. That had to be done two or three times a day, not once every two or three weeks. I felt he never achieved a proper feel for the file, but perhaps he did not need to as that may not have been the goal for the RCMP's management. It took a very long time, but eventually I would receive the documentation to show this.

It had quickly become clear I could not openly go against their ruling even though it was contrary to everything I had ever stood for in my career. While in New York to meet with the FBI, Karl had also met with representatives of the BATF, or the Bureau of Alcohol, Tobacco, and Firearms. He had enquired if they would be interested in viewing the aircraft reconstruction jig, and possibly offer their opinions as to the cause of the fire damage found on some of the debris exhibits of interest to the investigation. The engineers he spoke with were considered some of the best fire and explosives investigators in the US, perhaps the world, and they indicated their willingness and eagerness to attend Halifax if Karl could arrange it. However, Lathem, after he returned to the hangar, learned of this initiative and immediately prohibited their attendance.

After doing that, Lathem was not finished with him. Karl later told me that in an ensuing meeting, Lathem informed him he did not like what Karl had recorded in his investigative notes. Lathem presented him with what Karl described as an unconscionable request to change his investigative notes. Karl said he was insulted and incredulous by Lathem's actions, and he asked Lathem to withdraw the request, which he did. A few days later, Lathem acted to regain control by blatantly exercising what he seemed to believe was within his authority as the Officer in Charge. Karl said that in doing it, Lathem was visibly upset with the issue of the investigative notes and the potential invitation of the BATF fire experts. Lathem ordered Karl out of the hangar, to have no more association with the file, and to have no more contact with me.

As soon as Karl informed me of this, it confirmed my belief I had to be very careful with my investigation, including how I acted and what was said to others. Karl was conducting what we both believed was a criminal investigation in that he was an integral part of the fire team and was examining debris for fire evidence, and he already knew of the initial AES results. If Lathem could kick him out of the hangar, certainly he could have removed me and forced someone else to take over the Ident duties the TSB required.

Up until then, I, too, had been keeping excellent notes of everything I heard, saw and did. Now I started to keep even better notes. What's more, I now held numerous copies of those notes in various locations. I used Word to write my notes instead of the Force's data program, so making copies was an easy process. I had both a stand-alone desktop computer and a laptop for my use. The notes were copied to floppy disks at the end of each day and kept with me. Weekly, the files went to CDs and exterior drive cartridges that were then stored in safe offsite locations. After all, a dusty old 1950s hangar could easily have a wiring problem that could suddenly catch fire and destroy my Ident office and everything in it. I did not know what to expect or when the hammer might fall. I continuously hoped they would soon see what I already suspected, but I was not expecting that anytime soon. I did know I was alone when it came to Lathem's potential wrath.

Meanwhile, some of the TSB's hangar floor investigators quietly supported my endeavors. John Garstang, as my TSB supervisor and main contact, constantly informed me of important exhibits, test results, and what his intended plans were for the investigation. John was the TSB member who planned and undertook most of the specialized testing and procedures. Thus he guided the specialized areas of the TSB's physical evidence investigation. When the AES results showing magnesium, iron, and aluminum first surfaced, it was John who fully explained their connection to an incendiary device, and he directed me to a website providing detailed information on such a device and how to make it.

Don Enns, who became a good friend, advised me that when he learned of the magnesium issue, he had suggested the TSB should turn the whole AES matter over to the RCMP and let us run with it. He said Vic Gerden and senior TSB file administrators immediately rejected the idea.

Help also came from Larry Fogg. He was Jim Foot's main source of investigative knowledge in electrical components and related structures. Without Larry, Jim would have been lost. Foot failed to inform me of anything he had worked on unless he knew I already had the information. However, Larry almost daily waved me over to his office on the TSB side of the hangar to show me something of importance. Each time, I always came away with new material for my notes and numerous key photographs to be added to the main collection.

About the time that the visit of the BATF investigators was rejected, John attempted to bring in Dr. Quintiere, a US university professor and Ph.D. who was one of two world-renowned authorities on aircraft fires. John wanted him to view the debris and offer his opinion. His attendance never came to fruition because senior TSB management did not want to run the risk of having such a renowned expert provide an opinion of a fire of criminal origin. This was the same reason why the BATF investigators had been disallowed. The excuse given for the Doctor was that he had been hired by one of the partner companies as a consultant, and consultants could not be present for any of the investigation. I offered John a way of getting around that, but it soon became apparent Gerden never wanted Dr. Quintiere to step foot inside the hangar. I later received a copy of an email between Dr. Quintiere and Don Enns in which the Doctor wrote that the fire load in the aircraft by itself could never have produced the damage that was done. He felt the presence of an accelerant was most likely. He based this in part on the photos of the debris and reconstruction, and the rest was based on his extensive experience in aircraft fire investigations and knowledge of the materials that would have made up the fire load.

One question about the magnesium issue was how a criminal device could have been planted on the aircraft and where. During the second Zurich trip, I saw an innocent event occur that, under different circumstances, could have been the delivery of such a criminal device to the plane. While at JFK airport in New York, the aircraft's right forward door was always open to allow access by the service crews. Someone with criminal intent and minimal instructions could have easily entered under the guise of a service attendant to open ceiling hatches and deliver one or more criminal devices in the exact area where the most heat and fire damage had occurred.

A method of making an incendiary device was easily found on the internet using iron, magnesium, and aluminum as its ingredients. The small amounts of zinc could have come from the control mechanism or the carrying case. While in Los Angeles for the air flow flight test, I attempted to purchase the actual book by the same author. I was told it not only was sold out, but it was a popular book that did not last long on the book shelves.

As an indicator of what magnesium and aluminum can do in a fire, consider the space shuttle's solid fuel rocket boosters. They contained a solid petroleum fuel that, without magnesium and aluminum powders in the mixture, would have been unable to provide the required heat that in turn was thrust to lift the spacecraft into orbit.

Recently, an article by Howard Simon dated May 22, 1995, was found on the internet. It dealt with what was then a new and dangerous type of arson occurring in the USA, from the Pacific Northwest to the Atlantic states. Accelerated by high-tech chemicals, entire buildings were burning to the ground in a matter of minutes. Mr. Simon wrote that according to arson investigators, the fires were so intense they twisted and melted steel and made concrete crumble. A quote in the article stated: "The accelerant or accelerants, which have not been clearly identified, can be likened to solid rocket fuel that might be used to launch a space shuttle."

Everything known about the accelerant came from research conducted by the U.S. Bureau of Alcohol, Tobacco, and Firearms and the Seattle Fire Department. In each case, the building's fire load of materials was insufficient to create the temperatures of 3,000 degrees Fahrenheit experienced in the blaze, well above any temperature expected in a normal fire. The analysis of the accelerant indicated it probably contained an oxidizer, a combustible metal like magnesium and aluminum, and a petroleum-based fuel like diesel or kerosene. At the time, seven such major structure fires in the Seattle area were confirmed during the previous ten years. Later articles put the number of such fires nationwide at nearly four times that.

I remember having a discussion with a local Fire Chief in 1995 who had just returned from an advanced fire course in Chicago, Illinois. I recall him speaking about the use of this 'rocket fuel' for arson fires. So the method was important enough to be taught at fire investigation seminars in North America, including the RCMP's, and information material was widely distributed by both the BATF and the RCMP. Most likely Lathem had gained knowledge of this before the New York meeting by speaking with Wendy Norman, the Ottawa Crime Lab Chemist who was on the hangar sorting line. It would have been part of her job to know about it.

Unfortunately, I did not make the connection because when first informed of the matter in 1995, the accelerant's ingredients were unknown. There had been no device or residue left behind due to the amount of heat generated. The BATF chemists had deduced that magnesium and aluminum were the ingredients, and they called it HTA for high-temperature accelerant.

Lathem had been responsible for the delivery of the AES portion of the New York trip meeting. I would bet that the BATF member at the meeting was not told of the AES readings for magnesium and aluminum. I have no doubt that had I been there, or if the BATF members had been allowed to visit the hangar, HTA would have been an important topic of discussion. The petroleum product was added for ease of ignition, something that would not have been needed if a sophisticated dispersal and ignition system had been employed. The obvious importance of this article is the connection of magnesium and aluminum to arson fires, ingredients Dr. Brown found in the short-circuited wire beads.

As for delivering the material to the plane, consider this. Of the employees who serviced the aircraft just prior to its last departure, one was never found again. He worked the one shift to service this aircraft and left. He had provided fake identification to his employer when hired.

Just as disturbing, there had been Swissair-contracted security personnel stationed onboard Vaud during its last stopover at JFK. They were interviewed by RCMP investigators in New York just after the crash. It was learned that it was usual practice for these onboard security people, while the aircraft was at the gate and being cleaned and serviced by various contracted companies, to hide themselves in a bathroom enclosure. This provided unrestricted access to the hatches in the forward ceiling area above which the major fire damage had occurred, especially if disguised as an aircraft maintenance employee. A set of coveralls would not have been difficult to obtain.

These two issues were brushed aside by Lathem and all but one of the RCMP's backroom investigators. However, Karl was now being ignored and would soon be out of the hangar. They were never mentioned in Lathem's memo to Chief Superintendent Duncan that resulted in the closure of the investigation, what little his task force had actually done. There had been only limited passenger investigations or profiling, nearly no cargo identification or verification, and by June 30th of 2000, all the investigators were off the file leaving only three RCMP members on site. Cst. Andy Kerr handled exhibit control, Cst. Duane Cooper looked after computer data entry, and I was the third. My tasks were to continue the photographic and technical assistance requirements while seconded to the TSB. By December 15th, 2000, I was left to work alone with the TSB.

What Lathem would later condemn me for was that I continued my criminal investigation of the physical evidence. These bits and pieces of information came to me piecemeal while working more than ten hours a day and usually six days a week in the hangar. Pay for the overtime during much of this period was nonexistent. I worked alone. I knew there was a strong possibility the crash was criminal, and my management team seemed not to care nor did they want me to search out the truth. However, someone had to do the work or it would have been written off and the truth would never come to light. AES would be dropped or severely curtailed with the results downplayed, as indeed they were in the TSB's final report. Because of the workload and the meetings with Lathem and Gorman, the stress levels were high. Every day new things were being seen and learned that assisted my investigation, sometimes without me even recognizing it. However, whatever RCMP management was doing, I had no way to influence or control it short of going public, and I had nothing to go public with except the incomplete AES results. I had numerous other things to back up the implications of the AES data but nothing substantial or concrete. Going public was not even considered. As for my notes, there was so much going on that once details were recorded, only the essential facts of the actual day-to-day crash investigation remained at the forefront of my mind. I never stopped to put all the pieces together to show what Lathem and the others were doing to thwart the investigation, what few things I knew of their actions by December 2000. Communication with Lathem was by memo through Gorman or meetings where they reprimanded me for something or other. Besides, I considered Lathem to be incompetent and incapable of conducting the investigation. I thought that was the reason for his actions. At the time, I had no reason to believe he was merely following a well-laid-out plan.

The TSB also had their problems regarding the investigation. They had been given a closing date of September 30, 2000, by their management. That was just two years into what by normal standards should have been a three- to four-year investigation. In a TSB hangar meeting on the 25th of May, 2000, Gerden and the TSB senior management were openly criticized by the three main floor investigators. After ordering the secretary not to take notes of this part of the meeting, Gerden's response to them was that they did not conduct investigations the way the Americans did. He said that while there were only two Canadians on board, they had spent fifty-six million dollars on their deaths and that should be enough. He went on to state that the decision had been made and they would have the file wrapped up by the end of September 2000. He felt there could be some areas that might remain open, but the main report would be completed by then with subsequent follow-on reports for those areas still open. It was asked who had made the decision and how had the date been selected. Gerden stated it had come from a very high level. He said Mr. Bouchard, who was the TSB's Chairman, was very astute at understanding the political winds, and they wanted to have this wrapped up before those winds changed and support for the investigation was removed. The explanation he gave suggested the decision level was within the very top levels of the TSB and not in the government or the Treasury Board levels. He indicated they were trying to be prepared for what they believed would occur shortly. He spoke for some time about the loss of 'political interest' in the investigation and other similar statements.

However, a few days later, it was decided the end date was too early and the file would continue. Meanwhile, Gerden's statement did not sit well with the three investigators, each of whom discussed the matter with me over the next few days and made adverse comments about it. His remarks did not sit well with me either, including the fifty-six-million-dollar for two Canadians comment. If there had been four Canadians on board, would we have been able to double the amount? Were not the lives of so many other nationalities worth anything? It was quite simply a shocking and heartless comment. TSB management was stifling an investigation and curtailing their investigators. One of the other investigators, probably without realizing the implications of what he said, had suggested that the decision for the file had already been made, so they should accept it and finish on time. I put forward a copy of my notes to ensure Lathem read them. Gerden may have told his secretary not to take notes, but he had no control over me. By recording notes of it and forwarding them, I took the high and honorable road even if there was nothing else I could do. Later, Gorman and Lathem were highly critical of my actions. They, along with Gerden, chose to take the low road leading to the gutter. If nothing else, I wanted my management team to know I was keeping track of the TSB's actions. They would soon learn I was also keeping track of their actions, at least those I knew.

Periodically I helped John conduct burn tests of various items from the overhead and passenger cabin areas, and many were found to burn readily. Both John and I were of the opinion they should never have been allowed in the aircraft. A memo was forwarded to Lathem suggesting there might have been an aspect of criminality in how the materials came to pass the original FAA burn tests. The Federal Aviation Administration was the US Federal Agency responsible for the safety of all aircraft flying in US airspace. My suspicion was that years earlier, the tests might have been purposefully created to allow the materials to pass, and the matter should be investigated. I made the mistake of quoting John, thus revealing him to be my source of information. Instead of conferring with me, Lathem turned the memo over to Gerden who immediately became angry with both John and me. By his reaction, it seemed Gerden felt the TSB and their members were not even to think criminal, let alone speak of it. Gerden called me a mole in that I had embedded myself into the group of investigators only to feed information back to the RCMP. Some of my coworkers laughed at the idea I could be a cuddly and furry little four-legged creature. He ordered John to have no more conversations with me after reprimanding him for his actions. In turn, Lathem criticized me for the memo by suggesting I might have been trying to set myself up as a witness for the families in any future civil suit. However, nothing more was done about an investigation. Instead, the TSB handled the matter by working with the FAA to create up-to-date flammability rules for new aircraft materials. That people died because materials passed a possible fraudulent burn test was never investigated by the police because it ended at Gerden's desk.

The mandate of the TSB precluded any prosecution for past offences. They instead persuaded companies or agencies to change the defects in the interests of public safety. While this might at first look like a good way to improve public safety, it was after the fact and there was no deterrent value in this method. People usually died before faulty materials or procedures were fixed. Meanwhile, the companies made money by taking the shortcuts for which they knew they would never be criminally prosecuted, and any civil case would be difficult since the TSB members never appeared in Court. The TSB did not even have the authority to threaten prosecution because they could not consider anything that might be deemed a criminal offence.

AES examinations of various materials and test wires had by early November of 2000 revealed that the questioned elements were indeed present, and they remained as an unsolved problem in that there was no non-criminal onboard source for them. To confirm this, Dr. Brown had utilized several other highly advanced techniques to analyze the beads. Also, the results of burn tests completed at the Boeing electrical lab in Seattle confirmed the four suspect elements were not present in the flammables of the aircraft, including the paint.

With the AES results in mind, when speaking with Lathem on November 6th, 2000, I asked him what would happen if Dr. Brown's report indicates that a criminal device may have been the source for the questioned elements. His skating reply was it would have to be considered at that time, and he quickly moved on to something else. Nine days later in mid-November 2000, I learned he was in Ottawa in a high-level RCMP meeting to discuss the potential AES test results. Less than two weeks after that, Dr. Brown's report was received by the TSB, and it quite openly stated the presence of magnesium, aluminum, and iron could indicate sabotage. The report contained the opinion of a Ph.D. in the Geosciences who had done an exhaustive analysis of the aircraft wires and materials. Also, Dr. Brown had no knowledge of what other criminal indicators had been found. At that time, I had no knowledge of the contents of his report.

Starting in September of 2001, I made a series of three trips to the FAA Burn Unit in Atlantic City along with members of the TSB. As each trip came up, just as had occurred with each of the five AES tests, there was a question of whether I would be allowed to attend. Finally, Don Enns and John Garstang told Gerden that if I was not present, there would be no need to hold the tests as they would not be going. Since John could not be there for some of the tests due to his commitments to the Air India investigation, they had no one else who knew the plane's overhead layout as well as me.

Numerous tests were conducted by various means, and nothing that was tested was found to burn in an unusual manner. One method, though, was of importance. A piece of Boeing aircraft skin with the attached frames and two layers of insulation was positioned to replicate accurately the forward attic area of the MD-11 aircraft, the area where the major burn had occurred. Added to the bottom of the frame was a ceiling with mock ducts wrapped in insulation and Mylar material. The dimensions were equivalent to Vaud's burnt area. It also contained a special duct made of foam material unique to the Swissair configuration. One test was designed to see what damage would be done to this foam duct and how much it contributed to the fire load.

Once everything was in place and with cameras rolling, the first burn test was ignited. Then it was re-ignited again and again several times. The Mylar material supplied by the TSB refused to burn for more than a few seconds before going out. It turned out this Mylar material was a newer version that was non-flammable. A mistake had been made. This Mylar material looked identical to what had been on Vaud and many of the other examined aircraft.

On the next trip, the same test was re-run but with the flammable type Mylar like that found in the debris. This time, it burned but only slowly and without generating much heat. Considering the material, it was a slow burn and none of the aluminum frame melted. In fact, the burning MPET material wrapping the ducts on the bottom of the test frame failed to ignite the same type of MPET material in the frame's ceiling. Not only that, the material on the ducts had to be ignited in several different locations to try to increase the rate of heat gain in the frame. This slow burn rate was significant because it showed the MPET on Vaud was not as highly flammable as was previously thought. Perhaps the original FAA tests had been accurate.

For the next burn test, a high output electric heating unit was positioned in the frame to preheat the foam duct. Once started, the unit was so hot and close it caused the varnish-like coating on the duct to spontaneously ignite and burn. However, once that layer burnt off, the fire on the foam duct went out. Before it did, the burning duct surface and the hot heating unit caused the ceiling material to ignite. The result was a fire that burnt the insulation of the heater unit's wiring. The electrical wires shorted and showered the frame with sparks, many of which ignited the remainder of the Metallized Mylar. In the end, the foam duct suffered little damage and was only a minor part of the fire load. Again, no aluminum had melted. Even with an extremely high heat source near the MPET material, it took the burning surface layer of the duct and the sparks from the wires to cause all the dry MPET material to burn.

The last burn consisted of the simple addition of loosely packed and crumpled sheets of Metallized Mylar onto the bottom of the frame where it was ignited. This burn occurred in part because of a suggestion from the head of the FAA Burn Unit, Dr. Lyon. In a meeting with him and the TSB members during the second trip, Dr. Lyon was quite unambiguous in his comment that he did not believe the amount of Metallized Mylar in use, about 1000 grams, could provide sufficient heat to melt aluminum. He wanted to try a test in which all the Metallized Mylar in the represented ceiling area was placed in a loose pile in the frame and set alight. It would then be monitored to determine how much heat was released. He felt confident it would not do the damage we had seen in the aircraft debris. He went on to say he had been speaking with his team supervisor, and they both agreed that in all the years of burning materials in their mock aircraft, aluminum skin or frame had never melted unless they had used a petroleum accelerant. It was nine years for Dr. Lyon and sixteen for his team's supervisor.

Dr. Lyon went on to say he was not an expert in fires, but instead, he was a materials person. He knew what made up the materials that were in the airplane and how they each were affected by a fire. He was knowledgeable in how a fire burnt a material and what it produced, including the heat and gases, what heat it took to ignite them, and what heat they in turn delivered. He had created the equipment to measure the products of a burning material, and he knew what those measurements meant. While he might not have known how to investigate the fire scene, he knew more about the fire evidence in an airplane than anyone else.

He touched on the idea that something unknown could have been present above the ceiling. As no one commented, he went on to mention a thermite device. I spoke up to suggest that anything like a thermite grenade would burn through the ceiling and out the bottom of the aircraft, so that was unlikely. He went on to suggest some other sort of incendiary device, something of which he said he had no idea. Don Enns and Gus Sidla, both present for the meeting, said nothing while I told him to keep talking. Dr. Lyon certainly gave the impression he felt an incendiary device was truly a possibility, and later Don Enns agreed with my assessment of the discussion. Dr. Lyon was the other half of the team with Dr. Quintiere. According to many TSB members, they were the two people most knowledgeable in aircraft fires in North America.

At the end of the third trip, with four video and two infrared cameras to record it, the last MPET bulk burn test was started. Don had stuffed the frame with every piece of Metallized Mylar he had, his comment being he did not want to take any of it home. It was piled high in a loose bundle in the centre of the frame area, and the sight of it caused me great concern. There seemed to be no control over the amount nor was there any relationship to a real aircraft scenario. Much later I learned the Metallized Mylar for this test far outweighed anything that could have been burnt during the fatal flight by more than six times. What's more, this fire lasted for less than one-quarter of the time. That meant the heat generated, when considering time versus temperature, was increased by a factor of about twenty-four. Considering the material was dry and without any of the condensation that would have been on Vaud, the heat generated would have been even more for each gram of MPET. Also, keep in mind the skin of this frame was a small heatsink at a normal daytime temperature of twenty degrees Celsius while the skin of the aircraft during the flight was a gigantic heatsink at minus sixty degrees Celsius. Thus, it could absorb much of the heat from the onboard fire.

It would be an understatement to say the fire was spectacular. After being ignited from below, very quickly it all seemed to catch fire at once. The frame filled with gray-black smoke and within a few seconds, nothing more could be seen through the side and end viewing ports. The frame belched thick black smoke from every crack and hole. The smoke stack billowed forth like an old steam locomotive burning coal, and everything snapped and popped from the great heat. Part way into the fire that lasted about five minutes, the paint on the upper surface of the frame caught fire and was put out with a fine spray from a garden hose. The frame's skin had cracked due to heat stresses to create a narrow opening about a foot long. The cameras were all pulled back for their safety as there was no way of knowing if the frame could sustain the heat. The huge arena sized building filled with smoke, and the tempered glass of a viewing port shattered from the heat and flexing of the frame. Soon after, a piece of the frame's tin floor fell partly to the concrete floor, and we could see most of the material had already burnt. There were huge spattered areas of shiny molten aluminum on the tin's surface.

The examination of the test frame revealed molten stringers remarkably similar to those found in the crash debris. Later, the test frame was shipped back to Halifax and put on display beside the aircraft reconstruction jig for all to see. I offered to drive back the rental truck with the burnt frame, but I think John had been told to drive it himself. I was told Gerden wanted to ensure its safe arrival in Ottawa for all his bosses to see. Of course, I denied any intention to dump the frame in some salvage yard while driving through the State of New York, but John seemed not to believe me. Salvage value was all it was worth since the damage to the frame had been caused by a fraudulent burn that had failed to represent any true or legitimate test.

CHAPTER 3 – FRICTION

Back on day three of the investigation, profile examinations of the passengers by the RCMP were called to a halt. As in any death investigation, it should have been a routine procedure to question who the victims were, why they were on the flight, what work they did, and among other things, could or did they have any enemies. While names and addresses were initially supplied so each passenger could be identified for death certificates, the questions surrounding each person's details and why he or she was on the plane were never answered for most of those on board. For reasons that eventually came to light, those inquiries were curtailed by the RCMP's senior management.

The cargo was treated in a similar manner. Late in the investigation, Gerden asked for confirmation that diamonds valued at nearly half a billion dollars were part of the cargo. Cst. Cooper asked if I knew where the documentation was for the verification. As far as he could determine, no task had ever been created to investigate the shipment. Since everything was computerized, it seems the computer had not thought it worthwhile to create this as a task, and for sure Lathem would never have thought of it. Other cargo met the same fate. Just before the removal of the RCMP's investigative group in June of 2000, it was revealed there existed several pallet-sized tri-wall boxes containing dozens of pieces of unknown items that were believed to have been cargo. Most items remained unidentified at the closure of the RCMP's file.

During the investigation, considerable time and effort at great expense were put into the AES testing. As an investigative process, it was simple enough. Provide the required aircraft wires and elimination samples to Dr. Brown, monitor the process, collect the recorded results, and then wait for his opinion. That should have been all there was to it. However, from the very start, there were complaints the process was too slow and it would take too long before results would be known. Once they realized Dr. Brown's initial findings indicated a possible criminal cause, the TSB began a concerted effort to stop the tests. During several meetings, both Foot and Sidla indicated they wanted a preliminary report from Dr. Brown before continuing with any further tests. Since we all knew he had found evidence that could indicate a criminal device, I asked why they needed such a report and what would they do differently once the report was delivered. Neither had a definite reply except to skate around the questions. I countered their replies by stating that any expert such as Dr. Brown would never supply an evaluation of his data until he had completed his analysis and comparison. They knew I had taken a firm position on the opposite side of their argument.

Jim Foot was the TSB's electrical inspector, and while he knew how to be an electrician, I soon learned he knew very little about conducting a proper fire investigation and that he was ignoring the correct protocols for physical evidence and photographs. Jim had been with the Transportation Safety Board for some time and had been a commercial electrician before joining them. He seemed to have had no training in forensic investigative technics and, as far as I saw, no interest in learning. There was a saying that you do not know what you do not know, and this was the case for Foot and many of the TSB members when it came to conducting a fire investigation. Foot's methods frequently failed to follow the agreed upon MOU, and he showed no indication he cared. His expressed opinion was that the cause of the fire could only have been an accidental electrical fault, so there was no need to do anything differently. He frequently gave me the impression this was going to be the cause even if he had to ignore evidence to the contrary.

The other member was Gus Sidla, the TSB's metallurgist. Gus was extremely knowledgeable but was adamant the file belonged to the TSB and would be dealt with as they saw fit. Tall and thin, Gus had an Eastern European accent that added to his scholarly appearance and mannerisms. Gus provided some interesting times as well as many frustrating moments.

I attended meetings with these TSB members during which discussions could easily have led to severe arguments over whether correct procedures for the AES testing would be followed. My rule had always been that once a scientific process was started, it must be continued no matter where the evidence led. During any investigation, to conduct a test so it provided only a predetermined result was illegal. Winning the arguments was no assurance correct procedures would be followed. My notes contained many instances when the TSB members supplied improper test wires to Dr. Brown, wrong information about their source, and even incorrect test results to partner agencies. The ultimate disinformation occurred when the

TSB wrote their final report and discredited the AES procedure as providing unreliable results. They then pointed to a possible entertainment system wire as the accidental cause of the fire, knowing there was no reliable or verifiable evidence to maintain their theory. They had ignored significant physical evidence that supported a criminal incendiary device.

As part of the elimination process, Dr. Brown requested the preparation of test wires in a prescribed and controlled manner and then to have them submerged in seawater for a month. Jim Foot was adamant the AES process was a failure. He said he had several dozen wires, any of which might have been the cause of the fire, and there was no evidence of an incendiary device. He made a declaration that Dr. Brown had gone off track by looking for the magnesium source, and he threatened he would put him back on track. I was afraid the magnesium problem was going to disappear no matter what the physical evidence indicated, and there would be no salt water wire test. Only after Gerden realized I would not let the matter rest did he reluctantly agree to the preparation and sinking of the wires. However, when it came time to AES test those wires, again there were strong opposing arguments. Only after Larry Fogg provided his opinion and then Dr. Brown demanded the examination of the test wires did the process continue. It proved there had been no transfer of elements to the wire beads from either the seawater, a piece of pure magnesium, or from the aluminum alloy.

During these meetings, Lathem and Gorman were present and perhaps only for that reason the meetings remained civil. Several times I came close to telling Foot and Gerden just what I thought of what they were trying to do. As far as I was concerned, they were ignoring physical evidence of a crime and obstructing my criminal investigation. If I had said what I felt like saying, I am sure Lathem would have immediately removed me from the hangar.

Still, the disinformation continued as Foot cherry-picked the AES results. He argued that the beads were porous and contaminated by seawater, so the AES results were not reliable. He then took the same readings from the same wires to argue that certain wires were clean, or lacking the smoke contaminants, and others dirty, thereby showing the clean wires started the fire. He failed to realize that more than one initiation point in a fire usually indicated an arson fire.

Another area where Foot seemed to create his rules was with the placement of burnt wires in the reconstruction frame. The insulated copper cables had been burnt clean by the intense fire, thus leaving only the hot copper strands at the moment of impact. Immediately they were surrounded by tons of debris, including other insulated wires and plastics of the same chemical signature as was the insulation that had burnt away. Grabbed by the grapple bucket, they were dumped on the barge's deck, hosed with salt water, and placed in a large tub to intermingle with retrieved debris. Once ashore, they were again washed, remixed with more debris, and then subjected to a sort line. From there they were moved about in the highly contaminated hangar and placed on various grimy hangar tables. Months later, Foot decided to request an analysis of the cables' surfaces to determine the presence of insulation residue. Only after the analysis was complete was it realized that from those findings, he planned to position each wire in the frame. On learning the reason for the analysis, the Crime Lab Chemistry member refused to offer an evaluation of his data other than to say that many different materials adhered to the wires. Foot demanded the data printouts so he could evaluate that same information to determine the placement of the wires even though the wire's insulation and the tubes in which some of them travelled were of the same chemical composition. Foot boldly proclaimed to me that he was better at it than the lab member. The lab chemist, Jacques Rioux, had several science degrees and an abundance of experience while Foot had technical school as an electrician.

Even while the AES testing continued, Foot and Sidla told their TSB co-investigators as well as partner companies that there had been a transfer of the elements from seawater and the issue was no longer in question. TSB members informed me of this as well as a Swissair manager.

Most of these things I knew about while still in the hangar. However, there were certain occurrences I did not know until some ten years later. In speaking with Dr. Brown in 2011, it was learned that just after he submitted his first AES draft report to the TSB, he was approached by his CANMET supervisor who pressured him to alter his conclusions. In his first draft, he explicitly stated the source of the suspect elements was not part of the aircraft or its normal contents but an added source, and he called it sabotage. While I was aware of that pressure through an email in 2001, it was only in

2011 that I learned of the first report's contents and the actual extent of that pressure. Dr. Brown then submitted a second amended report in February 2002 and left out the word sabotage and some of his opinions about the source of the magnesium. However, magnesium and the other elements remained a problem with no onboard or any other legitimate source. So again, it was not satisfactory to the TSB. Jim was coerced into submitting a third and final report that was suitable to the TSB regardless of what the truth was. In truth, the magnesium issue remained unresolved and persisted as evidence of a criminal cause for the onboard fire.

Opposition to my involvement by certain members of the TSB began on my first day in Hangar A. When handling debris items in the many hundreds of thousands, correct numbering of the exhibits was an important aspect of evidence processing. Exhibits were to be documented in a particular manner, each with a new sequential number. However, the established evidence rules the TSB had agreed to were not being followed by some investigators. Several of the RCMP members had repeatedly tried to rectify the problem. On that first Sunday when I positioned my equipment between Jim Foot and Gus Sidla, John Garstang had put me between what I later considered to be the two worst offenders when it came to failing to follow the correct protocols.

Besides mishandling exhibits, photographs were being similarly mismanaged. The laws of this land demanded that every photo taken in a file by Crown investigators must be available for all parties in any potential Court proceedings. Protocols for photos had been developed but were not being followed. Jim Foot maintained his personal collection of digital photos without proper documentation and without ensuring their placement in the main file. By what he said to me when questioned about it, his attitude was that since the cause of the fire was due to an accidental electrical fault, he could look after his photo requirements and there was no need to document anything else. More importantly, he boasted his digital photo files were being selectively culled in complete disregard to those agreed-upon protocols. Even though a photo may have been blurred and improperly exposed, a lawyer could easily and successfully argue that the deleted photo was the key to the whole investigation. How could the Crown prove otherwise because once it was gone, it was too late to prove differently? By law, the onus was on the Crown to supply the photo, and Jim Foot worked for and was paid by the Crown whether or not he liked it.

John Garstang had a good understanding of how they should have been investigating the file and what he wanted done with important debris pieces and their photographs. For John, it did not matter what the cause of the fire was as their job was to consider the safety aspect. Since the TSB did not assess blame, why waste the time and effort going after something that might or might not have short-circuited to cause the fire? He felt that even if the cause of the fire was an incendiary device, the materials on the plane should not have burnt and a criminal device should not have caused the crash. So, by using state of the art technology and methods, he wanted everything of importance, including the melts on the wires, photographed by a new method so he could show the extent of the burn damage and prove certain materials were faulty. I worked daily with John to accomplish this, but working on the electrical wires brought me into Jim Foot's electrical environment. That was something that from the start he quite openly opposed.

Throughout the file, Foot continuously argued I did not need to attend various tests to record procedures and results with either photos or video. He fully challenged my attendance in Seattle, even though he gave no consideration to the exhibiting, storage, and transportation of the several hundred sensitive test wires, all without damage or contamination. However, after the second week, he commented to me that it was a good thing I had attended or the session would not have gone nearly as well. That was a major understatement.

When tests were conducted to see if molten aluminum would penetrate ceiling tiles, Foot again argued against my presence. Ignoring him, I videotaped the ceiling tiles as they repelled the molten aluminum at 1000 degrees F, a critical bit of information.

During one of the Zurich trips, several of the MD-11 aircraft were examined to determine the condition of one item called the smoke curtain. On the first plane, Foot jumped ahead of me to photograph the partially open curtain, and then he reached up to adjust it before I could photograph it correctly in a proper forensic manner. John, too late, told him to stop. Jim had allowed Larry Fogg, who was with us, to photograph it, but not me. So, Jim put the curtain back in what he seemed to think was its original condition. I now refused to photograph it. It had been adjusted and could never be shown to be in its original condition. I took John aside and told him this should not happen again. When it again occurred on the next aircraft, I took John aside again and suggested Jim Foot should be his official photographer. I would return to Halifax on the next flight as I was not going to work under these conditions. Luckily there were no further aircraft available until after lunch when Jim had meetings to attend. However, I had been adamant I would not record rearranged and fabricated evidence.

When Dr. Brown asked for specific test wires, the TSB supplied contaminated wires from the burnt area of the aircraft instead of the pristine wires specially prepared as he had requested. When relevant information was not forthcoming about the source of those wires and other exhibits, Foot appeared visibly upset when I provided the correct information during my discussions with the Doctor.

The TSB was not the sole source of opposition or attempts to control the file's outcome. After overcoming great resistance from Lathem, he finally authorized my attendance at the air flow flight test in Long Beach, California. It was Chief Superintendent Duncan, after coming back from a lengthy absence from the file, who told Lathem to allow my attendance. However, Boeing had a restricted crew list that did not include me until, at the last moment, a new position was required. Lathem had instructed me to call him if I was assigned a position on the flight. Because of time restraints, I could not make that phone call. It turned out that had I done so he would have ordered me to stay on the ground. Later, in closed-door meetings with Gorman and then Lathem, they demanded to know why I had not made contact before the flight. Their concern, so they said, was for my life insurance and potential civil suits against the Canadian Government had the plane crashed during the tests. They were bogus excuses seemingly designed to keep me off the flight and from learning too much about the aircraft and its air flow during flight. The hostility was not limited to Lathem and Gorman. Three of the five backroom plain clothes investigators offered their negative comments about the flight and the adverse consequences had it crashed. I knew their comments were bogus as no one seemed concerned about the potential loss of life, merely the repercussions. Furthermore, no one asked about the results of the airflow tests.

Two weeks after Lathem's group finished with the file, Gorman and another Ident Staff Sergeant, Neil Fraser, showed up at my office to conduct an equipment audit. After spending most of the afternoon going over every item and opening every unlocked drawer, Gorman tried to leave with a cartload of what he had determined to be surplus equipment. A severe argument ensued that ended with me forcefully taking back some of the equipment he had planned to remove. Video editing equipment, even though needed to copy my routine footage, had to be returned to the main Ident Section, yet it stayed on a photo darkroom counter top in a jumbled mess for another two years without ever being touched. A few days later when he returned to the hangar, I mistakenly thought Gorman intended to apologize. Instead, he had a written reprimand for my actions after his inspection. After a brief comment from him, he simply handed me the form. He said he sensed I had an anger about me. I did not even read his paper. Instead, I told him to get out of my hangar and not come back, but in a much more aggressive tone with a decisive choice of words. I had known and been friends with Vic Gorman for thirteen years, but his actions and statements put an end to that. Of importance were the lines that read:

"Sgt. Juby appears to have the position that the Swissair investigation is a criminal investigation, however, there is no evidence to maintain that position. To date there isn't any evidence of criminal activity."

This statement was clear proof my immediate supervisor as the second in charge of the RCMP's Swissair Task Force was stating there was no need for nor had there been any official criminal investigation. What's more, later correspondence from Gorman confirmed my suspicion that it was Lathem who had instructed him to remove my equipment from the hangar. Did they not read my reports? He sensed anger! Gorman had no idea how angry I was!

Another incident occurred just after preparing the wires for the seawater tests. The producer, Howard Green, was filming a documentary and wanted video of the process, so John and I set up a mock demonstration in the front of the hangar. When finished, Howard interviewed John to record a complete description of the theories and reasons behind the AES testing of the wires. He then interviewed me about the actual wire preparation. As soon as he was gone, Lathem in his usual black business suit and bright white shirt with a thin dark tie came out of his back office and quickly strode the length of the hangar directly towards me. While watching him purposefully advance, it came to mind that he was a ringer for 'Men in Black'. In his inside suit jacket pocket was his wand-thing-a-ma-jiggy. Reaching me, he immediately and authoritatively demanded to know what I had been doing with the film crew, why Green had interviewed me, and what I had said. After explaining what had taken place, he was assured I had released nothing controversial since John had already done that. I told him Green was smart enough to figure out what was happening. I reminded him Green was putting together a TSB glory film. Since Gerden had the final say in the editing process, it was most unlikely any RCMP member would appear in the final footage, least of all me. However, it was evident I was being watched very carefully. Lathem wanted to control what I did and to whom I spoke. He did not want the truth to be revealed by me to anyone, especially the media. However, he could not zap me because he had forgotten his sunglasses on his desk. I was sure the next time he would remember them.

CHAPTER 4 – THE RESPONSE

During the last week of November 2000, there was a general meeting of the partner investigators in the hangar to present and discuss the findings of the TSB's investigation up to that date. Attendees were from Boeing, Swissair, the FAA, NTSB, Transport Canada, and others as well as many of the TSB members. Sitting in was Howard Green with his video crew as he wanted to cover the meeting's details for the film. Since I was the only RCMP member on the fire committee, I had previously asked John about my attendance as it was by invite only. However, it became apparent the TSB's management did not want me there to hear and question or possibly influence what they were presenting. After all, it was just a few weeks since the incident when Gerden had called me a mole. No one for the RCMP would be present as only Cooper and Kerr were still in the hangar, and nobody else in the Force besides me knew anything about the discussion material.

During a morning break, there was a chance to speak with Pat Cahill, one of Dr. Lyon's FAA Burn Unit members with whom I had worked. She mentioned magnesium and that she had heard nothing on the subject in nearly a year. She asked what had become of it. I explained that the source was still unknown. She responded by saying she wondered why nothing had been said here in the meeting. I suggested to her this subject was not in the preferred domain of the TSB since it implied a criminal act and she would hear nothing about it at this meeting. She then asked an unusual question. She looked directly at me and asked if I had ever been told to keep quiet about certain things. I just looked at her. There was no need to say anything because she just nodded and said yes, she had thought so. In fact, both Gorman and Lathem had told me as early as September of 1999 that the AES results were secret, and I was not to discuss them with anyone, even in the hangar. As well, at the end of each of our meetings with the TSB members, Gerden always mentioned that nothing from the meeting was to be discussed with anyone outside of the room. As for our RCMP investigators' meetings, Lathem always began each by saying he wanted no notes of the meeting's discussions. That certainly did not deter me.

A few days later after Garstang asked, he was informed that several exhibits had been forwarded to Dr. Brown in compliance with previous agreements to find an onboard source for the questioned elements. He went on to say he thought Dr. Brown's AES report had been released and that Gerden wanted a meeting with the RCMP possibly to discuss it. He said I might be included. John did not mention anything more about it, probably because Gerden had already reprimanded him for telling the mole too much. The bridges were not yet mended.

Later I learned that on the morning of the 1st of December, 2000, Gerden did indeed have a meeting with the RCMP. He met with Lathem and another commissioned officer of the RCMP, Inspector Dan Tanner, who was what might be called the Intelligence Officer for the division. I was not invited.

After lunch, I was summoned to Gerden's office. At first, I thought I was late because Lathem was there with three other RCMP members, two of whom I worked with daily, Kerr and Cooper. The other was Neil Fraser, the Identification Section Staff Sergeant who had accompanied Gorman on his audit and who would soon receive his commission as an Inspector. For the TSB, there was Gerden, Garstang, Foot, and Larry Vance who was the Assistant Investigator in Charge and second to Gerden.

At the outset, it was quite apparent I was not late and this was not a friendly get-together. Taking the only available seat, I was now positioned directly opposite Lathem and Gerden who were seated side by side about ten feet away behind Gerden's office desk. As I sat down, they were silent, and both looked straight at me with a hostile stare. Lathem started off in a very intimidating tone with some direct and derogatory statements regarding comments having been made about the Force dropping the file and about its conclusion along with other misdeeds. These were all aimed right at me. Lathem made comments about going to the FAA, about the file being closed on the 15th of December, 2000, giving personal tours to outsiders and offering opinions to them regarding the cause of the fire, and submitting exhibits to Dr. Brown without authorization. Lathem was pointed and very aggressive in his remarks. It certainly seemed sources in the hangar had fed things to him which, when taken out of context, did not sit well with him. He was loud, aggressive, and not at all diplomatic in front of another agency and my coworkers. Glancing around the room, Garstang, Kerr and Cooper looked and acted embarrassed and intimidated. Foot sat to my left, and I could see he had a slight smirk on his face.

Vance's look was serious as if a major crime had been committed. It was as if they both knew what was going to be said. I was in the spotlight, and Lathem had an audience even if most were unwilling. He was making the most of it to show his authority. After another few minutes of spieling on about the investigation, he briefly mentioned the AES testing and the report. My activities after December 15th, 2000, were then mentioned, and Garstang provided some limited input as to what still had to be done on the file.

Gerden indirectly mentioned my latest burn memo by bringing up the subject of the TSB's approach to people or companies who might have known certain materials in the planes were faulty. He said it was his experience that it was seldom productive or beneficial to prosecute under such circumstances. He stated aircraft were much safer today than thirty years ago because they had dealt directly with the safety issues instead of prosecuting. He said such actions would cause irreparable damage to their safety investigations, and they certainly preferred not to go that route. No comments were added to Gerden's statement by Lathem or any of the others in the room, and for certain they were not there to debate the issue with me. So, the lid was now closed tightly on my report as far as the TSB was concerned. By Lathem's look, I knew nothing more would be done to investigate the matter by either the RCMP or the FBI.

Larry Vance made comments about too much cooperation between the two agencies. He said old timers with the Safety Board would be turning over in their graves if they knew of the level of cooperation that existed between the TSB and the RCMP on this file. Gerden added to this with some comments of his own, and then Foot made comments about the AES process, particularly that it was not supposed to be a search for the magnesium source and he was going to make that clear to Dr. Brown. He did confirm he had received the draft report from CANMET, but he did not reveal anything of its contents. He mentioned the latest exhibits to Dr. Brown along with comments that he expected him to take the costs for their testing out of the previous financial allotments. Foot then made comments about not knowing of their submission. Yet he had agreed to the process six months earlier, including my submission of exhibits as requested by Dr. Brown. His words brought out another cold stare from Gerden and Lathem along with further comments. No matter what he said, Foot had been remiss by not completing the task himself. However, I would never have trusted him to send Dr. Brown the correct uncontaminated materials.

Part way through one of Lathem's harangues concerning my short discussion with Pat Cahill, I managed to mention she had told me about an arson on board a Delta Airlines passenger plane while on the ground at Montreal's Dorval Airport in 1993. He had already been informed of it as I had submitted my notes including a copy of the TSB's report I had found on their website. It was of importance to me because I had been continuously told by Foot, Gerden, Lathem, Gorman, as well as three of Lathem's backroom people that no arson had ever taken place on a passenger jet. Therefore Swissair could not have been an arson. Their reasoning never made sense to me, but I had nothing to counter it until Cahill mentioned to me that she had worked on this one aircraft fire that was, in fact, arson. As I mentioned it to Lathem, he made a nodding gesture and then a further facial expression as if he did not want to open that subject. He immediately started to say something as though he was going on to another matter, but Foot interrupted and began to explain the incident. He was completely aware of all the details and described them to me, including that the Montreal Police had charged the suspect with arson. He knew all about it because he had been the onsite investigator for the TSB and had written the report. Cahill had been involved because it had been a US-based airline and she was the FAA's Burn Unit specialist. The culprit had tried to burn blankets in the overhead storage and garbage in one of the lavatories. However, it was arson, so the concept had previously been carried out.

Even though I had now presented them with an actual case, Foot, Gerden, and Lathem acted as though this meant nothing at all and I was the one who was in the wrong. When I looked at Lathem, he was straight faced, but his eyes would not meet mine as he tried to ignore the implications of this disclosure. It was as if it was of no consequence whatsoever. I had sat in meeting after meeting where Lathem, Gorman, and Lathem's backroom trio, as well as Foot and Gerden, had rebuked my suspicions that this file was arson. Their reason was there had never been an arson on board a passenger plane. The only other RCMP member who had ever had a similar belief as mine was Christiansen, and he had been kicked out of the investigation months before. Garstang had quietly supported me, and he had found one other example of a suspected arson on board a plane while in flight.

Lathem made some comments about taking over the investigation should something be identified as criminal by the TSB. Somehow I knew this would never happen. However, he emphasized that December 15th, 2000, was the end date for the RCMP in the hangar, and the complete file would move to his Major Crime Unit. The TSB would have to contract for anything more. John again went over his requirements for me to locate certain exhibits and debris pieces as well as a possible trip-note meeting in Ottawa, further photo processing, and lab report analysis.

Lathem continued by saying that nothing had been found during the investigation indicating any problems on board the aircraft, including any notes or photos on the bodies of any of the passengers. What bodies? There had been only one! He seemed to believe this lack of a message from the past authored by the victims proved nothing criminal had occurred on the aircraft. Lathem repeated this ridiculous statement he had made in previous meetings as though the passengers would have somehow known the cause of the fire and foreseen their deaths. He must have thought it had been like some Hollywood movie crash scene because my impression of him was he had absolutely no idea what had happened on that plane in the minutes before its crash or at the moment of impact.

Then three areas of concern were addressed. They were the magnesium levels, the burnt carpets at the forward galleys, and the high-temperature burns on the ceiling tiles above the right forward door. Foot made sure he added his two cents worth about the minute amounts of magnesium and that it meant nothing. However, there was no discussion on any of these issues. There was even a round table to ensure no one had any other problems, as useless as that was under these conditions. I was unprepared for the meeting, and the atmosphere was too hostile for me to raise any issues without them developing into a full-blown series of arguments. Those arguments could only end with Lathem expelling me from the hangar. Besides, I was so mad at Lathem and Gerden that I would not have been able to discuss anything. While they both had made it seem that everything was above board by going around the table to allow anyone to speak, any time I had tried to comment, I was either cut off or else the look from Lathem and Gerden was glaring and intimidating. They did not want to hear from me. Instead, I was there just to listen and be told. They had not intended for the meeting to be a forum in which to discuss matters. Furthermore, I had been given no time to prepare, nor did I have direct access to the test reports, especially Dr. Brown's. It would have been impossible to raise any questions. The tone and atmosphere of this meeting showed it was not a group discussion but instead a warning to all, and especially to me, to beware, that management had control, and I was only to do as I was told. It was best to keep my mouth shut and say nothing at all.

When the meeting finished, there was no need to wonder if Lathem was done. Both he and Fraser immediately followed me to the Identification office and there they let their true feelings come out. Lathem was furious and not bashful about making it known. He was mad about the exhibits to Brown, contact with the FAA, comments around the hangar, and contact with Karl just to name a few. Lathem felt I should have no contact with anyone or speak about the file at all. While it was a one-sided tirade with no room for discussion, a few words were edged in that I did not think I was being monitored for what was said and to whom. He blurted out that I was not, but I had no business talking to the FAA or Karl. Lathem was loud and aggressive in this tiny room, and he made the statement that I had never been told to keep my mouth shut about the file. These words were loudly snarled right after reprimanding me severely for talking to the FAA and Karl. Lathem continued by saying that he was getting complaints about my activities from various people, including RCMP members from the hangar.

Lathem went on to question why he was not contacted if I had any concerns or matters to discuss with him. He stated he had pagers and cell phones that he always wore. It was ironic this was put forward considering all the previous correspondence and severe criticisms about not going through proper channels to send reports to him. The instructions then were that I was to go through Gorman with my reports and not to submit them directly to him.

Lathem reprimanded me for showing outside people around the frame, and talking about hot spots and incendiary devices. That was ridiculous because I had never taken anyone around the frame and I certainly had not spoken to outsiders about those matters.

As for the FAA, they were just another source of information. Information sources were a required function for police all over the world and, as Gorman had already said to me, we were in the evidence gathering stage of the file. So, that had to include information about the evidence. As for telling her anything, it was Pat who had asked me if I had ever been told to keep my mouth shut. Why would she even ask if she did not suspect something? She obviously had gone to Gerden to confront him about the matter.

He asked what it was he had to do to get through to me, that we had discussed this three or four times. My thoughts were that any previous discussions were as one-sided as this insanity was.

Continuing, Lathem was again mad about contact with Karl and stated I had been told not to talk to him. Again, this was ridiculous because I had not spoken to Karl since he left the hangar except for a couple of emails. However, I had never been told not to converse or communicate with Karl, and what's more, it was none of Lathem's business with whom I communicated. Just who did he think he was in trying to order such a restriction? However, Lathem was literally bouncing off the ceiling so it would have done me no good to show my opposition to his demands.

Lathem then pulled a sheet of paper out of his briefcase and said when the file was over, everything was to be handed in. To ensure I did this, he demanded that I sign and acknowledge a direct written order under the RCMP Act to turn over everything by the 15th of December, 2000. Failure to do so would result in my suspension from duty without pay. As it was taken and read, he was asked if he had any reason to believe the notes and material would not be handed in. Lathem said no, but this ensured full compliance. This undertaking certainly was a threat and an attempt to intimidate. How else to take it, especially since the notes were already on the two RCMP-owned computers in the Identification office, and he had access to them at any time. When asked, he agreed I could keep a copy of all the notes. There was no way he could say no since they were my notes and required for the Identification file and any future Court. However, this simply made the point. I asked him about notes for the work after the 15th, and he said they could be added to the file later, and he brushed it off. Those future notes seemed not to be a concern for him. I asked about follow-up work regarding reports coming in, particularly the AES report. He said very pointedly that they would go on file and I would have nothing to do with them. He said it so forcefully that there was no room left for any disagreement by me. Much later, looking back at what he said and the way he said it, it was as if he was trying to ensure I would never learn what was in that AES report.

Neil Fraser made a comment that I had been the only one in the room who thought there had been an incendiary device on the aircraft, and he then asked why I thought I was the only one who was right. Looking at him, I managed to keep in check the urge to ask what he knew about the file and where he got his expertise. My thoughts were that I might have been the only one in the room willing to express the opinion that there may have been a criminal device above the ceiling, but the point was no one in the room knew for certain what had started that fire. At the very least, there was ample evidence now to suspect the presence of an incendiary device. I also knew two others in that room, at one time or another, held or had previously held suspicions about an incendiary device. They were John Garstang and Jim Foot. As for Gerden and Vance, they were pilots and not fire investigators, so they certainly had no expertise for any fire investigation even if they thought otherwise, and that included Jim Foot. He was an electrician, and if it had not been for Larry Fogg, he would have been totally lost on this file. The other two RCMP members, Cooper and Kerr, had never expressed their opinion to me, but they too had no expertise in the matter. As for Lathem and Neil Fraser, neither knew anything about fires, and Neil knew nothing about the file except what Lathem had told him. I felt their promotional desires so tainted their opinions that they were no longer trustworthy. My point of view was that when someone with adequate and acceptable expertise came forward with a reliable and credible opinion about the cause of the fire, we could then discuss and possibly determine the truth about its cause. Until that time, it remained up in the air. For now, though, the only person who could partially fulfill that role was Dr. Brown. I suspected that if Lathem and Gerden had their way, those answers would never be known. Too many of those in a position of control had already made up their minds for other reasons, and they were now afraid of the truth. However, I dared not say this to these two as they were in total control and I would have been out the hangar door in an instant. I kept quiet and just stared at Fraser, not answering his question.

Neil got into it further by commenting that there should be no need to assist Garstang with trip notes as those notes should be self-explanatory without any assistance from me. He said it in a kind of a flippant matter-of-fact manner as though he was expressing it solely to meet with Lathem's approval while knowing full well that indeed it would. I had to bite my tongue instead of again asking him where he had suddenly gained the knowledge to express such an opinion. He had other comments and demands, but they all showed his total ignorance of what was going on and his willingness to follow Lathem's lead blindly. He certainly did not wish to ruin any chance he had at his commission. He was going through the same process and was at the same point as was Gorman. They were vying for the same position.

Neil raised the topic of overtime by saying too much time and effort had been put into the file for my health. I told them this was an old story, but no help had ever been offered. Neil also made the statement that I should learn to say no to people who ask for things. I glanced at him and then at Lathem, and right then I decided I was fed up with their crap. I simply got up and walked out of the room, stating I had had enough of them. It was my way of saying no. As I walked out the office door and into the hangar area, Lathem shouted that he was not finished and for me to return. Continuing to walk away and without turning my head, my response was to say, too bad because I was done. However, he was shouting too loudly, and I was too far away for him to hear. My best option was to go somewhere and think things over because this whole session had added to an already high-stress level. Under the circumstances, I was not sure just what my reaction to more of this might have been. Perhaps that had been the whole purpose behind this effort by Lathem. Fraser was not needed except as a witness.

All Lathem had wanted was for me to fulfill the MOU as a simple photographer and exhibit taker, nothing else. He should have known better. I saw Lathem as nothing more than an amateur in a position of authority whose actions betrayed a level of competency that was insufficient to investigate properly a file of this nature or to stand up to those above him. However, this meeting showed he certainly could abuse those below him in rank. My opinion of him was that he was a thick-headed bully not unlike any street punk I had encountered frequently. The only thing different was that he had a badge and the rank to rule over me. As for Neil

Fraser, he appeared to me to be as two-faced as Gorman. Neil and I had worked together on the Halifax Ident Section for two years prior to Swissair, and he had looked after the DNA sample collection in the morgue. He, too, had stayed the sixty days that it was open. However, there was no use now in trying to explain anything to these two as they had their minds already made up. Any discussion would only have led to heated arguments, and Neil Fraser was there as a witness against me. The room was too small, they were too close, and the atmosphere was one of bullying and harassment.

One of the biggest problems in trying to respond to Gerden's and Lathem's actions was there had been no time to review the file and join the dots. I had taken extensive notes at every opportunity. I had monitored all the key tests up to that point, and one source or another had provided the results of others of less importance. Those observations and experiences had shaped my opinion without having to systematically and formally process the data. Once written, those notes had been set aside to be reviewed and correlated later. There had been no time to evaluate the recorded data because every day there was a continuous flood of new information. Besides, I had been concentrating on the criminal investigation of the fire, not preparing for what they were doing behind the scenes to impede that investigation while advancing their careers.

My experience of those commissioned officers for whom I had worked during my service was that about half of them were unqualified to fill their position. Corporals, Sergeants, and Staff Sergeants were no better. After all, Inspectors are commissioned from the NCO ranks. For many of them, there could never be any trust they would do what was best for the public or their subordinates, only what was best for their personal advancement and promotion. Many were alcoholics who found refuge and protection in the internal bureaucracy of the system. My first Inspector in Iqaluit told me, 'You don't smoke, you don't drink, you don't even swear enough to be in the North'. He was a drunk and should have been charged for impaired driving of the police vehicle on numerous occasions. He likely saw me as a threat to his alcoholic and playboy lifestyle because I would not lower myself to associate with him in the gutter. He demanded that I transfer south. He was abusive and belligerent with me for nearly the entire year that I worked for him. But everyone in the detachment was too scared to take him on due to his position of power within the system. Anyone trying to expose the misdeeds of a Commissioned Officer could ruin their career to the point that he or she might as well quit the Force. Those attempts would meet resistance from the more senior ranking officers who would never admit they had covered up the problem, sometimes for years. No Commissioned Officer would ever question the actions of another, certainly not openly, or that would go against the ever-present military-style discipline code of the Force. They feared it would cause chaos in the ranks. They had no regard for what harm it did to those working for the abusive member. What's more, there was no adequate system available to make a complaint about and then investigate such a problem member. The evidence of that would dominate and control this Swissair matter for many years to come.

But Iqaluit was not the only example. While in New Minas, my Officer in Charge in Halifax told my Sergeant that I was a disturber of unmentionable muck, but not in such dainty terms. I was trying to obtain a safe working environment within our Ident office. I had put a stop to our examination methods because we had to process crime scene exhibits with powders and chemicals at our office desks, the same desks where we sat to complete file notes and reports, or to eat our lunch. The chemicals commonly used on an Ident Section are toxic and present a serious health hazard unless used under proper safety conditions. With the support of my supervising Sergeant, we eventually received proper facilities after renovations to the building were made. The abuse abated somewhat until a new Sergeant arrived. He proved to me to be incompetent and a disgrace to Ident. Then for two years both the Superintendent and the new Sergeant conspired with lies and abuse to have me removed from Ident Services to a constable's position on detachment. The comment from the Superintendent was that I was a cancer and had to be cut out. They were nearly successful until I unwillingly transferred to Halifax. More than seven years later, the officer, now retired and in Alcoholics Anonymous, called to apologize for his actions. He said he had totally misread the situation and had made a serious mistake about me. He said that instead of pursuing me, he should have gone after the new Sergeant for his poor performance. I told him it was too late as the damage had already been done! I had retired six months earlier.

The good thing was the Commissioned Officers who replaced both were excellent, especially the Inspector in Iqaluit. He then moved to Yellowknife the year after I transferred there. He replaced another alcoholic Inspector. I had run-ins with that useless drunk on more than one occasion, one being a sudden death scene. He refused to believe my assessment of the body and scene physical evidence. When it was finally determined that I had been correct, he and his investigators considered it suspicious that I had known so much about the cause of death. When his investigator was shown a similar case in a Toronto Metro Police homicide investigation training manual, they backed off. They were incompetent amateurs!

Lathem appeared to me to be no different, and he seemed to have sold his soul for a promotion. There was not a thing to be done about it. He had bragged about passing his exams and he was now waiting to hear about his promotion to the next rank, possibly by two ranks. To receive that, he had to toe the line drawn by his superiors, and every officer's promotion had to be authorized by the Commissioner. While I did not yet know the role of Commissioner Zaccardelli in all of this, I would eventually come to understand just how involved he was.

This was certainly another of my twice as far moments. My old Norwegian saying came to mind once again to help settle things in my mind as I wrote up my notes for these two meetings.

On leaving the hangar, I ran into Jim Foot. Among other things, he mentioned the magnesium. As he had said in the meeting, he felt it was not their problem, that it was only a minuscule flag, and was not indicative of anything criminal. He based this opinion on the small amounts, a mere pinprick he called it. He said that what he had seen in the rest of the debris supported his belief. I wanted to ask him where he had suddenly gained his expertise in AES and fire scene examination and interpretation. He agreed that magnesium and the other elements existed and had been identified as a potential problem. He then again made his Zurich comment about initially thinking the cause of the fire was criminal. It was as if he had never said it before and he was only now letting me in on his little secret. Only now he sounded a bit more definite that the cause was not criminal. What had changed his mind, especially with the AES report now read by him? While I did not know what was in the report, I suspected a criminal scenario as one potential source. My opinion of Foot was that as a non-police and non-criminal investigator with no fire investigation expertise, where was his legal authority and mandate to determine if there was a criminal cause for this fire?

On Monday Cst. Kerr came to me to apologize for his part in what had occurred on Friday. Kerr said Lathem had ambushed me and he had received no forewarning it was going to happen. Lathem had come to him and ferreted information from him. He did not like what had happened, and he would never trust Lathem again. A little later Cst. Cooper had similar comments and said he was not happy with what had transpired after having information pried from him by Lathem. He also made some interesting comments about the meeting with the TSB. Cooper questioned Foot's argument that he was looking for the source of the fire. It seemed if it was an arcing event, Foot would put forth the effort, but he did not want the magnesium problem as a potential source. The other observation was Gerden's comment about safety concerns versus charges. Cooper indicated he felt Gerden had much more information than what was known by us and things were being hidden.

Now I knew how Lathem had obtained his information. I also learned that days before the meeting one of his backroom boys, Cpl. Peter Purchase, had made phone calls to solicit information from Kerr and Cooper. Purchase passed this on to Lathem who in turn used him as a third source of complaint, even though Purchase had not been in the hangar for months. So his comment about complaints from other members was a total fabrication. I would be correct in saying Lathem was lower than a snake in a swamp and could not be trusted.

Then in a conversation with John Garstang, without any prompting, he commented about Friday's meeting. John said he was very embarrassed over what happened in the meeting and it had not been handled at all well. John also stated he did not agree with Jim Foot in regards to the tiny amounts of magnesium being an insignificant event. When investigating explosive devices, trace evidence was minute in nature, and the pits caused on metal surfaces by the high velocity of minute fragments were microscopic in size but gigantic in significance. He also indicated that improvised explosive devices, or IEDs, as the name implied, were homemade and not dependable. Many such devices had been found to ignite and burn rather than ignite and explode, thus actually becoming an incendiary device. C4, the military explosive, was also used as a fuel for fires although dangerous to do so. It went without saying that when most incendiary devices burn, they seldom leave behind useable evidence. He indicated he would be discussing these topics with Gerden because of what had been stated in the meeting regarding causes. While John had not agreed with some of the comments made, he did not enter an objection at the time because it would have been a disagreement with his management. If John had taken my side in that meeting, he would have been out the door and back to Ottawa by nightfall. John also did not know what was in Dr. Brown's report. Because he was no longer on the systems committee, he had not been made privy to the report's contents. More compartmentalization by Gerden.

A few days later, on the 5th of December, 2000, when speaking with Gerden, he mentioned I would be staying on in the hangar for at least another couple of months. Then in a short discussion about AES, particularly magnesium, he again commented about the quantities being so small as to be insignificant. My response was that at least we would be able to say the subject had not been ignored and something had been done to look into it. Court attendance was mentioned, and he made a comment to the effect that they had no concern about Court as they never attended. He said he had no knowledge of what was in Dr. Brown's draft report, but he did say they wanted only the facts and numbers, no speculation. So, this certainly limited Dr. Brown's ability to interpret his results. It seemed their sudden expertise in Auger Electron Spectroscopy, the Anderson Theory, and some other fields would never need to be tested in a Court of Law or even the court of public opinion. However, I did not believe Gerden when he said he did not know what was in such a key report after having had it in their possession for nearly two weeks. Why did John tell me Gerden was seeking a meeting with Lathem about AES, a meeting that might include me? Gerden, as the Investigator in Charge for the TSB on this file, was required to know all about that report as soon as possible after its release. To not know implied he was derelict in his duty. That was not how Gerden worked. He chose to micromanage events as had been seen on many occasions. What's more, his Chairman of the Board had been in the hangar just days before this discussion, so surely Gerden would have been aware of the report's contents. He would have had to brief Bouchard before their big media conference.

Getting past this major confrontation was difficult, but there was no alternative. To cave in and quit would have been the end of everything I had done so far. I knew I was right, and that was sufficient for me to keep going. Besides, I owed it to John to complete what we were doing for the safety aspect of the file. When the 15th of December, 2000, rolled around, a CD of the notes and a stack of photocopied pages were handed over to Cooper to be passed on to Lathem.

Soon after this, Kerr and Cooper moved out of the hangar, taking with them the computer database. The working original went to the TSB in Ottawa while a copy was put on a terminal in Lathem's Major Crime Unit. I asked that another copy be put on my hangar computer since I was tasked daily with retrieving exhibits from the storage boxes. But Lathem refused saying the TSB had allowed him only the one copy. His response did not make much sense to me and it appeared to be a spur of the moment excuse. Perhaps there were notes, reports, and exhibits recorded in the database that I was not to see.

One day a bit later, I joined a conversation between Don Enns and the IFALPA representative who was a commercial pilot. IFALPA was the International Federation of Airline Pilots' Associations, the group who allowed cockpit voice recorders in the aircraft. They both talked about the effect that problems in the IFEN system would have had on the comfort levels of the passengers and flight crew. He said if a problem had occurred in the IFEN, the first thing noticeable would likely have been a loss of programming on the seat screens. Either the movies or games would have malfunctioned. This interruption would result in the passengers complaining to the flight attendants who in turn would verbally advise the captain either by entering the cockpit or by way of the intercom. However, there was no evidence of either of these on the cockpit voice recorder before or after the smell of smoke. Don said he agreed and thought the IFEN system malfunction was a secondary and not a primary event. This IFALPA representative had knowledge of the voice recorder contents as did Don.

Shortly after this on the 19th of December, 2000, Lathem showed up in the hangar to provide me with an official written reprimand for leaving the meeting. Ignoring it, I had a discussion with him. Among other things, my materials fire-test report that he forwarded to the TSB for their comments was brought up. I told him it should not have gone to the TSB in that manner, that what he had done was to burn John Garstang as my source and to expose me to Gerden's reprisals. I said no one would tell me anything now, thanks to his actions. With a fake look of concern, he responded by asking what he should have done and to whom I would have had him forward the report. I told him proper practice would have been to discuss it with me instead of going off to the TSB with it. I also said he was the plain clothes investigator and I was the Identification member. My job was to find the physical evidence related to the fire, its source, and any potential crime. His was to investigate for the possible suspects but not to turn a potential criminal matter over to a non-police organization. As well, I did not expect he would burn my source or me. Even though it would have been satisfying to do so, I did not say that as the Officer in Charge of the unit for major crime investigations, he was supposed to know the right thing to do. If he had to ask, then he should not be in charge. I told him there had been a failure to communicate. As the prime physical evidence investigator, I had been forced to go through other people with my reports and had never been able to approach him directly. There was plenty of paperwork to show it, and this was not the way to conduct a major investigation. It, of course, went unsaid that the reason for having to go through Gorman on everything was because he did not know or understand fires, physical evidence, or how to investigate this file.

While discussing this matter, Lathem made a comment that was of interest. He said he would not have the RCMP come between the TSB and the FAA. However, it was not the right of a police officer to decide against a criminal investigation when there were grounds to suspect a potential crime had caused the death of people. For him to refuse that investigation simply because he did not wish to hurt the feelings of a partner agency put him in a position of wilfully obstructing justice. No member of the police had that right. A fire on an aircraft had resulted in the deaths of hundreds of people, and what appeared to be flammable materials had been involved. Somehow those materials had passed the FAA safety test process and were allowed in the aircraft. It certainly seemed Lathem had allowed some ex-Colonel with no legal authority or forensic background to intimidate and harangue him into a position of abandoning his official duties as a police officer. However, raising this issue with him now in this manner would surely antagonize what was still a tense situation as it pertained not only to the FAA testing, but the whole Swissair file. So, there was nothing now to be gained and everything to lose by pursuing it further. Lathem came across as a conceited and arrogant officer who, in his mind, seemed to make no mistakes. As an RCMP commissioned officer, he was right even when he was wrong.

As for the official reprimand, what was strange was that there had been such a barrage of criticism over inappropriate and incorrect activities, yet the only thing mentioned on the reprimand was that I had walked out of the meeting. He did not mention any of the things he had complained about in the two sessions. At this time, I could only wonder why.

Soon after this, an interesting conversation took place while at lunch with John Garstang and Bill Ferguson. Bill was a CAD or computer assisted drafting instructor at the Nova Scotia Community College in Dartmouth. He had been contracted by the TSB to provide CAD work, and he supplied about six of his former students who worked daily in the hangar. Bill knew the plane structurally, having seen the drawings of nearly every piece of it. Working closely with John and Louis, the TSB's computer expert, gave him a good handle on many things in the hangar. This day John Britten of the TSB joined the lunch group. Britten had been setting up new flammability tests with the FAA for the new materials scheduled to go into the planes. During lunch, Bill asked questions about the former system of fire testing. The answers led to his comment about how incredibly inept the system was that allowed the placement of the Metallized Mylar and other flammable materials in the aircraft. Sitting to one side opposite Garstang, we both kept totally out of the conversation and had no influence on it in any way. Nor had Bill and I ever conversed on this matter. I had no idea he even held this opinion. Their conversation led to Bill's statement that the matter gave the appearance of corruption at one level or another, that materials were subjected to specific tests with what appeared to have been the intention of having them pass even though they would fail any new trials. On leaving the lunchroom, Bill commented further that it was criminal that people had to die in this crash before this re-examination took place. All I could think of were Lathem's written instructions in his memo to me.

"…. and there is no identified requirement for you to have any further involvement."

On the 13th of February, 2001, I received an email from Lathem to attend a meeting with him that would include Lee Fraser who was now the Director of all RCMP Forensic Identification Services across Canada. Gorman, Neil Fraser, and Peter Purchase would also be there. The meeting was purported to go over Identification methods for the file, probably for a best-practices review. I checked with Neil Fraser by email to see just what the meeting was to cover, and if it was for Ident practices, why would Lathem and Peter Purchase be there? His response skated around my question by being non-committal, but I noticed his reply was now added to my original, and a copy of everything was forwarded to Lathem. It had me wondering what it was all about, but I could never have anticipated what occurred in the meeting once it started.

I also received an email from Dr. Brown regarding AES and its use in everyday fire investigations. He was optimistic about the process and said it might be a viable method after further research. He also stated he had examined several wires involved in a short-circuiting event on another aircraft, and he had found little if any magnesium in those cables.

He then added the following line.

"As you had earlier suggested, some external and internal pressure applied to have me remove and/or alter commentary in my draft interim report (especially on sources for the Mg anomaly seen in many arc melt exhibits)."

Mg, of course, was the chemical symbol for magnesium. This comment seemed to relate directly to Gerden's previous statement of wanting only the facts and numbers, no speculation. While Dr. Brown had not elaborated, the question was if he would or had already succumbed to this pressure to limit his comments. After all, Dr. Brown was under a civil contract to the TSB. Also, I wondered if the report would be passed on to the RCMP, especially since Dr. Brown as much as said in this email that magnesium was still in question. It was exactly one year to the day since I had sent an email message to him suggesting he keep good notes and provide me with a warning if there was any pressure applied to influence him or to have him alter his work.

An email response was prepared to tell him if he felt he had evidence of a criminal device on the aircraft, he should make a formal complaint to the RCMP. Up until then, all I had were his initial three scenarios, but nothing more verbally and anything else was said indirectly in emails from him. Before sending it, I decided it should first go through Lathem.

Garstang then called to say they were once again planning an extension until mid-March 2001 for my work in the hangar. By this time, I had been the sole RCMP member on the file for three months.

CHAPTER 5 – CHANGE THE NOTES

On February 20, 2001, the 9 am meeting in Bedford began seven minutes late. Those present as expected were Supt. Lee Fraser as the senior officer, Insp. Andy Lathem, S/Sgt. Vic Gorman and Neil Fraser, and Cpl. Peter Purchase, the file manager. The meeting took place in Lee Fraser's former office in the tower in Bedford, a suburb of Halifax. Gorman had taken over the quite modern and large office when he had become the acting Regional Ident Supervisor, and since his transfer to Ottawa in July 2000, Neil Fraser had been filling the position along with his other duties. Only afterward did I realize that the seating arrangements had been orchestrated by Lee who was there when I arrived. We all sat at a large oval-shaped table about six feet wide and eight feet long. It was positioned off to one side in a small boardroom area with windows, something my office in the hangar did not have. I was seated with my back against the room's corner while Lee was on my left with the windows close behind him and Neil Fraser on my right. Close behind Neil was part of the wall and a shelving unit. Vic Gorman was on Neil's right while Lathem was directly opposite me and the farthest away. Peter Purchase was beside him and closest to the doorway. Because I was in the back corner, I did not have free access to leave the table. As well, I sensed an air of strangeness, a kind of tension about the room as they were all very formal with no friendliness or joking.

It started out with Lee stating the file would finish as of February 28th, 2001. That agenda quickly changed when I showed them Garstang's email for the extension. We discussed it for some time to decide what should be done and why. After what seemed like a ridiculous and needlessly lengthy discussion, they finally realized the extension was necessary to fulfill the MOU agreement. The Force was committed regarding that point. Lee then stated he wanted the Ottawa Identification Section to take over the work, and I would be removed totally from any involvement. I immediately questioned this by saying the work was here in Halifax, not in Ottawa. Lee stared at me with a puzzled look as if questioning my comment. Possibly he had spent so much time in Ottawa and was so wrapped up in the puzzle palace of the Headquarters bureaucracy that he seemed to think everything ceased to exist outside the Ottawa city limits. Perhaps, though, he was thinking seriously, and he had to make some quick changes to his plans. He certainly did not give me any clues. Since no one else said anything, I explained to Lee that the debris was still here in Shearwater, and the work still involved specialized photographs of the pieces, the frame, and the new exhibits I was finding and processing daily for the TSB. I went on to say they required someone with an extensive knowledge of the aircraft and its components as well as the ability to work the exhibit system to be able to retrieve specialized parts from the several million pieces in the exhibit hangar. I was the only RCMP member with that complete knowledge and ability. Only John Garstang had better knowledge of the entire aircraft and the debris. I did not say it, but I seldom had to refer to the database to find the pieces the TSB required. I knew the eight hundred boxes in the storage hangar along with their contents so well, I usually did not need that assistance. As for the burnt area of the aircraft, there were perhaps only two TSB members who had an equal or better knowledge than me. My thoughts were that if Fraser and Lathem wanted to fulfill the MOU, they had to keep me in the hangar to complete my present duties. This idea of Fraser's, who had so far been controlling the meeting, had me wondering just what was planned. I had known Lee for a long time and could usually read him well. What I was seeing and hearing I did not like, especially when Fraser again said they had to decide whether I would stay on with the file or leave it completely. Fraser's response had my attention, and I was worried.

A short discussion started regarding possible non-accident indicators. A list of items was briefly explained to Lee including the ceiling tiles, the bent door track, burnt and melted areas in the cabin carpet and curtains as well as seat cushions, and the large quantity of molten metal pieces that had been found. AES readings were quickly mentioned, including one that had been as high as forty-five percent magnesium with no aluminum present. This discussion lasted for less than five minutes, and Lee's response was to nod his head slowly. However, he did not appear to be listening, and it was as though I was boring him. The others said nothing.

The email from Dr. Brown was shown to them including the short paragraph about the interference. After reading it, Fraser started another lengthy discussion over how it should be handled. There was an opinion stated that Dr. Brown's credibility had been compromised by the interference of his supervisor. There came a comment from Purchase and Gorman that I had compromised it a year before by sending off the original email warning him of possible pressure to alter his procedures and findings. My email had come about after Foot's first of several tirades about putting him back on track, that Dr. Brown was not hired to search for a magnesium source. The idea of my having compromised him by sending the email had been raised several times in other RCMP meetings, and each time they were told their comments were ridiculous. It just proved to me they did not know anything about the players involved, Court expertise, or opinion evidence. As far as I knew, the TSB had no knowledge of my email, but perhaps Lathem had passed it on to Gerden just like everything else.

Then there was a discussion over how to go about this whole magnesium issue. At one point, Lathem made the brilliant comment that the presence of magnesium was a gray area, and he asked if it was science or merely an opinion. He had made this statement before in a meeting with Duncan and all the RCMP investigators when the spooling down of the file had been announced. This time, I just looked at him and wondered if he had ever taken a chemistry or physics course in his life. Dr. Brown as a Ph.D. had more education and knowledge of elements and chemicals and how they interacted than all five of these guys put together. Lathem was making a statement like this and trying to make it look as if he knew what he was saying. The others in the room all nodded and voiced their agreement. I wanted to say something, but this time my better judgment overruled me, and I decided to keep the insults to myself.

My proposed email response was presented, but Lee quickly rejected it. Lee Fraser suggested a face-to-face between Dr. Brown and Lathem to go over the AES methods and results and then to breach this question of interference. He said it would, of course, require an immediate follow-up visit to Vic Gerden to inform him of these actions. The look of surprise and shock on Lathem's face was very noticeable, and there was no doubt of what I saw there. A face-to-face was never going to happen because it could only result in one thing. Lathem knew Dr. Brown could supply a convincing argument describing the physical evidence that all but proved the presence of a criminal incendiary device. He would then have to act, something he and Force management seemed not to want to happen. After much discussion that did not include me, it was finally agreed I would send off a different short email message.

"Please clarify your last paragraph of your message of 01-02-13."

While arriving at this decision, there was again considerable discussion over the AES process and the findings in the beads, including the amounts of magnesium and other elements that were present. I again told Fraser about some of the readings reaching as much as forty-five percent with no aluminum present, and readings like that required a much closer look. My opinion was ignored. Any proposed action centred on Lathem and Fraser having to know what was going on regarding the message. Nothing, though, was said about the high magnesium and aluminum levels.

That all of this was just a false front would soon be revealed, proving that appearances can indeed be deceptive. Fraser and Lathem merely wanted to know what Brown's complaint was so they could pass it on to Gerden and the TSB's management. More important, the design of this whole discussion was to bait me to see what I knew about the AES reports.

Throughout, the atmosphere of the meeting had been very official, and everything was businesslike with no friendliness or cordiality. Looking back after what followed next, someone might even think Fraser and Lathem were following a script and the two email messages had merely interrupted their plans.

Lee Fraser now began to ask some very intense questions about possible indicators of a criminal device on the aircraft. The four distinct locations of molten metal were again described but this time in more detail as to location and amounts. Lee was provided the time/temperature amounts for the burnt ceiling tiles, but he probably did not understand the significance of any of it.

Looking around the room, everyone was quiet and not very attentive to what I was saying. Right then I had a sixth sense, a premonition they knew something was coming and I didn't. What I said generated more discussion with Lee. He asked me what I thought had caused the fire. He was told that to produce those temperatures and provide the AES readings we had obtained, an incendiary device containing magnesium, aluminum, and iron would have been necessary.

Lee quietly asked if I had any idea who might have placed such a device on the aircraft. Al Qaeda was mentioned, a vendetta against one or more passengers was possible, and the idea of the British MI6 agent Tomlinson being assassinated by the British Secret Intelligence Service was also mentioned. I said to Lee it was not my job to look for suspects, merely to identify the evidence. Lee just made a face, rolled his eyes, and grunted as if indicating he did not for a second believe any of this. I had the feeling they thought I was merely describing the far-fetched plot in a movie I had recently seen instead of an actual real life occurrence.

Lee asked the direct question of why I thought the TSB wanted this investigation to be a non-criminal matter. It rather caught me by surprise because I thought everyone knew the TSB could only investigate the file as a non-criminal accident. Lee must have missed that disclosure during our meeting with Garstang the week before I went into Hangar A. I told him the airworthiness directives would be worthless if a criminal action had been the cause of the fire. The airlines would never go ahead with the changes and would argue the fire was a criminal event due to a lack of security instead of faulty equipment. This important point would be raised again later. Possible locations in the aircraft for a device and how it could have been planted were also mentioned. The experience with the ceiling hatch and the SR Technics member in Zurich were described, including the hatch's location and size. Lee seemed to take heed of it asking if Lathem knew about it. I mentioned it was all in the trip notes on the Force's note file. Lathem slowly responded with a purposefully measured nod of his head that relayed in an arrogant and condescending manner that this was nothing new to him.

As I sat there looking at these two, part of my sixth sense was telling me this all seemed like theatrics. It was all surreal as Lathem, Gorman, and Purchase had full knowledge of all this, so why was it being explained again just for Lee Fraser. He ultimately should have had no seat at the decision-making table to determine how this matter was to be handled. His position was strictly administrative and non-operational in Headquarters Ident, Ottawa. Instead, he was acting as if he were the theatrical manager trying to cover all the preliminaries before the start of the performance that would lead in a prearranged direction to define my fate, all depending, of course, on my level of mental reasoning and how I responded to their demands.

A trip around the table was made to ensure there were no other concerns, for whatever value that may have been. After Peter Purchase was dismissed from the room, the meeting turned to take aim at my file notes. Lee Fraser did most of the talking once Lathem stated he had sent the CD off to Lee who gave it to Gorman to read. Due to the volume of material, Vic arranged to have eleven Identification members in Ottawa read those notes, well over a hundred pages each. Lathem said they had concerns with parts of the notes. He made it sound as if it was a unanimous finding and unprompted by Gorman or Fraser.

Now my mind was racing after hearing how the notes had been read, and I immediately realized there were two reasons for doing it this way. The first was to find certain specific areas or topics in the notes. The second was to keep the individual members from reading and learning too much about the file, or they might ask embarrassing questions. Later it was learned the first reason was the exact truth. The second was evident when all the notes were read. Instructions had been given to the nine other readers to locate and mark with coloured tabs the areas that included opinion, controversial entries that could embarrass the Force or the TSB, and any entries indicating the cause of the crash. Lee Fraser and Vic Gorman, both readers of the notes themselves, came up with these rules for their dubious undertaking.

I suddenly remembered that when Lathem arrived at the meeting, he entered a few minutes late and was carrying a tall cardboard box. He now retrieved that box and removed a stack of typewritten bond paper that looked to be well over a foot high. He stated they had the notes printed and this was the result. In that stack were pages marked with tabs of three different colours, probably four hundred tabs in all.

Lee Fraser now abruptly caught my attention when he forcefully asked if I thought the plane had been brought down by an explosion. For an instant, I thought perhaps he was joking. He was not! Both his attitude and the atmosphere in the room had suddenly become one of hostility. To reinforce his point, Fraser spoke of the explosive wires that were detailed in my notes and asserted I had alluded to a conspiracy in which the presence of explosives had been covered up. He demanded to know if I thought the plane had been blown up, speaking as if he was the bad cop in a Hollywood detective movie. However, I had not just suddenly materialized in the middle of some B-rated movie. What was happening was all too real, and as ludicrous as it seemed, I was being interrogated. At this point, Fraser had my full attention even though I could not believe the lunacy of the accusation. The whole issue was explained, including that Garstang wanted it all kept quiet as ordered by Gerden. Fraser argued that point and said he did not believe Gerden would have done such a thing. He accused me of saying it was a conspiracy to cover up an explosion. Several comments were made by the others in support of Fraser's attack, but because the notes were not available and I could not remember many of the fine details, it was impossible to offer a defensive argument other than what I had already said. Besides that, the whole matter had come out of left field, and to me, his accusations were so ridiculous I thought the notes had been misread. In my mind, that had to be the only reason. The answer I had provided to him was an explanation of what I remembered from the notes. The remains of explosive materials had been found on a beach during the initial shoreline search for debris, and they were believed to have been used by fisherman for illegal fishing. I happened upon the items one day in the exhibit room when photographing seat covers for Garstang, and he advised Gerden wanted their existence kept quiet. Neither Swissair nor Boeing knew of them, and it turned out that besides John, in the TSB only Gerden and Vance knew of the exhibits. Garstang told me Gerden did not want the TSB associated with anything as obviously criminal as illegal fishing with explosives. Since I had already explained it once, there was no need to go through it again, certainly not for these fools.

It seemed Fraser was on his personal mission and would not be deterred by the facts. He very nearly called me a liar, but perhaps he knew better than to do so. Instead, it was made to seem I was biased and alluding to a conspiracy. At this point, acting more like a pageboy providing a new sword for his knight, Lathem went to his pile of printed and tagged pages to try to find the notes for the explosives. His actions under different circumstances would have been comical as he grabbed handfuls of pages and flipped through them as if trying to find some code or marking. Whatever it was, it eluded him, and he became frustrated. Fraser finally told him not to bother with the notes, and he started to harangue and criticize the idea that the crash was criminal, and again he said the words conspiracy and cover-up. Fraser demanded to know why I alleged in the notes there was a conspiracy to hide something or cover things up. I told him the concern was things had not been fully and properly examined, not that they had been covered up. I had not alluded to a conspiracy except possibly with the FAA burn tests of previous years. Fraser turned to that subject by asking what should have been done about it. I suggested the FBI should have been contacted. Lathem quickly interjected almost defensively by stating that Gerden was looking into the matter and he had a committee set up to review it. He did not say it, but probably he knew the committee was only considering new tests and not how the old tests had come about or who had benefited after allowing flawed materials to pass those faulty tests.

Other areas were brought up after Lathem finally found a few things from the stack of notes. Perhaps a little bit of prior planning would have done wonders for this interrogation, but then Lathem had done nothing right on this file yet. He brought out notes for the 11th of April 2000, and the 16th of November, 1999. He read off the contents of the pages, and all the while Fraser interjected with the words 'shameful,' 'I'm ashamed of you', and 'you have let us down.' Fraser also made the comment I could no longer be trusted and my career was finished, I would not be going anywhere in Ident. I did not take it as a mere threat. It was a fact I could never alter. Fraser, as the Director of the RCMP's Forensic Identification Services, had the power, and he could reach out to any other Police Service or Security Agency in Canada. There would be no future promotions or advancement in Ident Services anywhere.

Fraser began another harangue over the contents of the notes, and whenever he stopped, Lathem took over. Everything from them was negative, and Fraser continuously interjected with the comments that he was disappointed in me, ashamed of me and I had let him down. It was only three years earlier he had asked me to write for my commission. Fraser had said then that of all the Forensic Ident people in the Force, if he had a crime scene involving one of his relatives, he would want me to handle it. According to him, I was one of the very best, I was extremely thorough, and I never gave up. Now things were different. As for Lathem, whenever he stopped to breathe, Gorman would add his few comments only to be interrupted by Fraser. Neil Fraser took notes, but I knew he was not there for my benefit. He even asked a few questions of his own. Lee Fraser made another comment that the notes indicated a conspiracy or cover-up on the part of the RCMP. Lathem immediately interrupted as if upset and offended by my implied accusation. He demanded to be shown where he was suppressing evidence as he thumped himself forcefully in the chest with his right fist. It was quite a piece of theatrics on his part, and he might have had a future on the stage. They paused as if to wait for an answer, but I just gave him a cold stare. This buffalo court was not a fair hearing. I was not prepared, and my stress levels were at an extremely high level. It was better to say nothing than to say what I thought of this bunch of idiotic clowns and their buffalo circus. Their minds were made up to try to discredit and intimidate me in any way possible.

As they went on, it became apparent their concern was how my notes would be torn apart by both the media and the lawyers in any Court cases. They seemed to think my credibility was totally destroyed because of the details included in the notes. Their problem was disclosure and having bits and pieces taken out of context. Apparently, they were experts in how badly the media would manipulate what was in those notes, and the material would not only embarrass me but both the TSB and the RCMP.

Fraser went on to question why the notes were not put into F&R, the Force's computer database for the file. The reason was explained as best as possible between the haranguing. The program could not accept the tables and columns of data that formed a large part of my notes, so they were written in Word. Lathem had agreed to this during one of our earliest meetings, of which there had been several and none of them could have been called cordial. Fraser commented that had these notes been submitted routinely every week, they could have been read, and the questionable parts addressed. I asked him if he meant edited, and he said no, but to answer the questions raised in those notes and address them. He came back to the explosive wires and the conspiracy as an example, but they still could not find those notes no matter how much Lathem again tried.

Fraser had been one of the eleven readers, and it was clear he had not read this section or he would have known he was wrong. He pointed out that the section he did read was very dull and boring. I saw this as a chance to explain to him that when anyone takes one hundred pages out of context, they would never have an accurate feel for the facts. Those reading their separate sections would know nothing of the environment or the participants involved. Fraser scoffed at this and several times he said he was very upset and disappointed. The tone of the meeting most certainly was that I was in trouble, I had done something terribly wrong, and my credibility for this file was finished. Lee again stated I would never be involved in any future serious investigation, and my career in Identification Services was finished, I was going nowhere. I took it to mean I would never see the rank of Staff Sergeant or higher. That was the wrong thing for him to say because there were only about two positions in the country I could ever hope to promote into and Fraser had already been turned down when he suggested I seek a commission. However, I was in trouble and they wanted to separate themselves from me just as far as they could, or so it seemed.

He asked if I would go through the notes to add clarifications to areas that were a problem. I asked if he meant the notes were to be edited. At first, he stated he wanted the questioned areas explained by adding follow-up details that related to the matter. Lathem immediately jumped into the conversation with a typed piece of paper and said no, he wanted the material edited out. I immediately questioned this, and at first, I thought Lee Fraser did not know this was about to happen. However, later when Neil Fraser's notes were reviewed, they indicated Lee fully supported the idea and led the demand for the creation of the second set of notes. Lathem was adamant the material must be removed and said he wanted an edited version of the notes with the 'personal opinion' material removed. He handed over the piece of paper that read:

> I, Sgt. T.C. JUBY, have reviewed all notes submitted by myself for filing as they relate to Operation Homage. These notes reflect my personal theories and speculations. They are not founded in fact nor is there any evidence to support them.
> Subsequently, by my own free will and volition without duress, I freely admit that my personal beliefs do not reflect the factual information found within the area of my responsibility – that being the identification, photographing, physical matching and physical examination of evidence.

Further, I agree to review my notes and to edit the non-factual information, knowing full well that the original notes will be retained on file. I will also take training to remedy this issue to ensure it is not repeated in the future.

T.C. JUBY, Sgt.
Witness
Date

 The page was quickly scanned to realize Lathem was serious about wanting a second set of notes without what they deemed to be the controversial material. However, this was wrong, and I quietly asked Fraser if this was legal. Fraser and Lathem both said to sign it, and I again spoke to Fraser, but this time to say this was illegal. He looked at me and again said I was a disappointment and had let him down, and then he confirmed it was indeed legal. Lathem made a comment that they had checked with Scott over at Halifax Headquarters, and he had agreed with it. This statement certainly did not alter the balance because my trust in Lathem and Gorman had run out long ago, and Lee Fraser's trust bank had suddenly developed a massive blowout. I told them that all of this questioned material could be included in the notes because scene notes were to include anything that reflected upon the matter at hand including the atmosphere during which the matter occurred. Lathem made the comment, "Oh, yeah, I've heard that one before". He went on to say the original notes would remain on the file, but the edited copy would be used for disclosure and access to information purposes.

 I did not heed what he was saying because I was thinking. These four had used their collective powers for over an hour to intimidate and pressure me. To a point, they had been successful. Every time I had given an explanation, they had mocked or ridiculed it only to build up to another criticism of something else. To say I had been beaten down was an understatement. Between Lee Fraser and Andy Lathem, they had the power, and even if they could not fire me, they could make life miserable for as long as I remained in the Force. What they did not realize was that they had underestimated my stubbornness. They had not broken me no matter how much they had tried. I realized this was all wrong, and I suspected this to be a criminal obstruction of justice even if what I had in my notes was improper. However, I had no proof outside of this office. I also realized these guys would back each other and all would be against me unless I had physical proof. To simply refuse their demand and do nothing would undoubtedly result in my expulsion from the file. To grab the paper and run was worthless because they could say I had made up the whole thing. What was needed was Lathem's signature, and he had provided that opportunity. When looking at the page the first time, a signature block had been noticed at the bottom for Lathem's name as a witness. So, it was decided to go for it. Looking directly at Lathem, he was asked if he would sign the page and provide a copy if I signed it. He almost excitedly said he would. As I again looked at the paper, there was something I did not like about it besides what was written there. It was the space where nothing was written. There was a wide space between the last line of the typed body and the signature area that was too wide for a normal note or memo. It was as if there was room purposefully left for something else to be added later once the page was signed. Speaking to Lathem in a manner more saying than asking, I said that it was a second set of notes that he wanted minus the personal material. He nodded agreement as he looked at me, not knowing what my intention was. In very bold handwriting, I scrawled the same words across the wide blank area:

"In other words, a second set of notes minus the personal material."

Then the page was signed, handed to Lathem and he was told to sign it, which he did in front of everyone. After going to the photocopier, I watched as he put the page into the machine and out came one copy that he brought back and handed to me. Before he did so, he again said he hoped to be able to get the edited version through any access to information requests and any following disclosure requests if it went that far. He had a look of satisfaction as if he had accomplished a major task.

There was some discussion for a minute or two between Lathem and Lee Fraser about how the changes would be made and how they would handle the note file. Once they finished, Fraser made the statement I would remain working on the file to support the MOU but only for that purpose. As for reports and results of tests, I would never know the details. For exhibits I may send out for the TSB or tests in which I might become involved, if reports were generated, they would be received at the Major Crime Unit and would go directly to the file. I would have no knowledge of them. I was there simply to do the work for the TSB and nothing else. Fraser was not asking for a comment. He was making a directive, and in no uncertain terms, this was the way it would be.

Well, so far during the file I had seldom received any written reports, so that would not make much difference. Moreover, he had no idea just how many contacts I had. However, I did not even nod. Instead, I just stared at him. This file had not only taken away any rapport I ever had with Gorman, but now vanished into thin air was a twenty-four-year-long friendship with Fraser. It went through my mind that power and promotion can easily corrupt some people, and I felt this indeed was corruption.

My stomach was now churning as suddenly I was unsure if I had committed a crime by signing or yet another by lying to a commissioned officer. I was now second guessing myself. For sure I had no intention whatsoever of following through with the demand. I never did intend to from the start. However, I was now worried. I had no plan other than to renege on Lathem's piece of paper, and I suddenly realized I had no one I could go to who could do something about this. I had a couple of members I could trust who could offer advice, but I believed these guys had just committed a serious criminal act. If I had arrested them, I would have been up against some very powerful enemies who had the ways and means to counter my story and who would have had me charged with some contrived offence. However, I had to do something, and Brian Flanagan was my first choice as he was the Division Staff Relations Representative.

I realized a few things about the demand while they talked amongst themselves. There had been no chance to review the notes, and they knew it. It would have taken days to go through the two-and-one-half years' worth of daily notes. Fraser was told when he questioned me about the explosive materials that I could not remember what I had written. It later was realized that short-term memory loss was one of the results of excessive stress and those stress levels during this meeting had been at the top of the scale. It was the fight or flight syndrome that had taken effect, and my instinct was to concentrate on those two actions. It was no wonder the finer details could not be remembered. As for the rest of

Lathem's paper, I was sitting in a room with two senior officers and two senior NCOs, one of whom was in an acting Inspector's position. For over an hour, they had repeatedly declared I had done a terrible deed. Any response I gave was ripped apart. Neil Fraser taking notes was intimidating enough, but it constantly reminded me to be careful of what I said.

Even so, in the back of my mind, I knew there eventually would be a settling of accounts for all of this. I had been asked to alter my official file notes by deleting important observations and details written at the time to describe the events and the circumstances. That was illegal. Notes were to reflect what was seen, heard, and done at any moment as a refresher to my memory at some later date. Considering my qualifications, my opinions were a necessary and integral part of those notes. Karl Christiansen had undergone something similar, but when he turned down Lathem's request and sought the paper's withdrawal, Lathem ordered him out of the hangar and told him to cease any further contact with the file and with me. My belief was that his actions were illegal. So what might Lathem have done had this paper not been signed? In effect, time had been bought so other resources could be contacted. However, who other than Brian Flanagan? As for the idea of getting up and leaving the meeting, to do that would have accomplished nothing and likely would have resulted in an immediate transfer off the file, possibly even a suspension and charges if Lathem had his way. As well, they had chosen the seating arrangements, and I was hemmed into the back corner of the room.

With this portion of the meeting at an end, Lathem had lived up to the name 'Ambush Andy' that I gave to him after the meeting of the 1st of December, 2000. Once the Frasers had gone, he and Gorman provided my annual assessment. Lathem started by handing me a written reprimand for the notes to make it official that I had done something terribly wrong. He then provided an interim assessment that committed to paper a description of the poor job I had done on this file.

The reprimand was dated for the 20th while the performance evaluation was dated on the 19th. Immediately I saw how the grievance for all of this would be won. Eventually, I would show he had broken every rule in the career management manual, thus making him look incompetent. This was something he had proven to me throughout his time in the hangar.

Because he had been my immediate supervisor for only five months, he did not want to complete the entire assessment. What he was doing was allowing Gorman to write the main assessment, thereby providing a second consistent opinion.

The evaluation Gorman had prepared was then read to me. When finished, they expected I would sign it as received. They both seemed surprised when I told them I would not sign until after I added my comments in a day or two. After all, I was entitled to do that much. While he had been reading the form, it came to mind that perhaps he thought reading it out loud amounted to a discussion, but no dialog took place at any time during the process. Assessments were supposed to be discussed and agreed upon if possible. It seemed as if he was showing off to Lathem like a little child to its parent, as though he was saying, see how good a job I can do, just like you asked me to do. However, at the time his words were a jumble and all I heard were the negative comments that went on and on for two long pages.

Much later when Gorman's assessment was analyzed for the grievance process, it was realized that much of the narrative was contradictory. An example was the comment in one paragraph that many long hours had been worked effectively with John, but in the next line, I was not a team player. This term seemed to be a common descriptor within the Force when someone in management did not want an independent thinker who had ideas contrary to those of the supervising member.

An assessment was to be written for a one-year period and must not overlap the previous year. Gorman had gone back to a year earlier and taken the same matters that he previously had written in glowing terms to apply a new spin and now write them in a very derogatory manner.

Once finished, other issues were raised. When the meeting came to an end, a quick exit was made, taking with me the proof of incompetence and corruption. I did not want Lathem to have time to change his mind after realizing I had an incriminating piece of evidence.

It was now becoming clearer what I had to do. When Brian Flanagan was contacted, the situation was fully explained to him. He was in total agreement with me and my actions. Brian had a lengthy history of detachment and investigative work and was highly respected for his experience and opinions on matters such as this.

He agreed the next step was to meet with Internal Investigations Section. First though, I had to start my grievances for the assessments. There was only one thing he thought I should have done differently. I should have arrested the four of them on the spot and put them in handcuffs to be led away to jail. Easier said than done! What I should have done was to get all four of their signatures on the demand as witnesses.

A short time later, I met with J.J. King of Internal Investigations Section. He had a slightly different assessment of the situation. I had known J.J. since 1988, and he, too, was very experienced in operational policing. I maintained a great respect for him and his opinion.

His first reaction to the change-the-notes paper and my explanation of the details was that, under the circumstances, there certainly must have been duress because of those who were present, what was being discussed, and the way the discussions were held. Second, with the volume of notes involved and the lack of notice given, there was no way the notes could have been reviewed, something that forms the very first line of the demand. J.J. asked what exactly was to be edited. There was nothing specific mentioned in the statement, only generalities. The idea of changing or editing was unclear. He was told that Lathem's intent, as I understood it, was to have two versions of the notes. J.J. assured me there was no way any material could be deleted from the notes. If there was something specific I believed to be wrong, it could only be corrected by making an addition with the appropriate notation specifying that fact. He stated that under no conditions can a police investigator have two sets of notes. To attempt to go to Court with two sets would only invite disaster. However, the key to any additions that altered the notes was I had to believe the particular notation was wrong and something added would correct the issue. Merely someone else thinking it was wrong did not count.

J.J. advised I should contact Lathem to request he specify what particular areas he had a problem with by page and content. The matter could then be clarified for him if I thought it necessary. If there was a mistake in the accuracy of the material, a notation of clarification to correct it could be added to ensure the accuracy of the notes. He thought I did not have the time to go through more than one thousand pages of notes to pick out areas Lathem might want to be clarified. I asked J.J. what would happen if Lathem ordered me to change the notes. He felt it would not occur as it was an illegal act, and I would then have every right to refuse such an order. If it went so far as to be a refusal, the matter would go to the IIS office. Of course, J.J. would have to bow out of the investigation because of this discussion, but he felt such an incident would not occur because of the obvious illegal nature of the event.

There was one thing that came out of this meeting with J.J. that made me realize the problem I now had. The only way to have Internal Investigation Section investigate the matter was if it came from the top down. An officer would have to make the complaint to IIS. For me to instigate an internal investigation without the assistance of an officer was impossible. So, I was on my own until I could stir the pot through the grievance procedure. That would take time, a very long time as it turned out.

Later, after thinking about the idea of contacting Lathem about the notes as J.J. had suggested, I decided against it for several reasons that would eventually be proven correct.

As for Lathem and Fraser, they had underestimated my firm belief that Court credibility was the mainstay of any crime scene investigator's work or, for that matter, the work of any street police person. Without it, he or she might as well quit because they were working for nothing. Everything that was done during an investigation could and probably would be scrutinized in Court, and my credibility in giving evidence was paramount. So, if I had done as Lathem demanded and had altered the notes, he would have created a situation in which I could never go to Court.

Two things needed to be pondered about Fraser's and Lathem's actions. The first was why he would want to create an edited note file unless Lathem had the intention of using it. The second was that the very act of editing the notes would totally ruin my credibility for this file, something they seemed to want desperately. Why?

There was such a thing as vetting of notes, but that was done by the Crown Counsel and was something different. It was the removal of names and details of a secret informant before disclosure for a trial. That was legally done by the Crown to keep the informant alive while convicting the accused. However, for a file like this, there was no reason for it. During the meeting, the discussion about Dr. Brown changing his report had led to suggestions his credibility for Court was ruined. However, he was under contract and was not a police officer. It was his report and not his notes that were to be altered, even though that in itself was illegal. Lathem and Fraser wanted my actual notes edited and changed. I suspected there was much more to this than what I could see at the time.

My role in this file had placed me in the position as the main witness in any Court case or hearing that might ensue. That was because the TSB would refuse to attend Court. However, once in Court, the public disclosure of certain details would destroy the TSB's plans for safer materials. It might even have created distrust and animosity towards the TSB that would emanate from the FAA and the NTSB. As for Boeing and Swissair, removing evidence of a possible alternate cause for the fire might have strengthened their civil case against Hollingsead and Santa Barbara, the two companies responsible for the IFEN and its installation. Added to that was the potential that the families might undertake a class action lawsuit. These were ample reasons for my potential evidence to be discredited and thereby keep me out of any Court case. Lathem's and Fraser's attempts, if successful, would have done that. It might make an unbiased person think Fraser and Lathem had been bought, or if not them, someone higher up the chain of command who controlled them.

A few weeks later, I received an envelope from Lathem containing instructions on note taking that he had pulled from the RCMP's data website. At the time it was merely set aside. Much later it would be analyzed line by line during the assessment grievance process to find that some of Force policy constituted instructions that likely would be deemed unlawful in a Court of Law in this country. This argument would eventually become very contentious in the upcoming battle with the RCMP, and subsequently, the Force would totally alter its note-taking policy to remove all the improper instructions. Of course, any connection between the reason for those changes and my complaint to the Force that pointed out the illegal policy was mere coincidence.

Moving on, Dr. Brown replied to my email requesting clarification.

"Hi Tom

1st: I've been misled repeatedly by TSBC about Swissair Fl111 with respect to onboard emergency flares (number, types, and locations). Only when confronted with info from other sources was their presence finally acknowledged and then only the existence of flares under doors in emergency chute/raft compartments (Other sources indicate airliners also carry flares accessible by the flight and cabin crew; TSBC says no). I'd like to believe them but experience makes me a skeptic.

2nd: My draft report has been heavily criticized because of comments on anomalous levels of magnesium in arc melt exhibits and possible reasons (my opinions). Some comments were justified and I've revised them. However, mention of the element Mg, presence of any pyrotechnic onboard sources and even the possibility that an enriched environment of magnesium existed in the vicinity of the wiring at the time of electrical arcing has come under considerable criticism. I have thus added a disclaimer that views and opinions expressed are those of the author and do not necessarily state or reflect those of the TSBC.

Regards,
Jim

Obviously, this reply should have been taken very seriously as he mentioned the presence of a pyrotechnic or, in other words, an incendiary or criminal source for the fire. Dr. Brown had previously expressed concern about the flares for the life rafts being the possible source, but they were all located in the door storage spaces with the emergency exit slides/safety rafts. There was no evidence to indicate the fire involved that area of the forward galley, and no flares were stored in the overhead area. The email was forwarded to Lathem, and I can only wonder if Gerden received a copy of it as was done with my memo about the faulty materials.

John was successful in continuously arranging for my time extensions in the hangar. He kept obtaining short one- and two-month extensions by not disclosing to Gerden exactly how much work was left to be done. Had management known, they surely would have called a halt to it. After the change-the-notes meeting, I would stay in the hangar doing a multitude of tasks for another year. His continuous short extensions showed how little Gerden and Vance knew about conducting such an investigation. Both John and I knew long before this there would be enough work to last more than a year, yet they had expected it all to be done in a month.

One such task was to go through nearly all the eight hundred large boxes in the storage hangar to look for pieces of Mylar material and record every stamp-mark indicating its date of manufacture, type, and series number. A retired RCMP member was hired to assist, and over several days we examined an estimated twenty-five thousand torn pieces of Mylar and created several hundred new exhibits. Each, of course, had to be numbered, documented, and photographed with special lighting to record fully and accurately the printing on each reflective surface. Then the information on each piece had to be transferred to a data table required by John. When finished, the process moved to seat foams and fabrics from both first class and business class seats. The several hundred blankets and several dozen pieces of shredded and cut up curtains that were on board were next on the list.

Eventually, I met with John and Larry Fogg in Ottawa for a week to formulate a trip report for the Zurich aircraft inspections. The report was based on notes the three of us had made along with the photos that had been taken. During the process, John and Larry provided an abundant supply of information regarding various components that had been present in the overhead attic area. By going through the photos and the equipment descriptions, it reinforced my knowledge that had been gained both from the trips and in the hangar. It was very easy to keep pace with the two of them and in most areas, I had significant and accurate information to provide regarding the equipment and materials that had been observed and photographed.

CHAPTER 6 – STILL MORE BAD APPLES

My involvement in the FAA burn tests in Atlantic City that began in September of 2001 has already been related in this narrative. Several things occurred around this time. First, Lathem took a back seat from the file's administration, and another Inspector by the name of Dan Tanner took over. He was the same officer who had been in the hangar for the meeting with Gerden on the 1st of December, 2000, the morning of the ambush meeting. The reason for the change was never made known, but right from the very start, I wished I had Lathem back, as bad as he had been.

Tanner, among other things, held up my expense reimbursements and overtime claims for no reason. Expense claims totaled in the thousands of dollars for some trips, all of which were on one of the two Force-issued credit cards. While the Force was liable for interest charges, late payments were reflected in my personal credit rating. Some payments would be as much as three or more months behind.

Typical of some of my interactions with him was a phone conversation held on the 3rd of January, 2002. When the phone was answered, he was loud and sounded enraged. He came across as very offensive and abusive. First, he demanded to know how time off for days I had taken had been looked after as, according to him, there was no time-off due. I told him it was time owed from the previous FAA trip. He abruptly responded I was to have taken that time off before going. He was furious when the matter was explained. He even read a memo from Neil Fraser that I had received only the day before. It said nothing about taking time off before the trip, an idea not only impossible but ludicrous and unethical. Tanner eventually deducted forty hours from my leave card for the twenty hours of time off I was owed.

Tanner demanded to know what was meant about a time extension in the hangar. When the latest TSB request was mentioned, he loudly declared there was no such thing. He finally stated he had not spoken to Gerden since early December 2001. The email from John advising of the extension indicated Gerden had contacted him on the 18th of December, 2001. It seemed Tanner either had a short memory or was not telling the truth. Gerden had no reason to lie to John. The latest message was read to him, and he shouted back that he was "running the show" and not the TSB. He loudly declared I could tell the TSB that any future requests for services had to come through him and I would not be making the decisions.

During his diatribe, he mentioned he still had the last overtime claim form on his desk and there was no explanation for the time. His comments about the shifts were insulting, and he even asked what SDO meant. SDO was the acronym for statutory day off. Likely every member of the RCMP knew what it meant, except, of course, Tanner. He wanted to know who authorized the shifts, what shifts were being worked, and why a ten-hour shift when I should be on an eight-hour shift. I told him I had always worked a ten-hour shift even before going to Swissair.

His rage continued only to end with his demand that I had to be at his office the next morning at 8 am. I told him it was my scheduled regular day off. That set him off again about shifts, and he commanded that I would be in to see him on Monday at 8 am ready to work an eight-hour shift. He added that I would from then on be working out of the Halifax office. Any further requirement to go to the hangar would be channeled through Neil Fraser. I interjected by saying the Identification Section worked a daily ten-hour shift, so he commanded that Neil Fraser would have to be spoken with about that. While I said nothing about it, I thought to myself there was no way either of them was going to change the shifts of the Ident Section merely because Tanner did not like the schedule.

During one of the two later meetings held in his office, Tanner informed me I had been mishandled by my management team. He said he had been seconded at one time to another agency for an undercover drug operation and, as such, he had a handler who debriefed him every day. A similar procedure should have been undertaken with me. I was speechless when he came out with this. There was no comparison at all. The two duties were so far removed from each other that anyone who knew what they were talking about would never entertain these ideas.

At one point in the discussion, Tanner was asked if he had any idea of the amount of expertise that had been gained in this file. Without discussing anything, his immediate reply was it was all useless for the RCMP to have any of that knowledge, and I should instead be working for the TSB. This single comment aptly illustrated what I believed to be his ignorant, narrow-minded and prejudiced attitude towards the investigation and me. There were many areas where the RCMP, if things had been handled correctly, could have advanced by what had been learned in this file. AES testing in fire scene examinations was one clear area. However, Tanner did not want to know about any of it because his purpose was to shut me down and get me out of the hangar by any means possible.

There was no sense saying anything more. It seemed that like most autocrats with excessive authority and a lack of leadership and managerial skills, he did not listen because he knew it all. I was about to find out that Tanner thought he knew so much that he was always right even when he was wrong. While he may have been the division intelligence officer, what I saw indicated he brought very little of it with him to the job. His tone was very aggressive throughout and at times offensive and abusive. During one of his outbursts, he was told his tone of voice was not appreciated. Several times he sounded as though he thought I was not telling him the truth. He commented about the amount of overtime that had been claimed in the past three years by quoting dollar values. Perhaps he was jealous, but it was none of his business as he had not been in charge of the Swissair file then or now. I asked what his problem was, and he blurted out I had a section to run and I was not doing as I had been told. I suggested to him there was a file to finish off. I had been provided a task, and that was what was being done. When finished, he did not sound any happier, and I thought it likely he would recycle it all at the next meeting.

Because of these meetings, I was able to advise him of the findings and latest test results, including the implications of the FAA burn tests and the magnesium issue. My due diligence in passing on my suspicions to my management team were done, for whatever that was worth.

Tanner subsequently wrote a memo to my new boss, Superintendent MacLaughlan, after I returned to the Identification Section. It would serve to taint the waters between MacLaughlan and me and would result in a complaint of harassment against Tanner. My complaint stated that what Tanner wrote was libelous and without foundation. In today's environment, it might have seen him fired for his abusive tones and outright lies and fabrications.

However, since commissioned officers like him were always right and could do pretty much as they wished, he got away with it.

Other things occurred to make life more noteworthy. During the 9-11 attacks, I was on the first test series at the FAA Burn Centre just outside Atlantic City. Having evacuated the Centre, when speaking with Linda Gray of the Halifax Ident Section around eleven am, she asked where I was exactly and what equipment did I have. It seems that Lee and Neil Fraser were trying to put together an Ident team and offer assistance to the US authorities. This never came to fruition as they had sufficient personnel to handle their three morgues. Just as well because I did not relish the idea of another morgue. However, it must have annoyed Lee when he learned that because I was centrally located, I would have been the lead person in for the RCMP's team.

Then on September 16th when coming back from that first FAA burn test trip in Atlantic City, N.J., it was just five days after the 9-11 attacks. The rental van was loaded with exhibits and gear from the first burn tests, and the plan was to take the ferry from Portland, Maine, to Yarmouth, N.S.

The ferry terminal was reached in plenty of time for the crossing. Before boarding everyone was notified they would undergo a customs check. I did not pay much attention to it until a uniformed Border Patrol Officer was seen with his German Shepherd dog. He was at the head of the lines of cars searching the area and then playing with the dog by bouncing a ball. I thought perhaps the dog was not performing as he should until, looking in the side view mirror of the van, I noticed another police dog at the rear of the parking lot, this one on a long leash attached to a plain clothes officer. They were at the tail end of the lines of cars. This dog was systematically going back and forth across the lines of vehicles smelling each as he came to it.

Now it made sense. Perhaps the first dog was a drug dog and right then they were not concerned with drugs being smuggled into Canada. No matter what the reason, he was a distraction, a decoy, and the second dog was most certainly an explosives dog. He was specially trained so when he smelled anything explosive related, he immediately sat. So, since my rental van was near the head of one of the lines, it would take some time for this second team to work their way up the lines of vehicles. The first dog was still attracting everyone's attention as he and his handler were putting on quite the show. However, he could, if necessary, easily outrun anyone who tried to bolt on foot. Eventually, the explosives team came to my vehicle and the words were whispered, "Dog, please do not suddenly sit beside this vehicle." The dog sniffed at my vehicle and then moved on to the next car.

Once finished, customs officers started at the head of each line to check the vehicles' occupants. Slowly the officer for my line made his way along, and suddenly I recalled hearing radio news reports that someone may have stolen aircraft debris from the twin towers site in New York. At the time, it was thought to be ridiculous. How could anyone locate and identify a piece of plane debris amongst the millions of tons of concrete and other rubble of the twin towers? With that amount of fuel on board, both planes would have melted within seconds. The window was down when he approached, and he said the usual. "Driver's license, registration, and state your business for being here." He was told I was a member of the RCMP travelling on duty from the FAA in Atlantic City to Halifax N.S. So far so good! Now I was dreading the next question. "What are you carrying in the van?" I made sure both my hands were visible on the steering wheel as I said "Aircraft wreckage". This guy immediately looked up from my driver's license and stared directly at me for a split second, just long enough to decide to take one step backward, move his right hand to his holster, and shout out for all to hear, "Guys, get over here, fast!" Before I could blink twice, four more customs officers encircled the van. Their boss came over to the driver's door and asked what the problem was. "This guy is carrying aircraft wreckage!" The boss now focused intensely on me as he told me to get slowly out of the van. I inched open the door while saying I was a cop, an RCMP member on duty. He told me to show some identification, and I reached slowly for the wallet I had just put back into my pocket. I knew I had better bring out that wallet and nothing else, not that there was anything but a notebook in the other back pocket. The Force would not allow members to carry a gun into the USA. The wallet was opened, and he was shown my badge and ID card. His response when he looked at the badge was a grunt and the words that he could buy one of them on the street in New York anytime. When he looked at the ID card, he said it looked fake. "What are you doing here?" he demanded. I told him I was working on Swissair 111 and had been down for burn testing at the FAA in

Atlantic City. His response was "What is Swissair one-eleven?" A quick explanation was given of the crash, including the date and a few details. His response was that he did not remember any plane crash off Nova Scotia. Immediately the situation had become very intense. I felt as if I had sunk six inches into the pavement from the weight of it because if he did not like my identification and could not remember the plane crash, there was nothing else he would accept to prove who I was. Anything I did have could easily have been falsified. About then the picture came to mind of me in a holding cell while these guys made phone calls to say they had apprehended one of the terrorists. I could envision the black steel door clanging shut. Just then my thoughts were interrupted as one of the agents came over to comment more than ask "Didn't we process a Navy ship full of divers back in the fall of '98? It had been up to dive on that plane wreck." I looked right at him and said they probably processed the USS Grapple because they were the US Navy salvage ship that had come up to help. Without thinking but more for good luck, the words came out "Fine bunch of guys they were, too!" Just then the female customs officer opened the rear doors of the van and shouted out "There are lots of bags back here of what appears to be aircraft parts, but all the bags have Royal Canadian Mounted Police on their labels." Hearing this, I immediately turned to look at her and again, without thinking and more as a command, I said she must be careful with them as they were potential Court exhibits and continuity of possession had to be maintained.

By now the boss was thinking hard and asked who my contact was with the FAA. "Pat Cahill" was the immediate response. He asked "What's his phone number?" and my reply was "Her! Pat is a woman!" His attitude immediately changed. He looked at his guys and signaled everything was okay. He turned to me and in a friendly tone as a fellow cop said he hoped I understood. They had reports of stolen aircraft parts from the New York site, and they had to be on the lookout. My return comment was it was all over the radio, but it was a wonder anyone could find anything amongst all that debris. He nodded in agreement as he said to have a nice trip.

That was it! They went on to the next vehicle, and I slowly got back into the van and sat there for a moment thinking about what had just happened. There was no way this guy knew Pat

Cahill. The odds against that would have been greater than winning the lottery. Maybe it had been the way I responded, especially about the bags of exhibits in the back of the van. Perhaps, too, it was that I worked with a female and the terrorists didn't.

Soon after, they then signaled to proceed up the ramp to the ship. Once underway, there was even a police boat escort out of the harbor. Things were very serious!

On the 18th of January, 2002, I officially moved out of the hangar and back to my Halifax Identification Section. Now I faced a massive problem. In my opinion, Lathem, Gorman, and both Neil and Lee Fraser had broken the law by obstructing a police officer and by obstructing justice in a potential murder investigation. They were far-reaching Criminal Code offences. What's more, I believed Tanner had also obstructed by knowing there was a need for an ongoing investigation and then ordering me away from the file by providing an official written directive under the RCMP Act. I felt at the very least they were all negligent in their duties. In the Province of Nova Scotia, there was a Provincial Statute that required any sudden death outside of a doctor's care to be fully investigated by a Coroner and the police, especially if there was any suspicion of criminality. It could be argued the Coroner had not been told the truth about the possible cause of death. I felt there had been ample evidence to suspect a criminal act, and the matter needed to be investigated. For anyone to argue the opposite and that there was a lack of reasonable suspicion, why did the TSB turn over Dr. Brown's AES reports to the RCMP? Dr. Brown had already communicated his suspicions of an incendiary device, and that information had been passed up the chain of command. For anyone to dispute Dr. Brown, they needed to show some credentials at least equal to his and a report to indicate they had performed the tests or reviewed his work. Then there were the burn tests at the FAA Burn Center, and they spoke for themselves.

What's more, it certainly appeared someone had not told the whole truth to the Americans. Duncan had told everyone in the meeting that announced the end of the RCMP's role in the hangar that, by the third day of the incident, he had correspondence indicating the Americans would handle any criminal investigation. In other words, the FBI would be involved. So where were they considering Dr. Brown's findings and all the other problem areas? I strongly suspected someone had told them there was nothing at all to indicate any criminal involvement. In other words, they had lied to them. After the disinformation provided at the New York meeting between the RCMP and the FBI, they likely had accepted this claim without question.

With all this going through my mind, Neil Fraser was now my Identification Supervisor. While he had no direct influence on me, to say I was uncomfortable with him was an understatement. Then there was Lathem, who was the Officer in Charge of the Major Crime Unit for the RCMP in the Province. Any major crime in my work area became his responsibility, and the investigators came from his unit. They were fine enough police officers, but I knew Lathem had attempted to obstruct both Karl's and my investigation because neither of us agreed with his view of the file. How could anyone be sure he would not do it again to other investigators? If he had overlooked a possible major homicide file merely for the chance of a promotion, what might he do if offered something more substantially material in value by someone in the criminal underworld? The ethics of the matter were such that I felt I could not work for either Lathem or Fraser without a major doubt about their honesty and integrity.

That was why I had been looking for a job outside the Force. I had applied to the Ontario Police College to be an Ident instructor, and to the Ontario Provincial Police to do a similar job as I was now doing. Both interviews had gone very well, but while Lee Fraser was in Ottawa, I could not get employment in any field of work related to Forensic Identification. I had reason to suspect each interviewer had contacted Fraser, and he had provided a negative assessment. Fraser's position as the Director of Forensic Identification Services for the RCMP was such that any of these agencies would have had him on their speed dial and, naturally, they would have consulted with him. In any event, I had concluded that after thirty-two years, it was time to leave and look elsewhere for a job. Because of the time in rank calculations, I would take a big hit on my pension, but nevertheless, I could not stay. Enough was enough.

Meanwhile, I was working through the grievance process. Lathem had ruined my chances of a promotion to an Identification Supervisor's position in Winnipeg, so I had added that to my list. In my submissions, I described the change-the-notes meeting and its implications. It caused Lathem to profess his innocence, even though he did not deny issuing the paper. In fact, he even supplied a copy of the demand for the process. His claim included a request for an internal investigation that was later conducted by a Sergeant in Internal Investigations Section. Lathem's boss, Superintendent MacLaughlan, who was also my boss, provided three questions for the IIS Sergeant. He was to investigate if Lathem:

1. Made Sgt. Juby falsify his police notes during the Swiss Air Investigation.
2. Made Sgt. Juby suppress evidence bringing justice into disrepute.
3. Acted in a manner that was construed as an illegal Act or improper.

When the memo was first read, it was thought finally something would be done. Then I had second thoughts. On re-reading the three questions, I realized the first two scenarios had never actually happened. Lathem was not guilty of any offence described in the first two. MacLaughlan used the past tense of the verb to make as if they were completed processes. However, each process only started during the meeting and had never been completed, certainly not by me as was asked in the questions. He had not 'made' me falsify police notes or 'made' me suppress evidence simply because the action of me changing the notes had never been carried out. If he had just added the words attempted to make, it would have been different. I felt what he and Fraser had done was to conspire to make me change my notes. Carrying out a criminal act was one thing, but conspiring to commit a crime was an entirely different action and, in law, became a critical point. Although related and illegal, it was technically not the same offence as described in the questions, and any internal investigator hoping for a further promotion would only answer what was asked by the senior commissioned officer. Although I believed there was sufficient evidence to support a conspiracy charge, the questions had not been asked, so they would not be answered. Besides, I suspected phone calls had been made and meetings attended to assure compliance.

As for the third question, it was ambiguous because the person who 'construed' it to be illegal was not defined. Obviously, Lathem would not say he had committed an illegal act nor would he say his actions were improper. What's more, since the first two questions were invalid, what was the action that was to be construed as illegal? Again, it was undefined. I suspected that within Division HQ where Lathem worked, there would be enough old cronies of sufficient rank that someone above him would make the same ruling. What would eventually be seen was those allies went all the way to the Commissioner of the RCMP. Indeed, the whole idea may have started with the Commissioner's office because a ruling would eventually emerge from there that Lathem's and Fraser's actions were legal and they were common and acceptable practices sanctioned under the RCMP Act. Meanwhile, I was never interviewed or questioned by the IIS investigator, and nothing more was heard in the matter until years later.

Once back on the Halifax Ident Section, there was yet more evidence of seemingly corrupt practices. The member who had been filling in for me while at Swissair was Sergeant Larry Kucey. Because of several alleged problems blown completely out of proportion, Neil Fraser was successful in removing him from Identification Services. Larry had become the security driver for the American Consul in Halifax and loved the job. In my opinion, it was a complete waste of a professional physical evidence investigator. Fraser was about to receive his commission, and one of the requirements had been to show senior management he could deal with a manpower problem even if it meant removing one of the best Identification members I had worked with to a non-Identification function. I felt his grounds for doing so were groundless and fabricated.

One afternoon soon after my return to the Ident Section, Neil Fraser came into my office to inform me that Larry's annual assessment was due. I was to complete it, and he described in detail how it was to be done so it reflected Larry's incompetence both in the work and his running of the section. After patiently listening to him as he described what he wanted, I simply said to Neil that he had several options as the acting Regional Identification Supervisor. The first was he could try to complete the assessment himself, something I knew he could not do since he was not in Larry's chain of command. He only acted as the regional advisor. The second was he could simply walk out the door, and I would disregard this conversation and what his prejudices showed. He was told obviously the second option was his only choice, and the assessment would be filled out as I saw fit and not as he wanted. He was informed he most likely would not like the results as the narrative would follow the rules as provided in the Force's Career Management Manual. Unless he had created the appropriate documentation, which I knew did not exist, nothing would be mentioned about an adverse audit. I felt that the faults he had found during his one and only review were Mickey Mouse complaints designed to make him look good as an auditor and to justify his biases about Larry. Fraser was told he was merely flexing muscle he did not have. He just looked at me for a moment, not knowing what to say, and then he just left, obviously not happy. Many other members if in my position might have succumbed to this not so subtle request, especially since Fraser was about to be our Supervising Ident Officer. I wondered if his request might have been an order if he had already been an Inspector. That would have provided me with just that much more pleasure and satisfaction while showing him the door.

Larry was pleased when the assessment was completed and so was I. Once again, I had kept my promise to commend at least some of the many members who worked far beyond any expectations that were required of them. Many performed their duties in indescribably extreme physical and mental conditions during a time of critical need and difficulty. After working some of the first weeks in the reconstruction hangar, Larry had gone on for three years to maintain the Ident Section. Only two or three of the positions were filled that just a few years before had been six, but the work had been no less during those shorthanded periods.

Over the summer, more items were located for the TSB members and shipped to Ottawa. However, by the 30th of July, 2002, the appropriate documentation for retirement had been submitted and the last day of work was to be September 2nd, 2002. The month of August was taken as annual leave. It was realized the wall had been hit. While I believed I had held the best job in the Force for the past twenty-seven years, there was no longer any desire or passion for that work. No amount of annual leave would fix the problems I had with the Force's management. My lack of trust in their ability to uphold the law stood in the way. As for my twice as far motto, it could not fix this problem, so it was time to get out.

The period of leave finished on the 2nd of September, 2002, exactly four years after the crash. The first thing in the morning there was a meeting with Supt. MacLaughlan in his office on the top floor of the 'H' Division Headquarters building, up where the air was rare and sound decisions even more so. After a very short chit-chat about the weather, he asked why I wanted to see him. My immediate thought was that a person knows he is not important when his boss does not even realize it is his last day of work! As he was being told, Neil Fraser walked in newly attired in his crisp white shirt with Inspector crowns and his neatly pressed blue trousers with yellow leg stripe and officer's brown shoes. I did not say anything except to offer my congratulations, but the thought ran through my mind to look at what the cat had dragged in! I would not have to put up with him, and too bad for those who did. The explanation continued about this being my last day until MacLaughlan blurted out, "No, it isn't! You're not finished yet! You have at least two months more annual leave to take!" I told him he had signed off on the paperwork over a month previously, it had gone through channels, and everything was set. He was visibly upset and did not know what else to say or do other than to insist I was staying and could not retire until my time off and leave were all used up.

I was not about to argue with MacLaughlan, so on his desk I placed my badge and ID card along with a locked box containing my gun and ammo clips. He immediately pushed them back saying he would not take them and I must keep them. He was told it would be illegal for me to be in possession of this equipment by the next morning as I would be a civilian.

He looked at Neil, and it seemed a light came on as he said to Neil that he must dust off the plans to increase the Halifax Identification position to a Staff Sergeant. Since the position was now vacant, the plan could go ahead. I knew what they were talking about as I looked at the two of them in disgust, glad I was finished with them. MacLaughlan still insisted that before I could retire, the leave must be used up. As I left, he was told I was on my way to see the Division Rep for clarification of the matter. Nothing more was said, not even by Neil. On the way out of the building, the thought came to mind that the air on the top floor was exceptionally rare this day.

The plan he had mentioned was quite simple. Back in October of 1998 when I had met with Inspector Robinson for an interview about my future posting, the plan had just been developed to increase the rank of the member in charge of the Halifax Ident

Section to the level of Staff Sergeant. He wanted me to remain in Halifax as I was in line for that promotion even though I had just been promoted to Sergeant. The new promotion would be based on my work in the Swissair morgue. Someone might now suggest this Staffing Officer did not know what he was talking about, but he went on to become the Commanding Officer of Prince Edward Island's 'L' Division. Lee Fraser confirmed all of this and gave an explanation as to why. Halifax Regional Municipality covered all of Halifax County. The old Halifax City, Dartmouth City, and Bedford, as well as other connecting areas, were policed by the Halifax Regional Police. The rest of Halifax County was policed by four RCMP sub-detachments. Over the years, various units had been amalgamated and, in so doing, one or the other police agency had taken charge of that unit. However, it had been decided by the RCMP's senior management that Forensic Identification Services would never come under the Regional Police. To ensure this, a plan was created to reclassify the RCMP's Halifax Identification Section position to a Staff Sergeant so the Sergeant in Charge of the Regional Police Ident Section would be outranked. That was the power politics of one police force against another. After I left, my replacement was promoted into a newly created Staff Sergeant's position. There would be no increase in the number of members of the Ident Section to justify his existence. Instead, it was claimed he supervised other Identification Sections in the RCMP's area of the Province.

When I met with Brian Flanagan, he stated that once the retirement papers were signed off by the line officer, there was no way it could be stopped or even postponed. He said to have a good retirement, and he, too, would be starting his very soon. So, with the road from Halifax in my rear-view mirror, I headed out to start a new career of retirement from the Force.

John Garstang did not make contact again until the 25th of October, 2002. His reason was to have me perform some follow-on work for them on a contract basis. Two members of the Halifax TSB office had failed to find one specific item. When he named it, I immediately knew what it was and in what box it was stored. It was in its correct location as listed in the database, but those searching for it just did not know what it was. If they wanted my help, they would have to hire me. In December 2002, I was hired back for a week to find items misplaced by the TSB members. More than five hundred exhibits had been moved between the frame room and storage Hangar J without anything being recorded. Some had been removed from the frame and just set aside while others were brought back from Ottawa and left in the frame room. Many could not be found as they were moved at the time of the TSB's relocation to Ottawa and nothing had been recorded. It was a general mess, and they wanted someone to organize things again.

John later indicated the rumor was I had failed to put in the proper exhibit updates. It was explained to him I had never handled the missing exhibits as those exhibit numbers were not in my notes. Instead most had been cleared out of the hangar during the rush to close things down, and the person who was putting out the rumor was responsible for that rush without keeping the proper documentation. He was now trying to cover his backside by blaming me.

John was told the TSB member had screwed up enough of the investigation during his time in the hangar to last a lifetime. I frequently saw that the method of close enough being good enough was the way he did much of his reconstruction work while in the hangar. One example was the forward drop ceiling mock-up table or FDCM table. It contained debris air ducts and other overhead pieces of equipment forming a reconstruction of the attic area of the aircraft. He had me photograph it on three separate occasions before he finally had all the pieces correctly placed, or almost all of them. Even after the third time, several ducts remained out of position on the table. He was in too much of a hurry to take the time to do things accurately. A computer scheduling program was utilized for all the projects, and everyone was expected to comply with his projected schedules when doing their work.

As for the FDCM table, each session had required two dozen rolls of film and a day to complete. Eighteen hundred photos had to be needlessly processed. The third set had to be accepted because I refused to do it a fourth time. Larry Vance happened by soon after I finished and made a comment to me about taking so long to accomplish the task. He was given a blast from me he likely did not forget for a long time. After explaining to him what had happened, I told him if the TSB ever got their ducts lined up in a proper row, I could do my job correctly. Vance rushed off to the other side of the hangar to likely berate the TSB member responsible. After telling John this, he just laughed, and nothing more was said about the matter.

By mid-December 2002, three-and-a-half months after retiring, payment for my lieu time off was finally received. When I had started in the morgue and again in the reconstruction hangar, Gorman as my Staff Sergeant supervisor had assured me there would be compensation for the extra time I was putting into the file. As time progressed, no compensation method was forthcoming and the extra hours kept building. To keep up with everything that was going on, I was putting in at least sixty hours each week, and usually seventy or more. When Lathem and Gorman started their closed-door meetings and their tactics, the subject was raised. Finally, through Garstang, the TSB asked the Force to allow me to submit overtime claims they agreed to cover. The claims lasted about four months until, during the ambush meeting, Lathem ordered them to cease. It was punishment for my actions. When Neil Fraser made his 'say no' comment and I walked out on them, I decided then I would add up my time and submit a claim. Lathem and Gorman refused it, so a grievance was undertaken.

The grievance resulted in an Alternate Dispute Resolution, or ADR. It was held in June 2001 with S/Sgt. White as the mediator and the DSRR Brian Flanagan sitting in to assist me. Brian was a super guy, and he expressed his confidence by saying I likely had all my ducks lined up in a row for this confrontation. What he did not know was all I had was a somewhat limp verbal agreement for compensation early in the file from Gorman. Added to that was Lathem's prior comment that I certainly deserved compensation for all the hours I had put into the investigation. Gorman had been transferred to Ottawa, and if present he would surely not remember such a discussion. So the room was entered expecting nothing.

The ADR began with White describing the process, and very quickly he related the general details of the matter. Because Lathem was the officer, he started first and described that there had been no written agreement in force. There was no documentation and Gorman had informed him he did not remember any verbal discussion. All of this information was recorded in a written statement, and Lathem merely recited the details for the record. There was not much to be done about his remarks, so it meant sitting quietly and listening. Lathem described the claim for sixty-six days of lieu time off, eight hours a day. He gave the impression he was shocked and astounded anyone would even think of making such a claim. His acting abilities were again coming to the surface. He said sixty-six days were beyond extreme even if it was for a three-year period. Lathem went on and on about the correct overtime process, and overtime had to be preauthorized, something I knew from experience was far from the truth. Most overtime on an Ident Section was never pre-authorized. He went on and on about every claim having to be fully documented and authorized beforehand and there was no way to authorize such blanket coverage as this. He then said half that amount would be more realistic, and he would be willing to grant it as he knew I had certainly worked many long hours on the file. However, five hundred and twenty-eight hours was out of the question, and he continued as though he enjoyed hearing himself talk.

For a second I was stunned. Then - Bingo! I win! I looked at Brian, but he had not caught on to what was going through my mind. I had just heard Lathem agree to half the claim. A bird in the hand! Two hundred and sixty-four hours was better than none. I just sat there with a winning hand until Lathem finished. What he uttered from then on was moot, and I hoped he did not realize the value of what he had said and renege on it. When he finally finished, White looked at me to indicate it was my turn to speak.

Looking at White, all I said was the offer of thirty-three days of lieu-time-off was accepted. Then I just sat there. White looked at me with a baffled expression. He obviously had not been listening closely to Lathem, and he was now confused for a moment. I continued by saying it was understood Insp. Lathem had just agreed to accept half the claim at thirty-three days, and those terms were accepted even though it was strongly felt I was owed the full sixty-six days. Flanagan reached over to get my attention as he still did not understand what I was doing. I added that, after all, this was an ADR, so both sides had to compromise. White looked at me, then at Lathem, and then back to me to ask more than say there was then an agreement. He was astonished, probably more so than me. I had entered the room expecting to leave empty handed. Now I had compensation for some of the extra time I had worked on this file. However, what was more important, I had beaten Lathem and Gorman at their own game.

151

The look on Lathem's face was priceless. It was surprise, then shock, and then anger. It seems he had not been listening to his own words, simply a talking head. White turned to Lathem to say that obviously, the ADR worked, and he thanked Lathem for his offer and turned to thank me for accepting it. White was so happy it was almost funny. He obviously had no expectation he would be successful. Later, I suspected it was just a formality for their statistics on grievances. He was delighted and felt he had brokered a deal. Good for him because I certainly did not want them to know there had been no hope when I had entered through the door. Brian asked if I knew what I was doing, that I was giving up two hundred and sixty-four hours of time. I simply said I would explain it to him later and yes, I certainly did know.

Within seconds Lathem was gone, obviously not very happy. He would now have to explain his actions and this new financial expense to his bosses. White lingered and thanked me again and then left. Flanagan was then told the situation that I had been in when arriving. For thirty-two months, I had worked nearly the same hours as had the TSB members who worked seventy hours each week, and who claimed everything over forty. However, for most of the time, I had been paid for only forty. The claim for sixty-six days was the result of going through my notes to tally up some of the time worked, and then making a one-for-one claim instead of the time-and-a-half or double-time rate as was the usual overtime procedure. So the sixty-six days came nowhere near what was owed. The correct tally should have been at least twelve hundred hours.

Now, finally those hours were to be paid, but at last year's rate when a new and higher rate was in effect for this year. When I questioned why policy had not been followed, Inspector Welsh of Fredericton commented that I had won the hours in the year 2001, and I would be paid at the rate in effect at that time. However, that was merely an arbitrary decision as there was other lieu time off that had been banked for more than twenty years, yet it was paid out at the rate in effect upon retirement. If still in the Force, this would have been a grievance as there was no date stamp on lieu time off. However, there was nothing to be done about it and they knew it. While they might argue it should have been taken as time off instead of payment, it was not part of the agreement. It was to be taken as I wished, either as time off or in payment. I chose the latter.

Their handling of this matter was another example of the abusive attitude of the RCMP's management simply because I would not toe the line and do as I was told in this investigation. During the first months, in several meetings with Lee Fraser and Gorman, it was very evident I was fulfilling a role the Force would otherwise have had a hard time to maintain. No one else wanted to take on the position, and the TSB were particular about the Ident member who did their work. However, even though the Division's Criminal Operations Officer, Chief Superintendent Duncan, had told me I must maintain contact with all the various tests undertaken on the file, Lathem failed to provide the means to do so without incurring extra hours of work. If he had handled it correctly, what later became an RCMP financial expense would have been absorbed by the TSB monthly in their manpower costs. He knew I was putting in the hours, but he expected I would do the work for nothing. When the TSB had asked if they could pay my overtime so I could work even more hours, it was granted, but only for four months until they deemed it necessary to punish my activities. Lathem's comment to me had been 'Officers don't get overtime either!' as if that made all the difference. As a Sergeant, I did not receive the abundant perks as did Lathem, and only half the salary.

As for who did the work for the TSB, Gorman was an example of why they were so particular. Garstang was an accomplished photographer and knowledgeable in the techniques and results he wanted. However, many of the photos of burnt exhibits Gorman took in the hangar were useless because he failed to utilize the proper camera settings to obtain the best possible results, even after being told what their purpose was. The CAD people complained to me about it when it came time for them to make use of his photos. Instead of using Gorman's photographs for their work as had been Garstang's intention, they required the actual metal exhibits. I had to remove and replace each piece from its position on the reconstruction frame. Throughout, Gorman expressed concern about expenses and it seems he did not want to use the extra batteries his camera's electronic flash would have needed to produce the proper results. He even reprimanded me for obtaining surplus studio lights. They cost virtually nothing, saved money in batteries and in time, and allowed for high-quality photos suitable for the CAD people.

During his time in the hangar, any new ideas or methods I presented to Gorman were always 'problematic'. He used the term so much, I called him 'Mr. Problematic'.

As for other costs, Gorman continuously complained that I was not authorized to spend any money whatsoever. He seemed not to appreciate that I designed and created several pieces of needed equipment for the specialized photography we were performing. One piece I put together on my own time using about fifty dollars' worth of materials. A comparable commercial version was later located on the web with a price tag of $14,000. When Lathem was confronted about Gorman's complaints, his reply was 'That's why you still have a Force credit card'.

So, it seems Gorman was merely treading water while in the hangar, waiting and hoping for the commission that never came. He then transferred to Ottawa where his future contributions to this file would eventually be disclosed through more access to information releases.

CHAPTER 7 – MERE SPECULATION

The release date of the TSB's final report for the crash was the 27th of March, 2003, amid much pomp and ceremony in Halifax. I was nowhere near as I wanted nothing to do with the report. I expected it to contain considerable speculation instead of fact. When the dust finally settled, it had to be admitted the TSB script writers had done an excellent job with the word craft. They suspected the cause to be a short-circuit on a wire in the aft cockpit area, possibly even an IFEN wire. The key word was suspect or, in other words, speculate, and no reliable or verifiable physical proof was offered. The report indicated there was no reason to believe the crash was due to a criminal act because the RCMP had not found any evidence of such a deed. However, the RCMP had closed their file based on the premise the TSB had not found any indication of criminality. That was the statement used by Duncan at the meeting on the 3rd of May, 2000, announcing the spooling down and parking of the file by the RCMP. Wordcraft was a nice term for it in genteel circles. It was two mongrel dogs running in a circle chasing each other's tail.

AES received short shrift in the report with only half a page stating it failed to provide consistent results. Magnesium was never mentioned, and incendiary was mentioned three times but only to say there was never any evidence of such a device.

While they pointed to a particular wire as the possible cause, I could only wonder about accurate wire placement when it was mainly based on Jim Foot's interpretation of the contamination on those cables. There was no way his findings would ever stand the test of a debate in a two-hole outhouse, let alone a cross-examination in a Court of Law. At least in the outhouse, the paper on which the report was written could be put to good use.

Even though their results provided an electrical fault scenario, other potential scenarios were not eliminated. A criminal device positioned overhead at the right front door would have been only a few feet away from the site the TSB had chosen for their possible initiating wire, and the smoke from such a criminal scenario would have been drawn into the cockpit. However, a criminal scenario was never investigated. Also, remember Gerden's statement that they did not have to be right so long as the safety aspect was addressed. Perhaps it was too bad all the Civil Court issues were settled without a trial because their findings would never have survived the test.

As for the safety aspect of their investigation, there were many recommendations, most of which were so obvious they should have been in effect long before the crash. Others never did come into effect. Like everything else, enough people had to die needlessly before the obvious became an acceptable practice.

After the media frenzy died down, I returned to the grievances. More than two-and-a-half years after the grievance process was started, the Commanding Officer ruled Lathem's and Gorman's assessments must be removed from my service file and sealed. As expected, nothing was done about the infractions of the Criminal Code except Lathem, Tanner, and MacLaughlan soon after retired, all within a few months. However, being a retired commissioned officer of the RCMP in the Province of Nova Scotia provided certain bonuses. One key perk was to be offered a plush government retirement job. Within another two years or so, Neil Fraser took advantage of this perk for his early retirement. While there was no proof, it would be somewhat satisfying to think Lathem and Tanner had been forced out to save their pensions in case some way was found to bring about an inquiry and criminal charges. I suspected, though, the internal investigation was a total cover-up ending at MacLaughlan's office after having been choreographed from Ottawa. One thing I had come to learn firsthand from the Force was an investigation might reveal one thing while the official report of that investigation could say something entirely different.

Once the assessment grievances were won, it created a situation where Lathem's and Gorman's negative comments on the Winnipeg position promotion forms had no basis. They had to be supported by previous documentation, and nothing existed once the assessments were removed. The adjudicator agreed with me and subsequently ordered a new promotion board for the Winnipeg Staff Sergeant's position.

It took twelve months before the board was finally held. When the results were finally released, I had tied with the member who had previously won the promotion. Time in rank then broke the tie as he had a few months longer in the Sergeant's rank. It did not count that I had twenty-seven years in Forensic Identification to his eleven years. So, he won.

However, on reading the board's comments, I felt there were grounds for an appeal. They had criticized me for having too many Swissair-related scenarios as my required examples. I could use examples only as far back as five years. Since for more than three of those five I had worked on Swissair, the sixty percent related to this file were a fair representation. Another thing was when I tallied the actual win/loss categories, I felt I had scored one more than the opposing member. This time around, he had acquired a category he had previously lost to a third candidate, but this board had been between just the two of us and did not include that third candidate. Technically, while he may have beaten me in that single category, he in turn had previously lost it to the third candidate, so it was not his to own. The correct score should have been 4:3:1 with me leading and the third candidate maintaining his single category. I felt the promotion board had overlooked something important, and it might be my winning hand. So after again going through the hoops and jumps, the arguments were presented, only to lose again.

That was it. After six years of continuously fighting the process and winning each battle, I had finally come to the end without winning the war. However, not so fast! My motto told me it was not over yet, that I had only gone part way.

About this time the head of the RCMP, Commissioner Zaccardelli, was in the news along with the head of Headquarters Staffing, or as they preferred to be called, Human Resources. She was Deputy Commissioner Barbara George. Zack was eventually booted out of the Commissioner's office in disgrace after misusing money from the Force's pension plan and for abusing the members who investigated the matter. Many people might have called it theft and abuse of authority. Barb received a judgment of Contempt of Parliament for having lied to them about her role in the matter. My feeling was if she had lied to the Parliament of Canada, then it was not unreasonable to think she had deviously controlled everything else in her department, including my grievance. After all, it would have cost them money in the form of back pay and a possible legal suit if I had won. Court would have put the whole Swissair matter into the media.

A new temporary Commissioner was named, and on the 3rd of April, 2007, another road was headed down with the hope something would be done about the Swissair file and justice would prevail. A memo of complaint was submitted to Commissioner Busson's office and, before the end of the month, a member of the Halifax Internal Investigations Section was in touch. I had known her for several years and considered her to be honest and forthright. In early May 2007, she met to discuss the file. She was astounded by what she was told and shown. There were numerous documents to substantiate the allegations along with a CD of notes. She seriously suspected the change-the-notes demand to be a criminal offence and the whole matter to be one obstruction after another. She confirmed Lathem was out of the Force and the only way to go after him was by criminal charges as he could not now be investigated under the RCMP Act. The thought of him sitting in the prisoner's docket as an accused went through my mind. That would certainly take the starch out of his white shirt! She was supplied with pages of material and a CD of files. My one stipulation was that this matter would no longer be investigated in Halifax. I did not trust anyone in a position of influence in the RCMP's Halifax Headquarters.

In mid-July 2007, Bob Elliott, a civil servant lawyer who had to be given quick lessons in how to properly stand, salute, and march, was named as the new Commissioner. He immediately set up an office for complaints by current and former members of the Force.

By August 2007, the IIS investigator had been contacted several times, and each time there were a series of excuses as to why nothing was happening. The initial meeting with her had been audio taped, and suddenly there appeared to be a problem with the transcript. She wanted me to edit the recording. "Edit" was a four-letter word I would not engage in, considering we were talking about evidence for a potential criminal investigation. Instead, another CD along with a binder of material were put together and provided to her with a demand it all be submitted to Ottawa. She had met with Karl who, in a one-and-a-half-hour meeting, confirmed many of the details of the complaint. By the end of September 2007, it was learned Ottawa had heard absolutely nothing from Halifax, and their file was at least three months overdue. Of importance, though, she was a Sergeant. Any submission to the Commissioner's office had to pass through several layers of commissioned officers above her. I was sure highly placed commissioned officers in Halifax

Headquarters had seen a review of my material long before it ever left their building.

By the 3rd of October, 2007, I felt I had waited long enough. In a memo to Ottawa headquarters, it was requested they turn the matter over to the RCMP in Vancouver. They were told it seemed no one in Ottawa was interested, but there were criminal investigators in B.C. who could and would investigate such matters. Within a week, a phone call was received advising that an Inspector Leduc in the Commissioner's office had the material and would be reviewing it. Meanwhile, it was learned Halifax had finally submitted their copy of the documents to Ottawa.

In one of the earlier meetings with this IIS member, I had asked for a copy of the internal investigation report that had been written back in 2002. She advised it was under lock and key and even she was not able to read it, but she did say it was a very thin file.

In November 2007, correspondence was received from Assistant Commissioner Sandra Conlin who was in charge of the RCMP's new Ethics Advisory Office. She had been tasked with the investigation of such matters as mine, and she wrote in her memo:

"Once we have had an opportunity to gather more information and have a thorough understanding of the issues we will be able to provide you with a more detailed response."

Something bothersome about her letter was that she had used the terms "review the file" and "gather" instead of the word investigate. I could only wonder if, like Gorman and Lathem, her office was in the evidence gathering stage rather than conducting a proper investigation.

Reading A/Commr Sandra Conlin's biography on the RCMP's website offered little encouragement. She had only limited Federal policing experience, no Provincial or municipal contract background, and she had worked in and around Headquarters Ottawa much of her service, as well as working for a retired RCMP Commissioner at Interpol. My impression was she was no street-smart policeperson. I thought she would not know where to start in a minor crime scene, let alone the obstruction of a mass homicide investigation. One of my non-rose smelling memos was sent to her office asking just who she was, that her rank meant nothing to me, and just because she had rank, it did not fool me into thinking she would do a proper job. I even questioned whether the Force could or should investigate this matter as it obviously encompassed the Commissioner's office. She was being given a warning that I was getting to the end of my rope with the Force on this matter.

Soon after this, I was informed the file would be handled by a lawyer specially hired for the job and she or he had at least five other complaints to investigate. This update failed to impress me. A newly hired lawyer likely meant someone without much experience. He or she would be both eager for a job, and wanting to keep that new government position. So, I reasoned he or she would toe the line and do as they were told. Second, it was still being handled by the RCMP in Headquarters, Ottawa. That was not promising at all!

One key event occurred that had me questioning the integrity of the Commissioner's office. It was the death of Robert Dziekański in the Vancouver Airport on the 14th of October, 2007. Four RCMP members tried to arrest this unarmed passenger on the inside of the airport's security zone by using a Taser weapon. His alleged weapon was simply a common desk stapler. Their actions resulted in his death. When the incident was first heard on the news, I questioned how four members could not arrest one unarmed male without lethal force. Four trained and able police officers had received no injuries, but one civilian was dead on the secure side of an airport! Something was terribly wrong.

Thousands of us over the years have policed some of the most violent areas in this country. On many occasions, while alone, we have arrested dangerous individuals willing to fight and armed with much more than a stapler, yet seldom did anyone die. One of many examples for me was an incident one night in Terrace, B.C. with three men and two women who all together were stupid enough to want to fight with me after they tried to bludgeon an old man to death. They had purposefully staged the initial event to lure in a lone policeman whom they then attacked. They all were in Court the next morning, albeit quite bruised, but nevertheless, they were very much alive. All I had was a now-broken two-cell flashlight, but not a mark on me. No baton or pepper spray, and certainly no Taser, just proper training in how to take down one or more suspects, armed or not. My gun never left its holster. While a police officer must never lose a fight, only if he is losing and in fear for his life is he justified to kill. With four-on-one odds, not one of those police officers was ever in fear for his life, no matter how big the stapler held by Robert Dziekański.

Within a day or two, there was a CBC news article on the web stating Commissioner Elliott had phoned three of the four members to offer his complete support. The prudence of this action was immediately questioned as he had not only influenced a criminal investigation, but he had committed himself before the matter had been investigated. Surely no one could fail to envisage the Constable sent to take impartial and factual statements from the witnesses only to be told the Commissioner had spoken with the members involved and had offered his full support.

When the video of the arrest hit the airwaves, I felt the Commissioner's office was nothing short of corruption in red serge for their initial actions and later attempts to influence and deflect the problems. What followed was a humiliation to all members of the Force, both present and former, who had stood for truth and justice over the many years. If I had been the Prime Minister, Elliott would have been fired within seconds along with several senior officers across the Force, especially those responsible for the Force's policy and training in confrontations such as this.

So between Zack and Bob, it seemed there was a lack of credible leadership. However, there was a ray of hope as one member of Canada's Parliament was in touch with just how Zaccardelli had operated as Commissioner. On the 7th of September, 2007, a CBC report read:

"Liberal MP Boris Wrzesnewskyj, a member of the committee, was not impressed.

'What he fails to understand is the culture that had developed within the RCMP — what's called a culture of corruption, a culture of intimidation,' Wrzesnewskyj told CBC News.

'The rank-and-file members were used to telling the commissioner what the commissioner wanted to hear. That's the culture that you had under Mr. Zaccardelli, and we've heard that when he heard things he didn't like, there were punitive transfers, etc.'"

An access to information request for the material of the internal investigation of 2002 was submitted. A package arrived with enough redacted areas to have used up a whole laser ink cartridge. Even copies of the memos I had already received from MacLaughlan were now blanked out. For sure somebody did not want me to know what had been written. I knew Lathem's request for the investigation had included bold terms like "offended by the erroneous and slanderous comments." He seemed to have put on the theatrical air once again to show he had done absolutely nothing wrong and he was falsely accused of illegal obstruction, harassment, intimidation, and abuse of authority. It seemed if he used his position of power boldly enough, he could make others think whatever he wanted, for a while at least. After all, one could say he had a corrupt Commissioner as a mentor.

Meanwhile, during September 2008, I met with Larry Fogg. He had contacted me to say he was coming to Halifax for a seminar and would like to meet for lunch. He was now semi-retired but still had his contacts within the industry and did part-time consulting work on aircraft materials. Over lunch at a downtown sidewalk restaurant, Swissair was on the menu. Larry was very surprised to learn about the treatment I had received from the Force during and since the investigation. He said Boeing thought the Force was investigating the magnesium question, and they were quite surprised to learn it had been dropped totally. Larry was asked if I had been wrong in pursuing the magnesium issue and he quickly answered "Definitely not!" He considered an incendiary device as a viable possibility for the cause of the fire. Larry was then asked if he felt the TSB had found a credible source for the fire when they located the wire event and burn area now proclaimed as the cause of the fire. He simply stated the event was the earliest electrical occurrence they could locate. He said it was "mere speculation" that this first electrical event had caused the fire. Since they did not do criminal investigations, an incendiary device could never have been considered by them to be an initiator. He laughed when he was told both the RCMP and the TSB had stated in their final reports that the other agency was the official source to verify there had been no criminal activity in the downing of the plane. While it was not specifically asked, it appeared obvious Boeing never received a copy of Dr. Brown's reports and they never learned what was in them. Larry would have said something if it had been otherwise.

The topic of the Metallized Mylar surfaced, and it seemed he had been fighting with Boeing for years before this crash to get rid of the MPET material. Larry said they knew it readily burned, and they knew of its flammability properties, but the engineers continuously cited that it had passed the FAA tests. He stated the tests were flawed, but they had been the standard tests in the early eighties before Dr. Lyon took over. He continued to say there had been nothing underhanded in the setup. The Metallized Mylar simply shrank away from the flame on being heated, and it had failed to burn because it was no longer in the flame area. Because it did not make sufficient flame contact and burn, it passed the test.

Other things were talked about, and then it was mentioned Lathem had been upset over my notes and had wanted material removed. Larry's immediate comment was he hoped I had not changed anything, and he just shook his head when I explained what Lathem had wanted removed from the notes. As for his notes, as I had suspected, Larry had recorded everything and then sent it on to Boeing. Larry laughed over Gorman's concern that everything was top secret and said Vic did little if anything around the hanger except express concern over secrecy. Neither did he have much good to say about Lathem.

Needless to say, it was an excellent lunch!

CHAPTER 8 – CONLIN'S REPORT

Returning to Conlin, she never replied to my memo. Over the next two years, four separate requests were submitted, but only twice were assurances received that the matter was still under review. Under the RCMP Act, I should have been updated by management every thirty days. Perhaps they hoped I would just go away or die.

Finally, on the 25th of March, 2009, a memo was received from Conlin's office. It had taken them two years less one week to create four pages of sheer rubbish. Some of the key phrases in the memo were priceless considering they had been written by a legally trained Canadian lawyer. This farce was then signed off by Canada's National Police Force. However, Conlin had not signed the document herself as someone temporarily in charge had performed that task. Nevertheless, as the Officer in Charge and due to the time involved, she could not shirk her responsibilities for this disgrace.

By the 4th of May, a rebuttal memo was completed and returned to Conlin's office. Her memo had been taken apart piece by piece, and ample material had been provided to counter every statement in her four pages. What they had written upset me to no end as I felt it was absolute garbage seemingly written by idiots.

After getting past some of the obvious verbiage written for the sake of using up the paper, several of their statements were key.

"RCMP management did not interfere with your activities under the MOU."

Then there was this line.

"The divergence between yourself and management of the RCMP originated when you came across information in September 1999, about a 'physically tiny bit of evidence' resulting from . . . . Auger Electronic Spectroscopy."

The words "came across information" and "physically tiny bit of evidence" immediately stood out. It was as if I had just happened upon it by accident, something otherwise easily overlooked. As for the second line, it was not the size but how it was used that counts. In this case, it was by whom it was used that counted. Dr. Brown was at the top of only a select few in his field in North America. There was no one in the RCMP or the TSB with any credentials that would begin to compare to his. Why did

Conlin call it this in a context so derogatory? Indeed, even Sir Arthur Conan Doyle's Sherlock Holmes said:

"It has long been an axiom of mine that the little things are infinitely the most important."

The TSB's John Garstang, a much better qualified physical evidence investigator than even Sherlock Holmes, said the following taken from my notes:

". . . . he did not agree with Jim FOOT with regards to the minute amounts of magnesium being an insignificant event. He said that when investigating explosive devices, trace evidence is minute in nature, and the pits caused in metal surfaces by the high velocity of minute fragments are microscopic in size, but gigantic in significance."

That was why it was called trace evidence. There was only a trace of it to be found.

John was speaking from experience because he had been the investigator who had located the microscopic evidence on the inside of an aircraft baggage-container when he was investigating the mid-air explosion of Air India Flight 182 over the Atlantic on June 23rd, 1985. The documentary showing it to have been the work of an Indian investigator and that the explosion was in the front of the aircraft was totally incorrect. I saw the reconstruction of the pieces of the plane and John's expert opinion evidence was accepted in a Canadian Court of Criminal Law.

Another of Conlin's lines was this.

"You became convinced that this magnesium may have come from an incendiary device planted at a specific location on the plane where extensive fire damage was found, although no physical evidence of an incendiary device was ever found amongst the debris of the aircraft."

This statement was such a dubious choice of words. A definite term "became convinced" was coupled with an indefinite term "may". As for finding the device, it was a good thing these guys were not running the Seattle Fire Department or the BATF. If they were, there never would have been such a thing as HTAA or high temperature accelerant arsons that used 'rocket fuel'.

A point of interest about bombs and incendiary devices came to mind. During the investigation of the bombing of Pan Am 103 over Lockerbie, Scotland, on the 21st of December, 1988, it was suspected a bomb might have been planted in a radio by a bomb maker in Germany. When arrested, a radio was seized along with his belongings. That radio was examined by some of the best bomb experts in the German security services, and nothing was found. They had it for a month before someone finally asked the right questions to reveal what was in the Toshiba Bombeat radio.

"The Bombeat measured just ten by seven by two inches. The model found in DALKAMOUNI's car had two sources of power, the standard batteries used to power the radio and cassette player, and four 1.5-volt batteries used to power a bomb. The bomb itself was a marvel: 300 grams of Semtex sheet explosive that had been shaped into a cylinder, wrapped with aluminum foil and decorated with a Toshiba label. Semtex is a most unusual product. Czech-made, it can be rolled like dough, molded like putty, or folded like paper. It is nearly impossible to detect by most conventional means. The Bombeat bomb had one standard electric detonator and two activating devices. In the parlance of explosives experts, it was a 'two-stop bomb'. It was state-of-the-art."

This paragraph is an excerpt from "The Fall of Pan Am 103 – Inside the Lockerbie Investigation" by Steven Emerson and Brian Duffy, page 168 and was published in 1990 by G.P. Putnam's Sons, New York. The writers may have got it wrong regarding the culprits, but their descriptions of the physical evidence and the search for the bomber by the British, American, and German authorities were accurate. A similar bomb in an identical radio exploded and brought down one of the largest commercial aircraft flying at the time. It was discovered because someone miles from the crash site picked up a tiny piece of the radio no bigger than his thumbnail. This piece was certainly a "physically tiny bit of evidence" among many tons of other physical evidence.

Conlin seemed to think something substantial should have been found as hard physical evidence. In a fire such as this, one can only wonder what could have been left behind as evidence since everything would have been designed to burn. However, that was where Conlin, Foot, and the others were wrong. It did indeed leave behind a trace of physical evidence. It was absorbed in copper just under the surface of some of the short-circuited wire beads.

Conlin's next paragraph began with: "In the absence of corroborative evidence,". That was quite a mouthful, but one can play with the words and allow a bit of symmetrical repetitiousness.

"The absence of evidence is not evidence of absence." US Secretary of Defense Donald Rumsfeld made this statement in 2001 when answering a question about the location of Osama bin Laden. If one knew anything at all about fires, it sure answered Conlin's comment.

As for "corroborative evidence", what qualifications did anyone have in the RCMP besides Karl and me or in the TSB besides John Garstang to determine anything about the fire on board that airplane. In a Canadian Criminal Court of Law, Karl Christiansen and I would have been the only RCMP members who could have given opinion fire evidence, and I was the only RCMP member who knew anything about the MD-11 aircraft and the actual fire load.

Added to that were the test wires specially created to locate an onboard source of the questioned elements. In fact, the seawater wire test was purposely slanted for contamination by a piece of magnesium, but it proved beyond a doubt a seawater magnesium source was not the culprit.

Just what did Conlin and her Ottawa crowd know about corroborative evidence? They certainly knew nothing whatsoever about the aircraft, the fire load, or the other physical evidence uncovered in the investigation. Besides, it certainly was not for them to decide. That was a decision to be made ultimately by a jury once all the evidence was accurately presented.

What were the indicators for a potential criminal device? The following were some of the points that made me suspect an incendiary device. Most of these points had been known before the file's parking date of June 30th, 2000.

1. During the Zurich 1 trip, John Garstang provided a list of things to watch for as the investigation progressed. It included burn damage exceeding the abilities of the fire load, burn through of the ceiling tiles, excessive molten aluminum, and molten aluminum and fire evidence in the galley area. By the parking date of the file, there was knowledge and proof of these things.

2. The Zurich 2 trip provided a potential scenario of how such a device could have been placed on the aircraft. A person receiving minimal instructions could have quickly and easily deposited one or more briefcases, satchels, tool boxes or lunch pails containing a criminal device and materials in the ceiling area where the most fire damage was located. It was already known the aircraft, while parked

at the JFK gate, was routinely serviced by catering and cleaning staff through the forward right doorway, and this corresponded to the potential scenario. One of those contracted staff who serviced this aircraft worked for only the one shift and was never heard of again after having provided false personal identification. Considering the now known habits of some of the contracted security personnel for the Swissair aircraft while parked at the JFK airport, there were sufficient breaches of security to allow for this to have happened.

3.   AES testing provided strong physical evidence of magnesium, aluminum, and iron within the short-circuited beads of the burnt wires. These were the three ingredients of a simple incendiary device. While initially this was no absolute proof of a criminal act, one of three source scenarios provided by Dr. Brown was for such a device. As time continued, the non-criminal sources for these elements were slowly but steadily eliminated until none were left.

4.   On the 7th of December, 1999, John Garstang displayed a piece of scorched and discoloured material that was either personal breathing equipment or smoke curtain. It initially appeared to be the former and the manufacturer advised it could withstand temperatures of 1700 degrees F. for five minutes without any degradation or discolouration. It proved to be the latter, and testing at the FAA Burn Center proved it to be equally resistant to fire damage.

5.   Two pieces of ceiling tile had been located showing evidence of extreme burning. After the parking of the file, it was learned from the manufacturer they were from the forward door area. The company estimated the tiles had burnt at 1700 degrees F. for 5 minutes. The TSB requested a re-evaluation for a longer period. They then provided a reading of 10 minutes at 1100 degrees F., yet there was little in the area to sustain a fire of such a temperature, let alone for that length of time. The tiles had been tested locally before June 2000.

6.   Investigators and engineers from the FAA, NTSB, TSB, AAIB, Swissair, and Boeing all expressed their views that the damage to the frame exceeded the capabilities of the fire load.

7.   Dr. Quintiere and Dr. Lyon as the two top experts in aircraft fires in North America expressed their opinions that the fire damage exceeded the capabilities of the fire load. During the later FAA tests, Dr. Lyon expressed the observation that he had never seen

molten aluminum after any of their FAA Burn Center tests unless they used fuel oil added to the fire load as an accelerant. The Swissair debris provided evidence of significant amounts of molten aluminum.

8. The TSB member responsible for the IFEN investigation expressed his opinion in October 1999 that the IFEN system was not at fault and could not have caused the fire.

9. During a conversation in December 2000, an IFALPA representative and Don Enns expressed the view that there was indirect evidence to eliminate the IFEN as the cause of the fire.

10. During the Zurich 3 trip and before the parking date, Jim Foot expressed the view that he initially felt the source of the fire had been an incendiary device. He offered no reason as to why he had changed his mind. He expressed the same opinion on December 1st, 2000. His opinion was without any qualifications, but he had Gerden's confidence throughout the investigation.

11. John Garstang, the TSB's principal onsite investigator, continuously offered encouragement and assistance to investigate the fire's criminal cause. At no time did he ever offer an opinion that the fire was not criminal in nature.

12. During the various trips, incidents were discussed, and evidence was seen of short-circuited wire events that had not created a fire scenario. With all the potential, there was no record put forward of any similar fire in any other commercial aircraft that was due to a short-circuited wire.

13. During the Zurich-3 trip, it was learned Swissair was about to install air dryers above the forward galley area. An average flight resulted in five hundred kilograms of condensed water on the cold above-ceiling surfaces including the insulation blankets. Any fire would have to contend with wet surfaces thus making it less likely mere sparks could be the cause. Any source would require greater amounts of heat to burn damp materials.

14. During the Seattle wire testing, purpose-oriented tests were conducted where short-circuited wires failed continuously to ignite nearby dry flammable materials.

15. Although incorrect, I was told there was no evidence to show an incendiary device had ever been previously used on an aircraft. Since this was a most unusual fire, both in intensity and in duration, never seen before, could not the first use of an actual incendiary device or fire bomb and the never seen fire damage be linked?

16.   Even after two years, the TSB failed to locate a viable cause of the fire other than their claim of short-circuited wires. AES data showed numerous possible initiating wires, the sheer quantity of which indicated arson. Add to that the AES test results of other wires that provided physical evidence linking them to an incendiary device as the ignition source.

17.   It was learned that during February and the fall of 2001, pressure was applied to Dr. Brown to have him adjust his AES report to show an accidental electrical cause. Later it was learned this pressure was so flagrant as to constitute a probable criminal offence by the TSB members involved. It seems the TSB felt the AES results were sufficiently viable to present a real and present threat to their safety recommendations due to their criminal implications.

18.   Discussions with Larry Fogg revealed the Boeing scientists were keeping a close eye on the AES readings. They had a concern over the magnesium and the associated elements that tended to indicate an incendiary device. The Boeing experts suspected an incendiary device and were surprised at the RCMP's withdrawal from the investigation of it as the cause.

19.   During the AES testing, CANMET's Dr. Brown and NRC's Irwin Sproule, the two Canadian Government AES operators in Ottawa, discussed the test results up to that date. Both agreed with the readings and the potential implications. Sproule's AES equipment had been used when, during one of the test sessions, Dr. Brown's AES unit required repairs.

20.   Test burns undertaken in the FAA Burn Center in Atlantic City resulted in the failure of the fire load to produce the heat damage as seen in the debris. Significant amounts of available material failed to burn even though there was an unlimited supply of oxygen and the frame was at normal temperatures, two factors that surely influenced the fatal fire. Only after filling the frame with more than six times the normally available amount of fire load in an advantageous manner was aluminum made to melt in a fire lasting one-quarter of the time as the fatal fire.

No one or two items or even all of them together served to verify the presence of an incendiary device. Nonetheless, these points offered an extremely strong suspicion when coupled with the presence of magnesium, aluminum, and iron in the quantities shown. To not act as I did under these circumstances would have been negligence. Also, that which forms a suspicion for one police officer need not be the same as that required by another. A background with knowledge and experience in fire investigations counted for much as did an understanding and appreciation of the fire evidence being examined. While my answers to questions asked in Court might be accepted as expert evidence, Lathem, Gorman, along with Neil and Lee Fraser would never be asked the questions as they had no expertise in the matter whatsoever.

As part of the rebuttal to these twenty points, reasons my supervisors provided have been put together to show why, according to them, the file was not a criminal matter.

1. No one had claimed responsibility for the downing of the aircraft.

Throughout the file, Lathem used this as his main excuse. Contrary to the opinions expressed by "media experts for hire", it was known some terrorist activities were not claimed. Their thinking seems to have been that many terrorist groups with sometimes diverse interests lay claim to most incidents. However, possibly a major group was experimenting with various methods to bring down several aircraft at a time? It was also a possibility that a non-terrorist group or an individual wanted to kill someone on board and make it look like an accident. This flight was dubbed the UN Special because it was routine to carry numerous United Nations personnel who were travelling between New York and Geneva and beyond. Several years after leaving the Force, information surfaced to indicate a terrorist group did indeed lay claim to the downing of this aircraft. Their claim was deemed not to be credible, so it was ignored. I do not know who made that decision, especially since, within a matter of days, the TSB determined it to be an accident.

2. There had been no physical evidence found resembling an incendiary device, and no other evidence of a criminal act.

Lathem, Gorman and Foot were fond of using this excuse, and it was used in the RCMP's concluding report. By its very nature, such a device would fully consume itself including its container. Perhaps it was more of Lathem's Hollywood-style theatrics, expecting someone to reach into a box of debris and miraculously pull out an item that was the remnants of a burnt-out incendiary device. Was not the presence of magnesium, aluminum, and iron in the copper beads the trace evidence of such a device?

However, the TSB was not responsible for finding evidence of a criminal act nor were their investigators trained to do so. The TSB later refused Dr. Brown's first two reports in which he gave a criminal scenario as the source of the suspect elements. They forced him to remove any reference to a potential criminal scenario before his report was accepted. At the same time, the RCMP's senior management was aware of the first two reports, yet they did nothing to initiate a criminal investigation of the matter.

3. Management claimed no other evidence had corroborated the AES findings.

Lathem held physical evidence in very low esteem as evidenced by his "folly and reckless" meeting of October 12th, 1999. How could there have been eyewitness evidence? However, there was corroboration, and that was the lack of an adequate fire load to cause the damage that was done, something shown to be true in the FAA fire tests.

4. There was "a loss of Government interest" and "no political interest" in continuing the file and the file "has lost its gloss."

These were the words of Chief Superintendent Steve Duncan on May 3rd, 2000. He said the file was being "parked" and only to be reopened if the TSB found evidence to indicate criminal activity. There were no reasonable and probable grounds to believe there had been a criminal act, certainly nothing that would allow the RCMP to obtain a search warrant. He went on to state there was no reason to believe there was any human intervention in the flight, and no one had taken ownership of the crash as being his or her act of destruction. He then went on:

"...even if an incendiary device were found, we will not be able to identify it to an individual at this late a date, so there is no use conducting such an investigation."

He also said the TSB had found no evidence of criminal activity, so there was no need for the RCMP to investigate.

These were the same comments Lee Fraser took offence to at the change-the-notes meeting. That these words were said by Duncan was immediately confirmed by Lathem and Gorman. After Duncan made these statements, he headed to Regina where he immediately took up his post as the newest Deputy Commissioner. There were six Deputy Commissioners in the Force, and the next higher rank was the Commissioner. When he spoke, he represented the Force's official position and attitude. One can only wonder about the timing of the file's shutdown and his promotion, and what pressure came from Ottawa to make him say these words. Only Commissioner Murray and Deputy Commissioner Zaccardelli would have had that amount of authority over him, notwithstanding that such an application of power would have been illegal.

5. No plane had ever been attacked by anyone with an incendiary device.

This was a favourite saying that emanated from the RCMP's back office, but there was indeed evidence. Cahill provided information of such an incident, and John Garstang uncovered information of a suspected arson on board a Gulf-area airlines jet.

Now it is time to go back to Conlin's memo to read this line.

"Although you were not discouraged to research the evidence of a potential crime,"

It seemed someone in Ottawa had a sense of humor. Surely Conlin referred to conducting a criminal investigation, yet I was told not to use the term, and Lathem, Gorman, and the two Frasers did all they could to bring a halt to any criminal investigation. Conlin was supplied the notes of the ambush meeting and the change-the-notes meeting. Did they read those notes? To illustrate my reasoning, I can simply refer to the incident created by Gorman in the hangar when he conducted the audit and removed some of my equipment. The ensuing argument resulted in a written reprimand that contained this line:

"Sgt. Juby appears to have the position that the Swissair investigation is a criminal investigation, however, there is no evidence to maintain that position."

Conlin's next paragraph dealt with the "group of eleven" and their findings.

"A group of eleven members trained in the Identification field reviewed your file notes. It was found that a large number of your notes were personal speculations and theories based on your belief that the Swissair Flight 111 air disaster may have been caused by a criminal act."

What immediately came to mind here was that even Canada's best painters were only a group of seven, and they produced something worthwhile.

The notes obtained from Neil Fraser, Lathem, and Gorman as part of the grievances showed the very same type of material for which they condemned me. The big difference was Lathem's notes were so sparse, they meant virtually nothing. It has always been common knowledge notes are made so years later the investigator as a witness can refresh his or her memory while giving evidence in Court. However, they must also be a verification of the witness's recollection and proof to the Court that he or she was not just spinning a yarn while making up details to suit the situation.

Some of Lathem's notes of 19th December 2000, are provided here. That was the day he delivered the reprimand for walking out of the second ambush meeting and the day I told him I was so fed up I could quit. His verbal response was he could expedite the paperwork for the retirement forms if I so desired. His notes held this line.

"I DEPART HOPING THINGS WORK OUT FOR TOM"

When Lathem left, he merely thought this statement without seeing, saying, hearing, or doing anything other than leaving. This was similar editorializing and no different to anything he was accusing me of incorrectly recording.

Something significant and central to the story happened later and must be added here. Without giving too many details, Lathem was visited by a CBC producer, Rob Gordon, and when he was initially asked if he remembered me, Lathem's comment was along the lines of

"Oh yes, he was the Identification guy who kept **such good notes.**"

The producer said he almost fell out of his chair. Enough said?

Conlin's next paragraph dealt with the change-the-notes demand.

"These findings were brought to the attention of Insp. Lathem. During a meeting held on February 20, 2001 in the presence of four other members, he formally asked you to read and sign a document by which you acknowledged that your "notes reflect [your] ... personal theories and speculations ...not founded in fact nor is there any evidence to support them". By signing the document you also agreed to review [your] ... notes and to edit the non-factual information knowing full well that the original notes will be retained on file. Furthermore, you agreed to "take training to remedy this issue to ensure it is not repeated in the future." You were then allowed to resume your activities with the TSB."

My worst fear was they would deny the change-the-notes document signing ever occurred. They made a mistake, though, as there were only three other members as accomplices to Lathem and not four witnesses as indicated. It would seem Conlin's lawyer included Purchase in the group, but he had already left the meeting by the time Lathem brought out this document. Perhaps if Conlin's lawyer had read the notes I supplied a little more thoroughly, this mistake, along with some of the many others, would never have been made.

Conlin's memo went on, and these lines are most important. They served to set the level of credibility for all of Conlin's investigation.

"After reviewing all relevant documents, I find that Insp. LATHEM acted within the purview of his authority by asking you to review, edit, and remove non-factual information from your notes. His request is in line with the correct reading of OM II.1 Investigative Guidelines / parag. G / Investigators Notebook, as well as other RCMP documents pertaining to 'Statement of Practice' on note-taking attached to the investigator's report."

Yes, indeed! What is written here is a verbatim copy of this part of the memo I received from Conlin's office. Reading it, I could only wonder who decided what documents were relevant and if they had read them all. Certainly they seem not to have reviewed the pages of the Criminal Code of Canada. To alter notes in the manner as described in Conlin's memo was an obstruction of justice and witness tampering, two very serious criminal acts. It also seemed to show Conlin had never given evidence in a Criminal Court in Canada or she would have known better. She was a commissioned officer of the Royal Canadian Mounted Police with nearly thirty years of service. She was in a position of extreme power with authority to make decisions on far-reaching matters. However, she seems not to have known the rules of evidence for the Courts of this land. Just what was her experience and what was her level of credibility to be able to offer an opinion on this matter? Shame on her and the RCMP! With these lines, a criminal act has been condoned. Does this not make her guilty of being an accessory after the fact?

If I ever went to Court and told a Judge I had edited my notes, two things would likely happen. The trial would be halted immediately with a stay of proceedings, and the accused might walk out the door as a free individual depending on my importance as a witness. Next, I would be charged with obstruction of justice. After the investigation, so would any of my supervisors who forced or condoned these actions. It would not matter what had been taken out of those notes. All that mattered was that something had been deleted.

Lathem made assurances the original notes would remain on the file. OK, which version would I use and disclose to the defense? By law, everything had to be disclosed. That meant both copies. It would be obstruction of justice to withhold any notes. Quite simply a defence counsel would ask which set of notes was accurate. If I said the first, he would ask why then was the second note file made if the first was accurate. Since I must have lied to create the second, was I still lying? If I said the second note file was correct, then that meant the first was inaccurate. So I would have lied in my first set of notes. Was I still lying now? Moreover, on what would I have based my second set of notes? Obviously, the answer would be the first set since there was a duplication of many of the details. However, I had lied in creating the first set as they were inaccurate, so then the second set was based on a lie. At this point, I might help my situation by saying my superiors had forced me to create the second set since they were afraid of what I had disclosed in my first set. Once the Judge finished sentencing them to jail, I might be lucky and receive a conditional discharge. I would have to be very cooperative for him to do that.

Even the proposal made by J.J. King to liaise with Lathem and add explanations to the notes would create a serious problem in Court. After being asked why I had made the additions, I would answer it was because my supervisor pointed out certain areas with problems. After telling him when this all occurred, the time between the initial writing of the notes and the writing of the clarifications would drastically reduce the credibility of any new entries. The very act of adding clarifications would discredit the original entries. Also, it could be argued the notes had ultimately been made to reflect the opinions and observations of Lathem and did not reflect my contemporaneous observations and understanding of the matters. Otherwise why change or make the additions to them? After all, when they were initially made, I certainly thought about and composed the notes to reflect what my knowledge and recollection of the subject matters were at that time, and they must have satisfied my requirements. In effect, the new notes were not my notes. They had become Lathem's notes because he had asked for the changes by way of the change-the-notes document, something that would be deemed to be an illegal demand. Their use by me would be disqualified, and my testimony disallowed. It would likely be successfully and correctly argued my evidence for Court had been tainted by what then had become Lathem's notes that now reflected his views of events and the file instead of my own.

It might never go to a Court case though, because the Crown Counsel might have already notified a Judge and an investigation would follow. I might be lucky and not have to share my cell with any of the co-accused after being charged.

However, this was all hypothetical because Lathem made one particular statement in the meeting to solve these problems. He simply said the original notes, although remaining on the file, would never be disclosed. In fact, later in Fredericton when I spoke with him for the last time, Lee Fraser argued it was unnecessary to disclose the old notes once the changes had been made. There, that solved the problem if I did not tell the truth in Court. I would have to lie when the Judge asked if the notes I referred to truly represented what I saw, did, and heard, and were made at the time of the matter in question. Unfortunately for them, I had a reputation with many Judges in this country. Whenever I took the witness stand, I would swear to tell the truth, the whole truth, and nothing but the truth, and I did just that!

The point of Conlin's paragraph seemed to be that since I had signed Lathem's demand, I must have agreed with it. However, I had signed the paper simply because that was the only way of retrieving the document as proof of Lathem's illegal actions. As well, it seemed no one in Conlin's office considered what was written in the demand. How could I possibly have reviewed all the notes that had been submitted? As for the next line, they were my notes, so they were not intended to reflect anyone else's ideas. The addition of theories and speculations were then criticized. Of course there were such entries. That was all anyone was doing with the file, theorizing and speculating. Was not Foot speculating and theorizing when he argued the cause of the fire was a short-circuited wire? I was dealing with theories and speculating on potential scenarios to "research the evidence of a potential crime." If not recorded, how could I have remembered the significance of various matters month to month, year to year? There was a need to put that material along with any associated influencing events in the notes as that was standard procedure for any police investigator. As for speculation, the TSB members did that very well, and they got away with it. After all, "why investigate when we can speculate?"

Continuing, just what specifically was it that was "not founded in fact nor supported by evidence". Surely not the exhibit and film details as they were obviously factual. There were notes of meetings and discussions that occurred throughout the file, and they were recorded as accurately as possible. On several occasions, Lathem read the notes and agreed with my memory of what had transpired at the meetings. When the three entries presented at the meeting were questioned, they were told they were accurate even if they did not like what was written.

Now the next line was the biggest joke of the day. "Subsequently, by my own free will and volition without duress, I freely admit that my personal beliefs do not reflect the factual information found within the area of my responsibility - ...."

The question of "free will" was whether and in what sense rational agents exercise control over their actions and decisions. What control did I have in that room? There were four senior members, all superior in rank to me, and each was attacking everything I said. I was at a table unable to leave because I was hemmed in by prearranged seating. The last time my "free will" was exercised with Lathem, I received a reprimand for leaving the room.

"Volition" was the cognitive process by which an individual decides on and commits to a particular course of action. However, there was no freedom of thought. As soon as Lathem stopped to breathe, Lee Fraser took over the harangue. Then it would be Gorman or Neil Fraser. I could not put a word in edgewise, let alone think or finish a statement. Lathem had reverted to Hollywood movie interrogation techniques, and between all of them, they were most intimidating. Lathem and Lee Fraser each had the ability to project a most threatening image, and they created an inhospitable atmosphere whenever they chose to do so.

"Duress" was defined as "any unlawful threat or coercion to induce another to act or not act in a manner they otherwise would not or would." From the start, Fraser held over my head that I was out of the hangar, finished with the file and the work was going to be done by the Ottawa Identification Section. If he had done that, it would have been an obstruction of justice and of a police officer. While I thought his statement was ridiculous, Fraser had the authority to do as he pleased, and it was certainly possible someone else could be forced to take over the Identification work in the file. Lathem solved the issue by stating that since it was staying in Halifax, I would continue with the photography and exhibit control but would have no further contact with any reports, meetings, other discussion groups, or access to the file materials. Since I was still involved in my criminal investigation, even if it was not sanctioned by the RCMP, or as Conlin wrote "research the evidence of a potential crime," just what part of duress does one not think their statements were? I was a police officer investigating a potential homicide, so there was a flagrant abuse of authority that led to a criminal obstruction by all four senior Force members, two of whom were commissioned officers of the RCMP.

The final part of the demand states: "Further, I agree to review my notes and to edit the non-factual information, knowing full well that the original notes will be retained on file. I will also take training to remedy this issue to ensure it is not repeated in the future." Okay, now I was to review the notes. What, again? A point of importance was Lathem never again mentioned the matter. He never met to discuss what areas were to be edited or how it was to be done. There was no follow-up except to provide a copy of the manual on notes. The question begging to be asked was what was so immensely important about the matter leading up to the 20th of February, 2001, that nothing was ever done after that date to correct the discordant notes already in existence or any of the notes that followed? It would be several years before I fully understood the underlying reasons for these actions, and it turned out this was all a sham, that he never actually had a technical problem with what was in the notes. He merely wanted to know if specific information had been received from Dr. Brown and, above all, to discredit my future testimony in Court. He very likely had someone else create a second set of notes for disclosure purposes that he then placed in the file.

What exactly made up my notes besides the one-and-a-half thousand pages in Word? First, there was the paper file containing a copy of all the hard documents, drawings and written notes in about eight three-inch binders. Add a copy of all the CDs and videos. There were more than eight hundred photo CDs by the end of the file, and they filled four file drawers. Each CD contained about one hundred and twenty photos. Then there were several thousand floppy disks, each with twenty or more photos. My videos consisted of more than one hundred hours of recordings. Since a photo was worth a thousand words, I had a lot to review.

Continuing in the demand, the next line was, "I will also take training to remedy this issue to ensure it is not repeated in the future." A month later, an envelope was received from Lathem containing a copy of part of the manual on notes. That material was all the training he offered. Of particular interest in the supplied material was a line on page two of the eight pages.

AN IMPORTANT INVESTIGATIVE TOOL

Your notes are one of the most valuable tools you can use during the course of an investigation. As a permanent, ongoing record of events your notes:

- serve as a record of your conduct should questions arise.

It stands to reason the notes would be used to show not only my conduct but the behaviour of others, including my supervisors, as well as the problems I encountered while trying to carry out an investigation. Moreover, the notes were intended to be "a permanent, ongoing record of events," meaning unchanging, unedited!

The next area of the training manual contained the following lines:

WHAT BELONGS IN YOUR NOTES

Essentially, your notes are a daily record of what you observe, hear, say, and do in the course of your investigations. . . . .

It is important to ensure that your notes are complete and accurate. You may need to rely on them years after the initial investigation. If there is any possibility that information may be relevant, make a note of it.

While the specific contents of your notes will depend on the type of investigation you conduct . . . .

The first line seemed to pass judgment on Lathem's notes. "I DEPART HOPING THINGS WORK OUT FOR TOM."

What one hopes appeared to be missing from the list.

Without any doubt, this was a unique investigation, a type that had not been undertaken by a member of the Force in a very long time, if at all. So, if that did not allow for some leeway in my notes, why then was this last line included in the manual?

Lathem stated my notes would be embarrassing to me if they were revealed in Court. I certainly agreed with that statement! It most certainly would have been embarrassing to reveal I was part of an investigative team that had acted as Lathem had directed. Instead, I tried to do the best I could by following my training, experience, and instincts and by doing what was morally and legally right. What was described in my notes and this recounting of events was what I had to put up with during the file. Management's negative and negligent approach to the important matters, along with their illegal and punitive harassment and abuse, were things that must not be covered up with correct words or with someone's ruling that they can be edited out.

Also, there was the sentence: "If there is any possibility that information may be relevant, make a note of it." That line carried with it a vast amount of latitude in what could be included.

There was another point put forward to Conlin in the rebuttal. The Identification process demanded the use of a specific methodology that turned out to be in complete conflict with the RCMP's manual on notes. This was elaborated upon in detail so there could be no misunderstanding by those in Ottawa who made such decisions. It seemed to have been somewhat successful as the manual on note-taking was totally changed and rewritten.

Going on with Conlin's memo, it stated:

"although the Ethics Advisor is not mandated to assess criminal responsibility, I fail to see how Insp. Lathem or anyone involved in the review of your file notes and subsequent recommendations made to implement appropriate corrective measures could have committed "deliberate criminal act by demanding that [you] ... alter [your] ... file notes", especially since you were never demanded to 'alter' or 'change' your file notes. I further fail to see how the legitimate demand that was put to you by your OIC could have been the expression of 'intent on the part of certain members to influence the outcome of the investigation ...'."

Several obvious things were wrong with this statement. First, the Ethics Advisor was a sworn police officer by way of the RCMP Act and, as such, had a responsibility under the law. If she refused that responsibility and hid behind her quasi-mandate, how could she possibly offer any part of the opinion given?

Next, closer inspection of Conlin's words provided the following adjacent lines:

"especially since you were **never demanded** to 'alter' or 'change' your file notes. I further fail to see how the **legitimate demand** that was put to you by your OIC ..."

Which was it to be, no demand or a legitimate demand? It was neither. Certainly there was a demand, but it was not a "**legitimate demand**". What part of "edit the non-factual information" from Lathem's form was not "alter" or "change" my file notes.

In looking up the word edit in the dictionary, it means "to modify or adapt so as to make suitable or acceptable." The notes were to be made "suitable or acceptable" to whom? Was it the two Frasers, Lathem, and Gorman since they were making the demand, or was it a higher level of authority in Ottawa?

If this was such a "legitimate demand", why did Lathem not issue an order under the RCMP Act for me to comply? JJ King in Internal Investigations said he would not dare as it would be an illegal order. If it was illegal to order it, why was it not illegal to demand it?

Why would Lathem want the notes changed in any other manner than as a training exercise? First, this was not and was never intended as a training exercise. With thirty years of attending crime scenes, I had made many hundreds of Court presentations of my evidence in five Provinces and two Territories. Many times, I had received commendations from lawyers and Judges with my memory refreshed by scene notes sometimes made two or more years earlier. I had been accepted as a Court expert witness in many areas of my work in each of those jurisdictions and had never had any problems with my notes and their presentation. I had more than enough experience to have easily written the book on what crime scene notes should include.

In contrast, my information was Lathem had several years as a Constable in Ottawa performing simple guard functions and then limited detachment time with little or no major investigative experience. He might have given evidence in Court, but not as an expert witness. Lee Fraser had possibly half of my experience. For the others, both Gorman's and Neil Fraser's combined experience might have been as much as mine. There was no comparison whatsoever. It was ridiculous for Lathem and Fraser to try to cover their actions by calling it a training exercise.

Next, when reading the notes that I suspected Lathem wanted altered, some of them were critical of certain members of the TSB and the RCMP. Those notes showed their total lack of sincere intent to impartially and scientifically investigate the cause of this fire.

Conlin's lawyer went on with more rhetoric about notebooks being the property of the RCMP and what they should and should not record. My response was to question the lawyer's and Conlin's qualifications to lecture me about notes considering their collective backgrounds.

Now came yet another line needing attention.

"Furthermore, a member 'may be expected to disclose [their] ... notes to [their] ... supervisor or legal advisor' and that 'if a change is necessary, the unwanted words should be struck out with a single line so they are still legible'. This is to ensure that 'a properly compiled notebook can provide corroborating evidence and increase the credibility of testimony' and that the 'notes may be part of the relevant information disclosed by the Crown to the defense, should a case proceed to trial'."

There were several things about this line. Where did it say to make a second set of notes if the first set had mistakes? The second was Conlin and her lawyer, with a minimum of operational experience, were lecturing me about notebooks and their contents. Considering some of the recent revelations about serious crime investigations by the RCMP, shame on them for the stand she, her newly hired lawyer, and the civilian non-police and inexperienced Commissioner of the RCMP had taken in this response to my complaint.

Conlin's lecture raised a point of contention for me, and she was notified of it in the rebuttal memo in no uncertain terms. It was the line "a properly compiled notebook can provide corroborating evidence" taken from the RCMP's manual on notes. According to the Merriam-Webster's dictionary, the words "to corroborate" meant "to support with evidence or authority, make more certain." This definition, applied as it was, implied all evidence presented must agree with the testimony of others that pertains to the charge, or makes the charge more certain. This question was put forward to her. Was it an improperly compiled notebook if it contained non-corroborating evidence that was contradictory? After all, the 'change-the-notes-four' seemed to think so as did Conlin's lawyer. If that were the case, then much of my daily work, along with that of the hundreds of Forensic Identification members across the country, was incorrectly recorded in notes.

Many of my Ident files contained notes describing the results of sometimes dozens of negative evaluations as it was typical to be given a list of suspect names for physical evidence comparisons. These results had to be recorded in my file's notes as opinion. However, a person whom I had noted as a negative comparison may have been charged with the offence. I might even be subpoenaed to Court to give evidence. This had frequently happened during my service. I had even provided evidence favourable to the defence in numerous serious Criminal Code cases including a homicide and a dangerous driving case. The evidence supporting the innocence of the accused was based on my scene work and recorded in my notes as non- "corroborating evidence" in "Notebooks ... property of the RCMP". That certainly contradicted the manual and Conlin's limited concepts of correct police procedures.

What about evidence exposing an investigator or supervisor who failed to perform his tasks in an impartial and diligent manner? What about the notes showing Lathem and Gorman interfered, hindered, and failed to allow me to carry out my responsibilities, indeed my duty? Notes that failed to corroborate the façade Lathem presented to his superiors, the public, and interested parties. In fact, if Lathem, Gorman, and others are ever charged in a Criminal Court for any of these matters, then my notes automatically would become "a properly compiled notebook" that "can provide corroborating evidence and increase the credibility of testimony."

As for her line "notes may be part of the relevant information disclosed by the Crown to the defense, should a case proceed to trial." By law, all notes have to be provided to the Crown who in turn must disclose everything to the Defense.

Recently it was revealed in the media that due to an audit within the Force, there was an issue about retired members retaining their old notebooks. It was suggested perhaps they should be maintained by the Force. In the Swissair matter, the Force did retain the materials, but luckily I made and kept digital format copies and photocopies. One must look at what happened to the material retained and stored by both the RCMP and the TSB, and can it be found today? Access to information requests revealed the RCMP had two hundred and fifty boxes of file material, all of which were totally unorganized and in a mess. Each request for material from those boxes would cost $2,200, or two hundred and twenty hours to search the boxes one by one. The carding system for each box was apparently in disarray, and the computer program for the data did not function. Many of the members' notes were in digital format only, so it would seem they can not be accessed. All these boxes in disarray and the faulty program made me wonder just what the material was Conlin's lawyer so thoroughly reviewed. The story for the TSB was the very same except they required a few more hours and when asked, they did not even know there had been a computer copy of their file. John and Louis will not be impressed.

Now to Conlin's next paragraph.

"Therefore, I do not find that Insp. Lathem or S/Sgt. Gorman abused their authority and/or harassed you by simply performing their administrative duties to yourself and the RCMP. It was within their authority to address you with verbal observations and to issue Performance Logs (1004) when they felt it was appropriate to do so. In addition, I find that your supervisors were obligated to record their observations in your Performance Reviews and/or PRP that were asked to be verified from time to time."

There was one very pertinent concept to know when considering these lines. Commissioned officers of the RCMP were never, ever wrong. That was especially so when they were indeed wrong. Add to that, any other commissioned officer in the line of command had to provide complete public support for anything done whether right or wrong. What's more, the policy of the

RCMP was once a member was commissioned and became an officer, she or he could perform any function within the Force, no matter what their qualifications. The one exception was in Forensic Identification. Lathem oversaw a major crime investigation unit even though he had limited, if any, previous experience investigating a major crime and knew little, if anything, about investigative techniques or physical evidence. Above all else, he impressed upon me that he had no human resource management skills. How does that make one feel about the credibility of a commissioned officer of the RCMP considering it remains as policy in the Force today? Indeed, that policy has even spread into the speciality jobs performed by some NCOs.

My response to Conlin was she wrote in her previous paragraph that she had no mandate to assess criminal responsibility, so just where did the ability and credibility of the Office of the Ethics Advisor come from to offer this assessment of the situation? It was evident to me the harassment and abuse were all part of covering up Gorman's and Lathem's failure to carry out their legal responsibilities and their attempt to have me conform to their illegal wishes. Two years had been wasted to tell me there was no mandate to assess criminal liability, only then to offer the finding of a lack of criminal responsibility on the part of Lathem and Gorman. This statement was an insult to me, other members of the RCMP, and law-abiding citizens of this country.

Continuing, performance logs were mentioned and that both Lathem and Gorman had a right to issue them. Look at Lathem's reprimand for the second half of the ambush meeting.

"During our meeting of 2000-12-01 and subsequent discussion, your conduct was not acceptable. You got up and left during the discussion at which time I said, "The meeting is not over" and your response, 'Well it's over for me' and you then departed. This type of behaviour will not be tolerated . . . ."

This performance log only mentioned leaving the meeting. Nothing at all was mentioned about why the meeting was held. This meeting was where I was in trouble with Lathem for what had been discussed with the FAA, for exhibits to Dr. Brown, and other things on a long list Lathem with the help of Tanner and Fraser had created after their meeting with Gerden. However, none of that appeared on the reprimand form nor was any of it ever mentioned again. Leaving the meeting was a trivial matter when compared to the other alleged problems.

Then we come to the performance reviews and promotion forms. The rebuttal to Conlin up to this point had been somewhat restrained. Now the boxing gloves were on, and the bell had rung! My comments to her were as follows:

"Let me be blunt! This line proves to me that the person who 'investigated' this matter and wrote the memo is totally out of touch with the CMM (Career Management Manual) and its requirements, and of the details of my file. Indeed, that person and by default, the Office of the Ethics Advisor is 100 percent out of line in making this comment. The Performance Reviews that were forced upon me on 01-02-20 by LATHEM and GORMAN for which you are obviously commenting upon were found to be improper and were removed from my file by the CO 'H' Div. when he upheld my two grievances. Both LATHEM and GORMAN failed miserably to comply with any requirements of the CMM. But your comment here is contrary to the CO's findings, and you have overstepped your authority. The comments for the PRP's were in turn ruled as improper by the Force's Adjudicator, and they were removed from the PRP's when they were presented to the 2nd promotion board. Again you have overstepped your authority. This comment alone establishes the level of credibility for this file by the Office of Ethics Advisor as being zero. An apology for these comments is now required as the writer has gone beyond reasonable ineptness in writing your memo. Obviously your lawyer doesn't know what he or she is talking about and for that matter, by allowing this memo to leave your office, neither do you!"

That was what I thought of Conlin and her buffalo court in Ottawa. There seemed to be ample to justify my feelings that she was just one of Commissioner Elliott's many fools. An apology was never received, not that one was expected. Honour and decency in the Commissioner's office seemed to have left long ago.

Skipping the next line, this followed:

"In response to the issues of harassment and abuse of authority, the allegations of misconduct laid against Insp.

Lathem in connection with the February 20, 2001 incident were found not to be substantiated."

Finally this was my official notification of the results of the internal investigation instigated by the grievance process during the summer of 2002. However, that finding certainly did not stand the test. If my allegations of abuse and incorrect behaviour had been unfounded, why did the Commanding Officer uphold my grievances and remove the assessments from my service file? The grievances centred on the abusive and inappropriate manner and circumstances in which the assessments were written and provided. Meanwhile, the internal investigator read the very same material and seemed to have come to a different conclusion. However, the CO 'H' Div. was an Assistant Commissioner. His rank trumped a Sergeant in Internal Investigations Section or even Superintendent MacLaughlan in Criminal Operations. He was the officer who called for the internal investigation and provided the three dubious questions. Now the Ethics Office had requested a copy of the internal investigation results and accepted their ruling that my complaint was unfounded. Perhaps they should have asked for the CO's memo, and that was made abundantly clear to Conlin.

The next lines were more meaningless rhetoric and then the memo concluded with:

"After a careful review, I am unable to find that the processes you engaged in or were submitted to were conducted in an improper manner. For these reasons, I conclude that an intervention of the Ethics Advisor is not warranted in the present circumstances."

Well, as is now apparent, the quality of this "careful review" was certainly in doubt, and Conlin was told it was unacceptable. I also requested a review by a competent investigative agency and an apology for this memo and the insult Conlin's office had delivered.

It was also explained to Conlin that when Fraser received Dr. Brown's report from the TSB indicating an incendiary device on the aircraft, there was then sufficient vindication for my actions on this file such that they should have reversed all punitive measures. Fraser did not.

Within a month of submitting the memo, I learned Conlin had been transferred from the Ethics Advisor's office to the Chief Intelligence Executive. There were jokes in abundance about the misnomer of such titles, and I had yet another. I heard nothing back from the new Ethics Advisor, and information was received that they had closed the file and were ignoring me. So the game was turned up another notch. Another formal complaint against the Force was submitted, this time suggesting Conlin lacked competence and had not faithfully fulfilled her job.

At the same time, a complaint was sent to the Commission for Public Complaints Against the Royal Canadian Mounted Police. It was an outside watchdog government agency dealing with complaints against the Force. I soon learned there would be complications. They could only investigate serving members, and the CPC could not touch those who had retired. The second was that when the RCMP set up the Ethics Advisor and the associated complaint system for members and former members, it did so in such a manner as to preclude the later involvement of this Commission. Therefore, the Commission soon advised there was nothing they could do to investigate any of this. At the very same time, Kennedy, the head of the Commission, was in the news stating the RCMP was incapable of investigating these complaints against themselves. I certainly could vouch for that.

During late August 2009, there was more evidence agreeing with Kennedy's claim. Staff/Sergeant Michael Robineau, NCO in Charge Professional Standards Unit in Ottawa called, sounding very young and inexperienced. At one point, he said he had been in Internal Investigations Section for several years. He said this after I made the point that even though this matter had been investigated numerous times, Lathem continued to get away with his wrongdoing. His comment was that in his years of dealing with internal investigations, he had yet to see anyone of any rank get away with anything. Obviously, he had yet to deal with Lathem and Fraser.

The phone call began with him asking for an explanation of the complaint and the procedure that had taken place. He was given a quick summation, but this was not a matter I could summarize in a minute or two. After allowing me a minute to speak, he asked if this was a legitimate complaint via Section 7 of the RCMP Act. This question caught me off guard because I did not know a thing about Section 7, nor did I care. This now became the focus of his attack including, "Why are you going through the CPC against the RCMP when there are other avenues?" He did not like my response that it was not any of his damn business, and he especially did not like my swearing as the word 'damn' seemed to offend him. I can only suspect he must have gone through recruit training during a more genteel time when instructors did not use the more aggressive verbal invectives and profanity. That was not the way when I went through Depot. He reprimanded me for going this route when I had other avenues specifically designed for members and ex-members. A rather heated discussion ensued. His comments were that I had no reason to go this CPC route. Again, he was asked what I was supposed to do when even the Ethics Advisor refused to respond to my rebuttal. His basic comment was the matter had been investigated and I did not like the results. So, I was seeking an alternate method. His comment was people over the years had seen the material, and no one had agreed with me. It was pointed out every grievance had been won, so several people had agreed. I suggested perhaps it was time for this matter to go to the public. He did not immediately respond, but it was apparent his design was to shut down the complaint before it went further.

At one point, I commented about the changing of the notes. Robineau said the RCMP Act allowed a supervisor to determine what should and should not be in notes and to put in anything else was incorrect. He asserted I had no business adding my opinion to my notes. He went on to say an officer had a right to tell a member what should be in his notes, and obviously my notes were incorrect. Robineau also commented that no officer would tell me to change my notes without pointing out exactly what it was he wanted changed. He made this assertive comment as though that action was most acceptable and standard practice. When I suggested Lathem might have had someone else edit the notes, he said, "you mean blank out pages." It had to be explained to him the notes were in Word format on a disk drive. That point alone confirmed he had not read any of the material except possibly Conlin's four-page memo. He asked if I had changed the notes, but I failed to ask him if it would have made any difference to him if I had. I then asked him if he honestly believed that any supervisor, especially in a major investigation, had the right to tell an investigator what can and cannot be recorded in his or her notes. He firmly stated he did. So as a Staff Sergeant in charge of investigators, he felt he had that right, and Robineau said the RCMP Act allowed for it.

At this point, I needed to hang up or I might have said something truly reflecting what I thought of this guy. Surely they could not all be like him up there in the puzzle palace of Headquarters, Ottawa. His responses revealed what I thought was more than just sheer incompetence because he had stated them so firmly and believed them to be true. Someone could expect this in a police state, but surely not in this country! Did they not understand the concept and the implications of what they were saying? How could any Judge in this country ever trust another RCMP witness?

I suspected he had been told to kill the complaint, so there was nothing I could do at this stage. He had made contact to establish the details, and he was likely trying to resolve the complaint informally. Once again, to say the least, I was dissatisfied.

Just over a month later, a two-page letter was received from S/Sgt. Michael Robineau. In it, he went to great lengths to explain why the CPC could not accept my complaint as it was an internal affair. He went on to state the complaint was terminated, but if I did not like this outcome I could complain to the Commission for Public Complaints Against the RCMP!

I tried once more with another letter of complaint, this time to the Professional Standards and External Reviews. The answer I received simply stated Robineau had terminated the file, and there was nothing further to be done. If I did not like the outcome, I could go to the Commission for Public Complaints Against the RCMP. This response was getting monotonous. S/Sgt. Michael Robineau had been very effective at doing what he was told to do.

A few years later, I happened on a transfer list for commissioned officers. In it was the name Insp. J.M. Robineau transferred from one office to another in the puzzle palace they called RCMP Headquarters, Ottawa. I could only wonder if it might be the same guy, as several years had passed, sufficient time for young Mikey to have been commissioned as Inspector Mike. If so, it was most ironic his new position was in Headquarters Human Resources, Employee and Management Relations, Officer in Charge of Respectful Workplace. Obviously, no swearing allowed. I just gave my head a shake and kept on going.

By the time I had finished with Robineau, I was fed up taking on the Force in a direct frontal assault. MP Boris Wrzesnewskyj was right except he should have said idiots barred the palace gates, and there was no way the Commissioner, King Elliott, sitting on his throne of scarlet serge could see or would be told he was the king who had no clothes.

The significance of the Conlin report was critical. When this matter was initially presented to the public, the RCMP described this report as being the result of a thorough review of the matter, and they went on to state my complaint was unfounded. While the report was not released publicly, enough details were provided to mollify the media so the matter could be put aside. As shown here, the Force's official report was just a selected series of worthless sentences adapted to provide the illusion of an investigation. The report did not reflect the truth, and its ultimate purpose was to fool the Canadian public and the media in particular.

There were other avenues of attack, and I was not yet finished. However, at the end of the day, all approaches made to any government agency failed. A copy of the material was sent to a Crown Counsel in this Province. Within a couple of months, I met to discuss it with him. He was astounded by the details and felt there certainly were grounds for criminal charges. The problem was that with this Province's present political circumstances, no criminal charges against these former members would ever pass through the Provincial Attorney General's office. The AG was a retired member of the Force, and the attitude of the NDP Government seemed to be that the RCMP could do no wrong. So that route had ended. Nepotism was flourishing.

A handful of MP's including Bob Rae, Don Davies, Joe Comartin, Jasbir Sandhu, and Scott Brison were sent a letter outlining the details. Some time later, a phone call was received from Scott as he was my Federal Member of Parliament. He said he would arrange a conference call with another member of the Liberal Party, but they never did call back. It seemed he too had been told to back off. After all, the Chretien and Martin Liberals were in power in Ottawa when the initial decisions were made about the file and its finances. The rest seemed to be too busy to become involved in the old news until it became new news. When it finally did make the news a few years later, the NDP members got in some licks for a day or two in Parliament until the whole matter was smothered by the disinformation supplied by the TSB and the RCMP.

This attempt ended my efforts to handle the matter through channels within the RCMP. I had met a total roadblock, and what I had uncovered I found disgusting and disheartening. It made me question why I or anyone else would ever aspire to become a Mountie. There was no truth or justice in the office of the Commissioner of the RCMP, merely corruption and nepotism.

I had run into problems along these lines before but on a much smaller scale. In 1979 I had a case where a male had been charged with several criminal code driving offences after being involved in a pedestrian accident. My investigation revealed that road and lighting conditions were crucial mitigating factors in the incident. The detachment investigators refused to provide my evidence to the Crown, so immediate steps were taken to notify the Crown Prosecutor through alternate means. The evidence included night-time photos, a three-dimensional sketch made from a transit surveyed scene, and an opinion of the driving conditions. This evidence resulted in all but one of the charges being withdrawn and a subsequent plea of guilty. When the Prosecutor informed the Judge of the reasons for the withdrawal of the charges, the Judge wanted the members charged in Criminal Court for obstruction of justice. Instead, the matter was handled internally, and the members were transferred and eventually fired after more problems arose in their new detachments. Later, the experienced Crown Counsel shook my hand while making the comment that he was glad to see there was still some honor and decency left in the Force. However, the detachment Sergeant who was fully involved in the matter was never touched and, instead, he was soon promoted and transferred. His very words had been, "If you can't give evidence for the prosecution, you won't give evidence at all."

I was told the matter was closed and to pursue it no further. When an incident with a Coroner occurred several months later in the same area, perhaps that was why senior RCMP managers in Fredericton were eager to charge me under the Provincial Coroner's Act. I had barred an incompetent Coroner with no forensic training from a potential homicide scene until I could secure the physical evidence he would have otherwise destroyed. They failed in their attempt to prosecute me, and they had to settle on a written reprimand, likely because no Crown Counsel would pursue such foolish charges. The senior officer in Fredericton who pursued the matter had ambitions for promotion and did not want problems with another Provincial agency. The Chief Coroner should have been told to clean up his department. Local Coroners performed their duties on a part-time basis with only three days training. Some Coroners were a Deputy Sheriff while being an Auxiliary RCMP member. No conflict of interest there!

On the other side, the following was another matter where evidence was provided that totally exonerated the accused, and the Force gained praise. It also showed the value of minute physical evidence. The incident took place during the short summer in the High Arctic of the Northwest Territories. A young Inuit female was charged with killing her brother by shooting him in the forehead with a .22 caliber rifle, killing him instantly.

The scene was a remote beach campsite with a heavy canvas tent consistent with what the Northern Inuit used in the High Arctic. She would not offer any explanation of what had happened, likely due to her culture, young age, religious beliefs, and certainly due to her mental condition and absolute fear. During the brother's autopsy, I noticed on his face four tiny and very slight puncture wounds only barely breaking the skin and with nearly no blood being drawn. The pathologist confirmed the wounds could have been inflicted just before death. Three were in a straight row with the fourth offset just slightly. The contents of the tent had been closely examined, and it was remembered there had been numerous metal eating utensils present. One of the forks had one of the four tines slightly bent. As far as could be determined at the time, it was a possible match. That would be confirmed later back in Iqaluit, but in the meantime, an immediate phone call was made to Norm Fradet, the Corporal in Charge of the detachment. Norm had an abundance of detachment and investigative experience. He was the type of street police officer that every day set the example to which others should aspire. He agreed it was likely a defensive wound inflicted by the accused. It had come to light that the brother may have been sexually assaulting the sister on a continuing basis.

Eventually, it was determined her brother had indeed attacked the young girl while out on the beach, and she had sought refuge inside the tent. No one else was around for miles, just foxes, northern hares, and polar bears. When the brother started through the tent's entry flap with the intention of continuing the sexual assault, she stuck him in the face with the fork, and he backed off. He then returned with a vengeance. The tent as typical was a heavy canvas-walled type about ten by ten feet with the long canvas wall flaps weighted down by heavy rocks. They now prevented her escape. The rifle, handy because of bears, was her last resort.

My Court brief was presented to the Court by the Crown. Due to weather, I could not attend. The Judge accepted my written evidence along with Norm's testimony, and then he offered his commendations to the RCMP for their diligence in determining the truth of the matter even without the cooperation of the real victim.

As shown in this last instance, observation, memory and careful note taking were major parts of this profession even if it created notes of physically tiny bits of non-corroborating evidence that failed to support the criminal charge. The first instance illustrated that one's integrity was paramount and that truth and honesty must prevail. After all, the Force's motto was and still is "Maintain The Right".

Others have argued an aircraft fire is different to a normal structure or vehicle fire. That is bunk designed to protect the TSB's turf. If it were true, why was John Garstang the only TSB investigator with fire investigation skills. He has now retired. No other TSB member had even a fraction of John's fire investigative skills or abilities. Perhaps that was because, in most aircraft crashes, the plane usually burnt up due to the fire that started upon impact with the ground. Or perhaps it was because they never go to Court. There was no need for the expertise. Besides, everything was deemed an accident and never due to a crime. The last thing they would want was for one of their own to have the expertise to determine that a fire was due to a criminal cause. After all, they did not need to be right, just safe.

Nevertheless, a fire was a fire, and I had an extensive background in those investigations. Luckily, Lathem seemed to have been unaware of my fire investigation qualifications or I would have been expelled from the file along with Karl. Additionally, in four years, I had developed a thorough knowledge of the forward section of the aircraft and the materials involved in the fire. I liaised directly with the scientists who analyzed those materials to determine their various characteristics. Later I learned of their test results. No one else in the RCMP had that total experience, and indeed no one else in either agency except John Garstang equaled or surpassed my experience to investigate this fire. Without equal fire investigative qualifications, Jim Foot, Vic Gerden, Larry Vance, and Gus Sidla could not provide a reliable opinion about the fire. Neither could Lathem, Gorman, or the two Frasers.

What was most noteworthy was that John never once suggested to me that magnesium and the other elements were insignificant or a non-factor in the cause of the fire. John, of course, had to be careful, but he worked around the issue by suggesting to Gerden that whatever may have been the cause of the fire, a large amount of magnesium had initially burnt near the short-circuited cables. He suggested we should continue the search for that on-board magnesium source to assist in locating the ignition point of the fire. Gerden reluctantly agreed that continuing the AES testing could be of value to them. All the while Garstang knew there was no such legitimate source.

CHAPTER 9 – GOING OUTSIDE

Before taking the next leap, some research was done to ensure the legality of what I had planned. The Security of Information Act of 1985 was examined. Since nothing in the RCMP's Swissair file had been officially deemed secret, there was nothing to consider here. If someone were to suggest the contrary, Section 15 provides for the disclosure of such information. The section's provisions had been fulfilled by going to the Ethics Advisor, A/Commr. Conlin. What's more, a letter of complaint had been submitted to the Attorney General of Canada, so the Act's requirements had been met twofold.

The path was clear to go outside the Force. The problem was now there were two issues. First, there had been the shoddy crash investigation performed by both the TSB and the RCMP along with all the associated issues. That seemed to take second place now to the attempt by RCMP and TSB management to keep the matter quiet.

The question might be asked as to how so many could be involved in a potential cover-up. As shown in the recounting of these events, there were not many who knew all the details. Within the TSB, John and Don were no longer on the systems committee with Jim Foot. They only knew what they were told at the weekly meetings, and they would reasonably have believed the TSB had complied with the requirements of the MOU. Then there was Sidla spreading the word that Dr. Brown had decided the magnesium was no longer an issue. If he knew the truth was never revealed, but he was likely just passing on what Jim Foot and Gerden had told him.

As for Lathem's back-office investigators, they were either removed from the file before substantial evidence surfaced or were totally out of touch and chose not to learn the facts. The information would soon surface revealing that even the member who maintained the documents and computer data for the file knew nothing of Dr. Brown and his reports until just before the third and final report was issued. Even then, he likely never saw the reports.

Regarding my grievance processes within the RCMP, the details I had revealed were minimal and pertained more to the procedural methods used by Lathem and Gorman than the results of the crash investigation. What's more, it would still be several years before I finally learned of Dr. Brown's three reports and how the TSB had abused him. For management's purposes, Conlin's four-page memo had enough standard catch phrases and keywords available at a glance that it could be used to quell any inquiry into the matter by someone without knowledge of the full facts. Indeed, it was likely written with that in mind as it certainly did not reflect the truth of the actual file. Additionally, those few in the know within the RCMP were all commissioned officers and, as such, their level of expected secrecy was far above mine. The same pertained to the TSB. Besides, who would dare to doubt the word of Assistant Commissioner Conlin or Commissioners Zaccardelli and Elliott?

In June of 2009, Mr. Paul Palango was contacted and supplied with Conlin's memo, the rebuttal memo, and other material. Paul had written three books on the Force. He said that when he started, the books were not intended to be a critical evaluation of the RCMP, but the details he uncovered led him in that direction. When Paul and his wife were first met for an interview, it lasted three hours and not nearly everything was covered. It quickly became apparent they both believed me, and they completely understood the circumstances of the complaint. Over the next two years, extensive work was done with a view towards Paul writing a fourth book about the RCMP, this time based on the Swissair investigation or lack thereof.

At the same time, a submission was made to the CBC's The Fifth Estate. Nothing was heard back until February of 2011 when Paul called to say he was bringing Rob Gordon of CBC Halifax for a meeting. Apparently, Paul used to be involved with the CBC and still had good contacts with them. He was trying to put together a documentary in conjunction with 'The Fifth Estate' program. Rob had a bevy of questions that were answered to his satisfaction in a series of meetings and phone calls. A further meeting was arranged, this time with Linden MacIntyre. Linden, too, had a bevy of questions, but they were because of his having read the material and understanding what it all meant. The questions were professional and to the point. He knew the material and what the story line would be. He just wanted to confirm I was truthful and up front with them, and that I would provide a credible presence on camera. As events showed, obviously he was satisfied.

Over the next few months, there were a series of videotaped interviews and scenes. Morris Karp, the program's senior producer, would prove to be a true professional. Considerable time would be spent with him at videotaping sessions, on the phone, and in emails as explanations were required for many of the details to be revealed in the upcoming program. The lawyers for the CBC were a demanding lot, and many details and explanations were necessary for the program with each having to be verified by documentation. Unfortunately, there was only a limited ability in the short lead time before the broadcast, and with only forty-four minutes, there was little airtime for details. Because of that, many critical parts of the story could not be told. What's more, there was too much information in my notes that I had not yet fully deciphered, and other relevant documents were yet to be received even at that late date.

As part of an attempt to balance the presentation, both the TSB and the RCMP in Ottawa were approached by Morris and Rob for a video interview to present their side of the story. Lathem was approached, and he offered his acknowledgment of who I was with his answer – "Oh yes, he was the Ident guy who kept **such good notes**". Both agencies refused to be interviewed on camera. Morris and Rob knew why, but there was nothing they could do. Neither agency wanted to put their spokesperson in front of a camera to try to explain embarrassing questions from an interviewer who knew the story. Just imagine what Linden MacIntyre or Rob Gordon could have asked. Answers would be required the RCMP and TSB senior management would be unwilling to give. No member of the Force such as Conlin or of the TSB such as Gerden or his boss, Executive Director Ken Johnson, could withstand such a confrontation. They risked revealing more by their answers than could ever be shown in the short time frame of the episode. The standard practice of any organization was to refuse the pre-story interviews and then do a follow-up interview to balance the story. Their media relations people only then needed to respond to the material that had been raised in the program and could do so in a manner that was ambiguous while sounding righteous and innocent. Those balanced interviews seemed to be selectively provided so only an uninformed interviewer who could easily be controlled asked the questions.

Gerden did respond off camera by saying the evidence contributed by both Dr. Brown and me was so trivial as to be virtually non-existent. Perhaps that was true, particularly since the AES material in the TSB's report was indeed non-existent. As for his opinion of my involvement, Howard Green's final video showed it all. I could be seen in the final footage but only if the viewer did not blink at that moment. Gerden made the comment, again off camera, that I was out of the loop and did not know all the facts. This attitude was common for Gerden as he frequently made the statement that because I was not a pilot, I could never understand certain details of the investigation. Some of them would soon come to light, and I appreciated he had removed any implication that I was associated with their underhanded dealings.

Attempts to contact members of other agencies involved in the file met with a brick wall. I was told they had been ordered not to speak with me or the CBC on the threat of being fired from their job.

The program aired on the 16th of September, 2011, as the second episode of the new season. There was a flurry of news activity for several days before its airing, and numerous reporters contacted me. Morris wanted nothing revealed before the program aired. As part of their policy, I had no knowledge of what would be shown, yet the reporters seemed to know the story already. Since to deny their statements would be a lie, the no comment answer gave them the go ahead to air their version of the story.

Once 'Swissair 111, The Untold Story' aired, there was another bevy of communications. The Fifth Estate website received comments both pro and con. In general, the cons were comments from people who, contrary to what they wrote, had no idea how the investigation had been handled or what the materials were that made up the airplane. Others felt that because I was a Forensic Ident member, I was not an investigator, so I had no knowledge of the actual investigation. However, the majority were pro comments, and they were astounded at the potential cover-up, and many wanted to know more. Some, especially other police officers, commented about the illegal demand to change the notes. My website received a multitude of search hits, and numerous people sent emails favourable to the story, especially regarding the illegal activities of my supervisors. There were several requests for interviews that were fulfilled, but generally within a few days the hype was over. The RCMP and the TSB provided their carefully edited response, and no one seemed to press for more. The program had been too limited to present all the facts, and no one knew enough to counter the half-truths and lies put out by the media relations people.

One interview was conducted by the local CBC Halifax morning radio program. In the interests of providing a balanced coverage, Jim Foot provided his version of events. The host seemed to have failed to prepare himself with the proper questions. Possibly because he had received a radio news award for covering the initial days of the crash, he seemed to think he had full knowledge of the story. Foot just used him to put forth a fresh version of the same TSB disinformation.

As planned, the RCMP spokesperson in Ottawa knew nothing whatsoever about the file and simply stated the RCMP had fully investigated the complaint, and they stood behind their concluding report. That, of course, was Conlin's memo. Well, now that the lies and double-talk making up the Conlin report have been finally disclosed, I can only wonder what their response might be the next time this issue is raised in the media.

In February of 2015, I finally received by way of access to information documents shedding light on how the Force reacted to the program. Lathem, after his contact with Rob Gordon, notified the Force of what was coming. Briefing notes were prepared for the Commissioner outlining the matter, and preparations were made. Only specially trained members were to deal with the media. What were called media lines were prepared to provide answers to any expected questions. It was interesting that this paragraph appeared in the material.

"No media interviews will be granted prior to the CBC Fifth Estate broadcast. RCMP will respond in writing until such time that all details and allegations being put forth are known and will allow us to properly respond.
'H' Division Communications and Media Relations will prep the spokesperson for the interviews prior to there (sic) completion."

It rather seemed this document was prepared in haste as they did not bother to spellcheck. A further line read as follows.

"Contact with the Transportation Safety Board Communications team should be made and media lines should be shared to ensure a coordinated approach.

The retired IDENT member will be seen as a credible source given his role in the investigation and specialization as a Forensic officer."

After several lines of verbal rhetoric, the document provided one line of importance.

"If pressed on the direction provided to the employee:
It is not uncommon for an investigative report to be reviewed by a senior officer before being filed/closed to ensure the content is fact and evidence based. If a report is plagued with opinion and does not focus on the facts/evidence the author of the report may be asked to remove it."

What was important here was the word "report". A report was different to notes. Notes were written during the investigative process to record details of events so a report could then be written. When giving evidence in Court, a police officer did not refer to a report to refresh his or her memory. Notes were used, and it was the notes the change-the-notes-four wanted me to change. What happened here was that somewhere between the complaint to Conlin and this set of media lines the concept of what was to be altered had conveniently been falsified. Every police officer knew 'reports' may not reflect what the individual investigator thought of the file, especially if there were multiple investigators. 'Notes', though, were his or her personal record of their individual portion of the investigation. They were sacrosanct and could never be altered. Convenient, was it not, that this falsification of the truth had occurred for the writing of the media lines, and now the complaint concerned a 'report' instead of 'notes'? Someone in the Commissioner's office had decided they could pull one over on the Canadian public by feeding disinformation and lies to the media. By doing that, they controlled the public. It was an art learned by Government agencies after years of having been made to look like fools.

As for the complaint to the Force's Ethics Advisor, A/Commr. Conlin, the following was offered in the media lines.

"Q: What can you tell us about Mr. Juby's Ethics complaint?
A: The RCMP Ethics Officer independently reviewed the complaint and concluded it was not substantiated.
Q: Did the RCMP take the concerns brought forward by Mr. Juby seriously?

A: The RCMP Ethics Officer independently reviewed the complaint and concluded it was not substantiated."

Strange how the addition of one adverb affected the meaning of the whole sentence. The word 'independently' tended to give Conlin's report an air of honesty and integrity when, as shown, it was nothing but controlled words polluting white paper and written by a lawyer trying to keep his or her job. What's more, these lines proved the previous media lines indicating a 'report' instead of 'notes' were purposefully written because they knew of my complaint to Conlin.

There was another line as follows.

"Q: How do you respond to Mr. Juby's allegations that the investigation was conducted improperly?

A: The RCMP completed an extensive and professional investigation. The evidence was reviewed before a determination on the cause of the crash was reached. The RCMP and the Transportation Safety Board of Canada both concluded that the cause of the crash was accidental and not criminal."

This "extensive and professional investigation" must have taken place during the first two weeks of the file because that was when Lee Fraser offered the information that Ottawa had determined the fire to be accidental in nature and there never would be a Court case. It was Ottawa's senior TSB and RCMP management and not the onsite investigators who came to that determination.

As for the last line, it was a bit high and mighty considering the file was entirely a physical evidence file, and the RCMP's physical evidence investigation was conducted with me as the main and, for much of the time, only investigator. Who in the RCMP knew better than me what the physical evidence was and what it meant?

There was one more line of interest.

"Q: What was the role of the IDENT officer?

A: The role of the IDENT officer was to gather all evidence at a scene that may be relevant to the investigation. The body of evidence was provided to an investigative team and a scientific team for review. They both concluded that the cause of the crash was accidental, as did the Transportation Safety Board."

Just who were the investigative and the scientific teams reviewing this "body of evidence"? The investigative team obviously was Lathem and his backroom people. The New York trip report was a prime example of the work done by much of that team, and it was amateurish. The only investigator Lathem had with any capability, expertise, common sense and independence was Karl Christiansen, and he was kicked out of the hangar even before all the debris could be examined because the results of his investigation were not what Lathem wanted. Because he had severe doubts about the amount of burn damage versus the fire load, Karl had to go. If they wished to call those few who remained Lathem's investigative team, then I considered it an insult to real police investigators. Brian London with his dust balls was just one example of their level of competency. When I asked him, he indicated he had never dealt with any fire in his life, not even a campfire. As for dust balls, I suggested that if he felt they were a contributing factor in this fire, then he should sleep with a fire extinguisher beside his bed in case any dust balls under his bed suddenly ignited due to static electricity. My remark was not intended as a joke. Those who were left had nothing whatsoever to do with any of the physical evidence that was gathered. I suspected they would not have known what a piece of physical evidence was even if it had jumped up to bite them on the backside.

As for the scientific team, the RCMP's Crime Lab refused to conduct many of the requested tests and for good reason. They were useless tests asked for by a TSB electrical investigator and an RCMP Inspector who knew nothing about physical evidence. However, the Crime Lab certainly had no insight as to what was going on in the file and had no "body of evidence" to examine. Sure there was an Explosives Disposal Unit (EDU) member and a Crime Lab Chemist on the sort line every day. The EDU member found no evidence of a bomb. Even if he had been looking for an incendiary device, what would he find considering the purpose of such a device and the high temperatures involved? The Chemist, though, found traces of military type explosives, but it was written off as coming from the ordnance previously housed both onsite and on the ships. What is interesting is that Dr. Brown, during one of the AES test sessions, stated he had found elements indicative of plastic explosives. Nothing further came of it because the magnesium, aluminum and iron question overshadowed everything else.

In fact, the real scientific team consisted of Dr. Brown and John Garstang. While Dr. Brown's initial report revealed his true opinion, Garstang was kept from providing his opinion by his position in the TSB. Thanks to an ATIP release after the program aired, further members of the RCMP's 'scientific team' and their actions were revealed to me. However, no matter who or how many reviewed the scientific evidence of Dr. Brown, only he had the qualifications and expertise to offer an opinion. No one else with comparable qualifications was ever asked by the RCMP or the TSB to review and either verify or disprove the results.

As for the TSB, they simply pointed to a wire and speculated it was the cause, but they offered no scientific proof. An accidental cause due to wiring was the most convenient and the least controversial decision they could make and, of course, it was the only one permitted by their legislation. That seems to be the TSB's way of doing things, and unfortunately, it appears to have become the RCMP's way of doing police work in too many instances.

Before the airing of the program, an RCMP internal email was sent to every member of the Force. It played up the hard work done by all members and that their dedication to that work was still recognized. However, my complaint and the CBC program were never intended to discredit that work nor those members. It seemed to me the email was sadly lacking in the facts while being cloaked in what can only be called a false sense of gratitude to the members. The truth was the hard work of so many was tainted by corrupt RCMP and TSB management practices.

As for handling the media, the RCMP and the TSB did an excellent job with their media lines because it put a large wet towel of disinformation on the flames created by Linden, Rob, Morris, and Paul. So much so the matter was just as suddenly dropped.

While I was not expecting any communication from the Commissioner's office, I did hear from a Sergeant in Headquarters, Ottawa. The Force had a unit monitoring for any copyright infringements of its image. Years ago, the RCMP's image had been sold to Disney in the US, and they held the copyright. I have had a website for years containing photos depicting various facets of the Identification function, and one showed two uniformed RCMP members working in an arson scene. I knew both and took the photo myself. Soon after the program aired, I received an email indicating the photograph must be pulled because I had not received permission to display it, thus there was a copyright infringement. I solved the problem by using Photoshop on the yellow stripe on the members' pant legs, and there was nothing further heard from Ottawa. Perhaps someone might think the 'Mickey Mouse Club' had taken up part-time residence in the RCMP's Headquarters building in Ottawa and Goofy was in charge!

Stepping back a bit in time now, just after Paul Palango arranged with the CBC for The Fifth Estate coverage, it was decided to renew contact with Dr. Brown to see how he was making out. Contact had been lost for several reasons. His clarification email on the 20th of February, 2001, had been turned over to Lathem, expecting him to do something about it, but not convinced anything would be done. Once it was realized the latter was correct, it was felt Dr. Brown had been let down and abandoned by the Force. As for contacting him myself, what was I to say other than sorry but my RCMP management neither trusted nor believed him? Perhaps it was that they just did not care even if he was right. Besides my guilty feeling of having let him down, there was the fact that I had been beaten down so badly by Lathem and Fraser. Add to that all of the TSB's disinformation they had spread around that Dr. Brown had determined seawater to be the cause. There was so much of it that I was going through a stage of severe self-doubt and self-denial. That was the reason why I did not want to go through my notes. What was the use? By the summer of 2002, everything seemed to indicate I was in the wrong, and there was no one to go to who could or would do anything about Lathem's misdeeds. Once I retired, there was nothing further I could do directly. There were battles of credibility to be fought on my front without getting involved with more TSB-related matters. What's more, deep down I had a faint but unending hope legal action would occur, and the last thing I wanted was to be accused of tainting Dr. Brown's evidence. Then things changed. I had beaten Lathem's and Gorman's assessments, I had reasonable proof of a cover-up by way of Conlin's memo, and I had people who believed me. It was now time to learn what had happened and to see if he was willing to assist in bringing the matter to the public.

On the 2nd of February, 2011, Jim Brown was contacted by phone, and during a long conversation, some important details were learned. By this time, he had been retired for almost a year, but he remembered everything about the Swissair file. The most important piece of information was he had never found seawater or anything else to be the source of the magnesium and the other questioned elements. Next, it was his supervisor who had applied pressure to him to make him soften and change his first draft report as was indicated in the email from him in February 2001. She seems to have been successfully influenced by the TSB. A short time later the TSB's chief scientist, Gus Sidla, retired. That she became his replacement perhaps should not be held against her by any outside observer. She, of course, would have had excellent credentials and would have come highly recommended both by CANMET and, of course, by the TSB's management.

However, even the second report was not acceptable. Jim said the TSB director told him they were going ahead with the safety recommendations. They did not want anything to muddy the waters, or none of the airlines would fall into place with the changes. This reason was precisely the point I had made to Lee and Neil Fraser, Gorman and Lathem during the change-the-notes meeting. They had said I was nuts to think it.

Jim Brown told me he had no idea of the problems I had encountered or that RCMP management had obstructed the investigation. During my work with him, I had not told Jim anything of the investigation outside of the AES area or even how RCMP management had reacted to the AES findings. There was a need then for him to act only on his AES evaluations and not be influenced by other parts of the investigation. That was the way evidence of this sort had to be handled so it could carry its weight in a Court of Law in Canada.

He went over some of the details of the testing and stated he had accurately identified the wires that had been made during the Seattle wire test. The problem was some of those wires were unsuitable because carbon from the smoke had been deposited on the bead to such an extent it interfered with his tests. Those wires had to be removed from his test results. The TSB used those numbers against him saying it proved the method was not feasible as an investigative tool. It was pointed out to him the TSB's comments about the AES testing had tainted the whole process and RCMP management had refused to consider it as an investigative tool for fire investigations. At one point, the comment was made to him that the TSB wanted the physical evidence to match the results they had previously decided upon, and he fully agreed their whole approach to the AES testing was precisely that.

Jim stated he had submitted a total of three reports, the first two having been rejected by the TSB. After the second, he was approached by a TSB director whose name he had forgotten. He was told to read the contract between CANMET and the TSB. They had the final say in what went into the report and, if not satisfied, they would not pay for the services that had been provided. Dr. Brown was forced to submit what in effect was a false report, and he was still upset over it.

During our conversation, there was a strong hint Dr. Brown felt a certain amount of guilt at his having to give in to the TSB's demands. However, there were several things for him to keep in mind. Jim had taken it upon himself to reveal to the RCMP exactly what his findings were, yet they did nothing about it. Having done that, he then submitted reports that eventually went to the RCMP. Again, nothing was done, and the RCMP did not contact him. Jim was neither a police officer nor in any way a person with any legal authority in the investigation. His actions went beyond anything a normal citizen was required to do, and thus they freed him from any moral or ethical responsibility to breach his worksite obligations. CANMET had a binding civil contractual agreement with an independent non-judicial federal agency to present AES findings. Some official in CANMET had already agreed that the results must be to the satisfaction of that agency. If there were any fingers to be pointed, they certainly must be towards the TSB for such an underhanded and immoral, if not illegal, contract. Nonetheless, the onus was on Lathem as the Officer in Charge of the RCMP's investigation to speak with Dr. Brown to determine the truth. It would appear he knowingly and purposefully failed to do so, something that possibly made him derelict in his duty as a police officer as well as culpable in obstruction of justice, and it freed Dr. Brown of any criminal or civil repercussions or responsibilities. Eventually, evidence would surface to suggest both Lee Fraser and Gorman shared that same guilt with Lathem.

What was of importance here was that Dr. Brown did not have a copy of his reports readily available and neither did I. More importantly, Jim did not realize I had never seen those reports, and, therefore, I did not know what was in each. Had I known, the CBC's story certainly would have taken on a different slant.

It was explained to Jim what had transpired recently, and he was asked if he would agree to disclose his details publicly. He said he had not thought about it, but he was now retired, and nothing was stopping him. He was told someone from the CBC would be in touch with him shortly, and he commented he would welcome the phone call.

By the end of March 2011, Rob Gordon had spoken with him. Rob's comment was that he was on track and very willing to be interviewed by the CBC. Dr. Brown was an important source for revealing the AES findings as his material was an essential part of the story. The problem was no one in the CBC knew what was in the reports as they had not seen them.

When the program aired in September 2011, the only concern I had with it was that Jim used the term pyroclastic to describe what normally would be called a criminal incendiary device. While technically correct, the problem was many people did not understand he was indeed talking about a criminal device or firebomb used to cause a fire and murder the two hundred and twenty-nine passengers and crew.

As part of the preparations for the program, Morris had decided to seek a second opinion of Dr. Brown's AES findings. Of course, they were unable to examine the actual cables, and they did not have the actual reports. Thanks to Larry Fogg and Dr. Brown, during each testing process we had copied all the AES readings as they were displayed. Those readings from my notes were valid and suitable for interpretation by other experts. One was easily found at the University of Toronto. Morris explained that after the Professor had checked the readings as a blind examination, he was surprised and concerned about the high levels of magnesium and the associated elements. He wondered if further testing had been undertaken to look deeper into the problem. Morris was told it definitely should have been a matter of concern.

Now there was another filament of the story that warranted telling. About the time Paul Palango was making arrangements with the CBC, he also encountered Mr. Fritz Muri, a producer for Swiss Television. Fritz intended to produce a parallel program in Switzerland like the CBC's The Fifth Estate. In early December 2010, he flew over to Canada, and Paul brought him to meet with me. Fritz had many questions, some of which I never actually had a chance to answer. An example was he questioned the validity of the notes and how did he know they were not made just the previous year? Paul jumped on the question and commented that all anyone needed to do was read them. There were far too many minute details for them not to have been written throughout the investigation. Although Fritz was not familiar with all of the story's details when he started, by the end of the meeting he knew much more.

On the 8th of August, 2011, Fritz called from Switzerland and talked excitedly for three-quarters of an hour. He had been conducting considerable research for the story. Lausanne and a city in France each had a University with an outstanding Criminology Department. He had been speaking with some of their leading professors and had provided them some of the AES readings along with photos and the TSB report. They had found so many loopholes in the report they called it a sham. They said the TSB's findings would never be allowed in any Court anywhere in the modern world as they were not objective or verifiable. Commenting about the actual fire and the melting of aluminum, they stated that under these conditions they strongly doubted any aluminum would melt unless an accelerant had been present. They explained to him the cold-sink value of the aircraft, but he had not understood what they meant. I explained to him the plane's skin had been at minus 60 degrees C. for an hour, and it would have sucked up extreme amounts of heat from any interior fire before any of the interior metal could have melted. Fritz went on to say they could not understand how such findings and such a report could be released and why no one had stood up to question it. The professors also commented that nowhere in the democratic world was it legal for a police officer to be told to alter his or her notes. It was one thing to comment on the contents, but no one could have them altered or ask for them to be modified. The professors were apparently willing to be interviewed on TV, and Fritz planned to do so that same week. The tape was to be included in The Fifth Estate episode.

Fritz mentioned the figure of 98% of the aircraft being recovered. He questioned why there were so many holes in the plane's reconstruction frame. He was told the material had all been weighed while wet, so all the absorbent materials were waterlogged and heavy. Two percent of two hundred and fifty tons was five tons of material, a significant amount. Because the heaviest items such as the engines, undercarriage, and the main frame materials had been retrieved, the five tons were a disproportionately higher amount of the lighter materials such as the light alloy skin and frame pieces. He was astounded they would do it this way.

Fritz asked some technical questions about the short-circuits, and then he said his professors had commented that the mere presence of a short-circuit was not an automatic indication of a fire cause. He also asked if the magnesium was burnt when found in the beads, and he was told about the oxygen levels. He lacked a technical knowledge of chemistry and physics but seemed to make do sufficiently.

Fritz then had a few more questions about the actual investigation, including how many forensic investigators were involved for the RCMP. It was explained to him what had happened and that I was the only RCMP forensic physical evidence investigator attached to the file on a full-time basis after about one year into the file. He asked what the standard procedure was for crashes, because the police automatically started a criminal investigation into any plane crash in Switzerland. Even if it was deemed to have been an accident, there still could be an investigation to determine who was responsible and if there could then be criminal charges. The process for Swissair was explained to him and that it was left in the hands of the TSB.

When commenting on the amount of fire and the evidence of Dr. Brown, he added that he was shocked no one else in the RCMP had grasped the situation. He wondered if any of those senior people were still in the Force. He was told they all had retired.

He also wondered why it had taken so long for me to come forward publicly. He was told there were certain legal procedures for someone in my situation to follow before going public, and it had taken until 2009 for that to be completed. He was again shocked it would take so long. I assured him copies of all the documents had been kept, and a continuous effort in trying to have the matter investigated could be shown. Even after deciding to go public it had taken a considerable time for things to arrive at this phone call from him.

Fritz planned to interview his university professors that week, and then he intended to come to Canada during the third week of August 2011 to interview Dr. Brown and me. His comment was he wanted the two most important characters of the story. Even though he had the CBC material, he had his questions to ask.

Fritz sounded very excited about the whole matter and was no longer hesitant about the story. He could not understand why no one had questioned the TSB's findings or the lack of a criminal investigation. Fritz was asked if he still thought the notes were made just a year previously and he commented about the number of note files he had received. It was explained that copies of the backup CDs were provided to prove nothing in the notes had been changed.

By the third week of August 2011, Fritz had decided he would use the CBC's material and forgo his interviews. Fritz seemed to think he could prove an incendiary device downed the plane, but he gave no indication of how he planned to do it. By the time the CBC aired their program, the Fritz connection had fizzled out. It seemed Swiss TV had looked at the overall situation and decided that to attack the Canadian investigation and its outcome meant criticizing procedures in a friendly foreign country. Because of the embarrassment they might cause, they would sooner drop the program and allow the Canadians to do it themselves. That ended the Swiss TV connection for the time being at least. I could only wonder what back channel dealings might have occurred between certain agencies in each country.

Coming back to the investigation in this country, just what did Dr. Brown provide for his preliminary report? I finally received a copy of all three of Dr. Brown's reports using Access to Information, but only after the CBC's program aired. A copy of the first was sent to Dr. Brown who confirmed it was his initial report to the TSB. While it contained details about the testing, the wires, and the methods used, the conclusions were of interest.

CONCLUSIONS

The Auger electron microprobe has analytical capabilities uniquely suited for determining the surface and near-surface chemistry of Cu arc beads and melts. This information is critical to the arson investigator trying to determine if an electrical short (arc) caused a fire. Very little calibration data existed prior to this study to support the applicability and reliability of AES in typical residential or commercial building arson investigations. More importantly it had never been applied to aviation wiring arc melts salvaged from an atypical marine environment (i.e., the crash site) and after being submerged in sea water for many weeks.

Eight (8) arc melts from seven (7) exhibits have near-surface chemical profiles that suggest they are possible ignition sources of the on-board fire. The likelihood of eight electrical shorts on 7 separate wires (of four different gauges) occurring in a relatively clean atmosphere (i.e., prior to the fire) is difficult to reconcile however. If a massive shorting event involving many wire gauges did occur nearly simultaneously then one is lead to speculate the cause as either: (a) a short exposure to a strong electromagnetic pulse (very high induced current) or (b) a deliberate act of sabotage. For example, fine Mg metal wire/ribbon wrapped around a wire bundle(s) and remotely ignited could cause multiple, nearly simultaneous arcing. Alternatively, the AES protocol, developed for classical arc beads, is providing a positive ("cause of fire") reading in some cases due to unknown factors/artifacts. Additional experiments and analytical studies are currently being performed to determine the morphological properties of these arc melt exhibits and the effects of sea water exposure generally (chemical and biological) on Cu arc melt surfaces.

That was all there was for conclusions. Cu was the chemical symbol for copper and Mg was the symbol for magnesium. Any arson investigator would be alarmed at the statement that eight melts could be simultaneous initiating points, because more than one fire source indicated arson in 99.9% of fire investigations. Since that number tended to indicate a set fire, it might be reasonable to assume the Anderson theory for finding the single initiating wire did not work for this file likely because the excessive heat caused re-melts of the wires.

However, that did not change the fact that the beads were examined by a sound scientific process, and hard data of real physical elements other than copper were found. The wires were normally of pure copper with a tin or nickel coating on the outside covered, of course, by insulation. As Dr. Brown indicated and as could be seen in the data readouts, magnesium, iron, and aluminum were real and present. After exhaustive searching, no legitimate source was found in the airplane, and seawater had been ruled out. One had to be naïve to believe Dr. Brown, with his knowledge and experience, would hit minute cracks and fissures in the beads' surfaces during each examination that revealed these elements, yet only they showed up and not the wide range of elements normally found in seawater. As for the seawater test wires that John, Larry, and I created, they underwent similar conditions and circumstances, and they all failed to show any of these questioned elements. One would have to argue the aircraft wires had cracks and fissures and selective absorption while the seawater test wires did not. That goes beyond credibility since they were duplicate wires in nearly identical circumstances.

The electromagnetic interference or EMI theory was something easily ruled out as the initiator of the eight clean wires. If that had occurred, then how did the three elements come to be in the other wire beads as there would have been no onboard source? Since in theory it would have affected at least eight or more wires and, therefore, most likely other electronics on a modern fly-by-wire aircraft, would it not have been recorded on the Flight Data Recorder, the FDR?

Dr. Brown's magnesium ribbon was only an educated guess since he had no idea of the layout of the overhead equipment. Nevertheless, between Dr. Brown's opinion and that of all the other experts who were consulted, such as Dr. Quintiere, Dr. Lyon, the CBC's metallurgist, and Fritz's two independent university professors, there was more than sufficient expert opinion to suspect a criminal scenario as the cause of the fire. At the same time, there was no expert opinion or scientifically proven physical evidence to support a short-circuited wire as the cause. Jim Foot had no qualifications to say otherwise.

CHAPTER 10 – MAKE IT SO

What now needs to be presented are several seemingly unrelated threads and events that occurred to influence the investigation. Even though they might seem entirely unconnected and inconsistent, they will all come together to show what happened behind the scenes. That apparent disconnect provides the reader with the main reason why this whole underhanded scheme took so long for me to decipher.

Continuing with Dr. Brown's report, let us examine the timeline and how the document was handled. By November of 2000, it was known his report was about to be released, and there was a good indication that at least one possible source for the questioned elements would be a criminal scenario. The TSB had decreed only they would receive any report from CANMET, and I was told the contract stipulated total confidentiality of the results. That was why I had no idea the main scenario of only two would indicate sabotage as the cause of the fire. I would be retired for ten years before learning this. Now one might think that upon being presented with Dr. Brown's conclusions, Lathem, who probably thought he was a legitimate police investigator, would want to examine the matter further. Surely any police agency worthy of its name would demand control of the file. The timeline tells a different story.

Dr. Brown's first AES report, dated November of 2000, was received by the TSB before the end of the month. Emails from Dr. Brown and words spoken by Jim Foot on the 1st of December, 2000, confirmed this fact. So during the 'ambush meeting,' Jim Foot contributed to the abuse thrown at me, all the while knowing the implications of this report that he had already received a week earlier.

Who else in the room knew? Gerden as the TSB's lead investigator had to have known as Foot could never have kept that information from him for any more than a few hours. Gerden wanted a meeting with Lathem to discuss AES. Why call the meeting and what would he discuss if he did not already know what was in the report? Gerden made a comment to me a few days later that he was not aware of the report's contents. Preposterous! To say he had no knowledge of something that important was ridiculous. This report affected the TSB's future fate in the file, yet he did not know its contents! The truth was the report was to remain a secret and was not to be leaked to anyone, so I was forbidden to know its details. It was easier to tell a lie to the only full-time police investigator on the file because he could not risk an explanation.

Remember, too, Pat Cahill had already confronted the TSB on the matter of AES, and Gerden, in turn, had made his complaint to Lathem about me. Gerden most certainly told Foot to keep the details of the report quiet. If he did not know the exact wording of the report, Gerden surely knew enough about the conclusions to realize the implications if the truth ever got out. After all, what was there for him to know or pass on to Lathem and Tanner? The simple statement that Dr. Brown said the cause of the fire was sabotage covered it sufficiently.

As for Larry Vance, he had to have known as he was Gerden's right-hand man, Assistant Lead Investigator, and he was present at the meetings. Garstang did not know the report's contents as he was off the systems committee and out of the loop, although he may have suspected something. Neither Don Enns nor Larry Fogg knew about the report. Boeing could never know. As for John, it would be the 28th of June, 2001, before he would inform me indirectly that he knew of the report's contents and that he had advised Gerden of the need to notify the RCMP. John did not say what the contents were because he likely had been sworn to secrecy. What's more, the report he then knew about was probably the second and modified or softened report from Dr. Brown. It was entirely possible he never knew about the first report.

Who in the TSB and when they knew of Dr. Brown's report was important. Foot and Sidla received the initial report, and it might be argued they performed their job as required by their Act. However, I would have to hold my nose while saying it due to the smell of it. As for the actions of Gerden and Vance, they were another issue that soon will be examined.

What was more important, though, was that my RCMP management already knew of the report's contents by the time of the afternoon ambush meeting on the 1st of December, 2000. I know that Insp. Dan Tanner was in the hangar on that morning to meet with Lathem and Gerden. Tanner was the Division Criminal Intelligence Officer and had direct connections to his counterparts in Ottawa. What possible reason did he have to be there other than to discuss the file and Dr. Brown's first report with Lathem, Vance, and Gerden? Remember the meeting took place in Gerden's office within a week of the TSB receiving the report, and, according to John, Gerden called the meeting to discuss AES. He thought I would be included, but I was never invited.

Lathem and Tanner, both being RCMP commissioned officers and police officers, were told of Dr. Brown's conclusion of sabotage during the morning meeting. Then during the afternoon meetings, Gerden, Vance, Foot, Lathem and Neil Fraser tore strips off me for my work with Dr. Brown and the continuation of my criminal investigation. Did Neil Fraser know of the report's findings? His notes gave no indication of it, but he was now Lathem's Identification contact and the acting Regional Identification Supervisor. Fraser had to have been told something to make him hurry back from a file in Northern New Brunswick, and merely that I was a loose cannon in the hangar was not news to him.

What transpired during the morning meeting, a meeting called by Gerden? Could anyone not think it was convened to discuss Dr. Brown's first AES report and the future of the file? Some points of possible additional discussion could be considered. Of course, my memo regarding the requirement for a criminal investigation into the flammable materials in the aircraft might have been mentioned. Gerden and Lathem had already discussed and decided on that topic as I had already received a memo telling me to back off, so surely there was nothing more to talk about on that matter. However, I had been talking with Pat Cahill of the FAA and sending more exhibits to Dr. Brown. Speaking to the FAA about the magnesium issue would soon be shown to be forbidden when Lathem made the comment to me that he would not have the RCMP come between the TSB and the FAA. Remember the timing of this incident. By sheer coincidence, I had spoken to Cahill about the magnesium problem within days of Foot having received Dr. Brown's first report. It would be interesting to know what Cahill was told when she confronted them about the matter, although I am certain it was not the truth. This whole incident must have rattled Gerden and Lathem. Added to that was their worry of outsiders being shown the frame and any discussions I may have had with them. As for work extensions and the turnover of the file's database, they were merely housekeeping chores. Surely those matters could have been dealt with over the phone, and they certainly did not involve Tanner and his area of work. No, the significant and pressing topic involved the AES report and how to handle it along with both Dr. Brown and me.

They must have had some serious concerns, and my earlier conversation with Cahill would have fed their suspicions. Gerden and Lathem must have been worried about what I already knew of the AES report and what I would do about it. Because of my previous memo about the faulty FAA burn testing of the materials in the plane and then my suggestion that the FBI should investigate, how far would I go with Dr. Brown's sabotage report, something that was much more serious? They could not provide an answer because they did not know if I had contacted Dr. Brown about that report. Keep in mind I had recently sent off more test materials, so they must have been thinking we had discussed his findings over the phone. What Lathem did know for certain was that I had mentioned to him I thought a criminal scenario would be included in Dr. Brown's report. Now they needed to know how much I knew, and the best way to find out was by reviewing my notes.

Why the concern? Dr. Brown's criminal scenario created a major problem. The very word 'sabotage' left no doubt in anyone's mind that it meant a multiple homicide or mass murder, a deadly criminal act, a police matter. What might it mean for the TSB? They, of course, would lose the file. However, at this late date turning over the file to the RCMP as a criminal investigation would cause irreparable harm to them, a total loss of face and credibility. The safety concerns would be out the window, and the reliability of the TSB to conduct such investigations would be severely questioned. After all, they had spent more than fifty-six million dollars, and they would have nothing to show for it. Also, they had already told everyone the magnesium problem had been put to rest as a seawater issue. For those seeking their promotions and their annual bonuses, they could kiss them goodbye. Within a few days, the Chairman of the TSB was scheduled to be in the hangar for a media conference where he would announce several safety-related recommendations. What prospects would Gerden and his bosses have if they had to notify Chairman Benoit Bouchard they had lost control of the file because of this report? The media scrum, of course, would be canceled. However, after inviting the world's media, canceling because of anything short of a hangar collapse would trigger a public relations disaster.

Surely Mr. Bouchard would never allow himself to be placed in such a position without certain safeguards. He was a very politically savvy bureaucrat having been a Member of Parliament for years and a Cabinet Minister of several departments, including Transport, in the previous Mulroney government. After a period as the Canadian Ambassador to France, Prime Minister Chrétien had appointed him in 1996 as the TSB's Chairman. To say he had influence in every direction of the compass would be an understatement. He had much more than the Solicitor General from PEI, Lawrence MacAulay, whose area of responsibility included the RCMP.

At the time of the crash and the initial decision-making by Commissioner Murray, Andy Scott had been the Minister at the helm. Soon after, he had to resign due to a scandal over the investigation into the APEC conference in Vancouver. He was overheard on an airplane making the statement that several RCMP members who had overused pepper spray to disperse protesters would take the fall for any wrongdoing even though they had been ordered to use the spray by some very senior officers and politicians. It seemed manipulating the outcome of investigations in an underhanded manner came naturally to some of our high priced leaders.

What was interesting was that two months after the crash, a lawyer in Switzerland, on behalf of one of the families, lodged a complaint resulting in a criminal investigation of the air crash in that country. That led to a request for assistance from the Canadian authorities. In a news conference in early November of 1998, the RCMP's media relations representative in Halifax, Sgt. Bill Price, told the media the Swiss investigation was not entirely unexpected. Price was quoted as saying:

> "That doesn't really surprise me. I'm sure the American authorities are probably doing the same thing. Canadian authorities continue to view their probe of the crash as a criminal investigation. Although everyone is fairly certain it was an accident, we still have to treat it as a criminal investigation until such time as we have been told that it is definitely an accident," he said.

It was reported that Price went on to say investigators would co-operate with any requests made by the Swiss authorities. When he said these words, Sgt. Price, as the Force's main media relations representative, was not just the RCMP's conduit to the reporters. He was also a police officer. He may have been briefed in what to say by senior commissioned officers, but here he was stating what should have been obvious and normal investigative procedures under such circumstances.

The news article also included a transcript from the American NTSB website of a speech given by Benoit Bouchard as the Chairman of the Transportation Safety Board of Canada while attending an NTSB/TSB symposium in 1999. He totally contradicted Price's statement.

"Two recent accidents come to mind. We saw the intense interest of the FBI in the TWA 800 accident. In the Swissair 111 accident near Peggy's Cove there has been, in Switzerland, an allegation of "manslaughter through negligence". An investigating judge has been assigned in Switzerland and the Canadian Department of Justice has been asked to obtain our files. While we like to cooperate, we will resist the use of our information for the purposes of prosecutions with extreme vigour. For the crews and the companies involved, this interest in criminal charges must be alarming. From the perspective of the accident investigation agency it is very worrisome.

The effect of bringing criminal charges against crews and companies can be very detrimental to the investigation and to safety. If crews and companies are fearful about speaking freely to investigators, the investigators must necessarily take longer and may not even succeed in identifying safety problems. So, what is required in the coming months? The accident investigation authorities need to explain clearly the ground rules and the protections for information that are in place. The accident investigation organizations will need understanding and support from the industry to defend the protections that exist for important safety reasons. The investigation authorities must explain that some information that is wanted by the industry will not be available if we are to protect the principles that support getting complete safety information to the investigator by the quickest means available.

. . . .

The Board believes that almost everyone in the transportation community is objective and forthright. It presumes that people who work in the transportation community are generally competent, they like their work and they try to 'get things right'. That when there is a safety failure, it is likely because there was an absence of knowledge or training or understanding. Those inferences are reflected in the legislation and practices of the TSB.

. . . . we should do everything possible to separate our gathering of information from accidents and incidents for non-regulatory safety purposes from the activities of others who gather information for their own purposes which often conflict with safety."

There was more to the news release, and it is available on the website for this book. A very similar speech was listed on the TSB website and attributed to Gerden's boss, Ken Johnson.

Price's statement showed what had been presented to the public by the RCMP. Those outside of the investigation were being mollified and fooled into believing everything possible would be done to investigate this crash fully and comprehensively. I remember the comments and obvious concerns of some of the TSB members about the possibility of their involvement in a criminal investigation. That lasted for only a very short time. Bouchard's speech, because he was merely a figurehead, had been written by very senior and experienced members of the TSB. Long before the words were spoken by Bouchard at that symposium, they had been expressed by Gerden and Vance to those in the investigation who wore a TSB shirt. I was quietly informed no information would be forthcoming unless ordered by a very senior Canadian Judicial authority, something that would never happen due to political interference.

To say there was extreme resistance by the TSB to any criminal investigation into this crash by any criminal investigative agency would have been an underestimation of the political resources available to Vic Gerden and his managers.

Gerden's concern, nonetheless, must have been that this was such a minute amount of material, merely a pinprick providing an insignificant indicator. After all, those were the words from Jim Foot on several occasions. If these AES results ever became public knowledge, it would be the ruination of their ambitions. Something must be done about it, and he had to meet with Lathem and Tanner so a prearranged contingency plan could be put into action.

Lathem had attended a meeting two weeks earlier in Ottawa where he had discussed AES and Swissair with his superiors. It was just two weeks after I had asked him what would happen if Dr. Brown's report contained a criminal scenario. It certainly must have started him thinking, possibly even worrying, and within a few days, he was in Ottawa to brief the Commissioner.

After all, just seven months earlier in a memo to Duncan dated the 20th of April, 2000, he had written his opinion as an officer and a gentleman that the fire was not of a criminal origin. That, of course, was all he could base his opinion on because he had no expertise and no factual foundation on which to write that memo, notwithstanding that he was merely following orders to write it. My belief is that, in submitting it, he was derelict in his duties as a police officer by closing a necessary investigation.

As for the meeting with his superiors, on the 15th of November, 2000, I received his secretary's phone call asking for a copy of Sieverts' law so she could fax it to him. Her words were that he was "in Ottawa on business". I was instructed to fax the material to her and not directly to Lathem myself. At the time, I thought it strange because she stressed this point several times even though she had provided me with no Ottawa fax number. Her insistence had been excessive, so much so it raised my suspicions that there was a very high-level meeting going on about the file in the RCMP's Ottawa Headquarters, and it was most likely in the Commissioner's office. His fax number was not given out to mere run-of-the-mill file investigators. AES, of course, must have been on the agenda because of the Sieverts' law request. No other RCMP investigation in the country at that time involved AES, or Dr. Brown would have known of it. AES was a new investigative tool never before used in this country.

Details of the meeting are not completely known, but the new Commissioner of the RCMP was Giuliano Zaccardelli. His requirement to control operational situations in a slightly underhanded way would soon come to light. It was reasonable to assume it was he who chaired this meeting so he could be updated.

After all, top-level decisions had to be made about the future direction of the file. He and less than a handful of very senior officers would have had any knowledge of the decisions already made for the file back in the fall of 1998.

This meeting was held in Ottawa for several reasons. Perhaps he was not such a fan of east coast lobster as was his predecessor, Phil Murray, so he did not want to come to Halifax for the meeting. Murray had been down at least twice and had toured Shearwater both times. The first time included the morgue about ten days after it had opened. He passed through it so fast his shadow had to run to keep up with him. His actions were embarrassing for the RCMP members who were working so closely with all the other civilian and military staff. However, Murray, as the Commissioner, had his fingers in the file, and his replacement was now Giuliano Zaccardelli.

I would be very curious to know who else was in the room with Lathem and Zaccardelli. Keep in mind this Commissioner of the RCMP did not speak directly to an Inspector, the most junior of the officer's rank. He only seldom spoke to those in Lee Fraser's rank of Superintendent. However, as the Director of Forensic Identification Services, I suspect Fraser was indeed there. After all, I was part of their problem and I belonged to Ident, Fraser's domain. Soon it will be shown it was Fraser who orchestrated the next series of events. Probably the CO of HQ Div. was there. As a Deputy Commissioner, he had taken over the Division from Zack and likely had maintained control of the file. For the TSB, surely someone very highly placed was present besides Vic Gerden. Possibly his boss, Ken Johnson, was there. However, due to his position as Commissioner of the RCMP, I am certain Zaccardelli controlled the agenda and the outcome. Their concern was if the AES report was not handled correctly, the Force would soon be saddled with this file.

Now I have no evidence of exactly what plans were made or who was present at the meeting to give their input, but I am convinced Lathem and Fraser were there with the Commissioner. Access to information requests were submitted, but nothing was received. Certainly, there should have been a file with minutes of the meeting that Zack would have kept, but it may have been destroyed by Elliott when A/Commr Conlin investigated my complaint. Nevertheless, remember everyone was in a very precarious position. The stand had already been taken that the cause of the fire was non-criminal. Now a credible scientific test result that stated otherwise was about to be delivered. Something had to be done about it or there would be a disaster. If it ever leaked to the media, it would wreck the planned outcome of the TSB's investigation and ruin them as an agency, and it would be a major embarrassment for the Force.

Obviously, there was an agenda, and it included AES and Dr. Brown's report. Why else did Lathem ask for Sieverts' rule? That very request seemed to show Lathem could not find his notes, a common occurrence for him. What's more, of all the people to give a science lesson! Of course, his AES-101 lesson would have been his limited knowledge of the process and might even have included key points about how an incendiary device required a secondary fire to cause any damage. This comment was Lathem's favourite whenever he spoke about incendiary devices. Surely Zaccardelli found that most informative and was probably impressed by it. Whatever minor value Lathem may have given the AES results, Gerden, along with his boss, Johnson, would have seen that the magnesium and aluminum issue was further trivialized. After all, that was the intent of the meeting. Had their plans been otherwise, there never would have been such a meeting. The file would have been turned over to the RCMP as was legally required.

Lessening the value of the AES results accounts for Lee Fraser's question to me when I saw him in Fredericton on June 19th, 2001.

"How could we conduct an investigation based on such controversial and trivial evidence that only amounts to a bit of high magnesium in one or two beads?"

Nearly two years earlier in September, 1999, I had told Fraser of the AES process and its preliminary findings, but I had provided merely a brief description with only limited details and that suspicious elements had been located. Fraser brushed it off with a "so what" comment and likely he never gave it a second thought. Then in Fredericton when he made this comment, Fraser seemed fully informed on the subject. After all, he had the benefit of Lathem's AES-101 science lesson. Ignorant of the process, they did not realize Sieverts' rule was sound science while the Anderson theory was the controversial and unproven theory that interpreted each bead's contents to determine if it had caused the fire. Sieverts' law firmly stated that elements in the air were absorbed by the hot liquid copper no matter what had caused the fire.

Nevertheless, a successful meeting meant a plan had to be decided upon, and Zack was one who strove for success. There was no need for anyone else to know the reasons behind his decisions. It seemed to be common knowledge that no RCMP member under the rank of Deputy Commissioner ever dared to ask this pompous little bully to explain his reasons. Those present were commissioned officers or their equivalent, and all were 'yes-men' or they would not have been where they were in the promotion pyramid. So it was simple. There was no verifiable physical evidence indicating criminal involvement. By Zaccardelli saying it, as surely as if the words were spoken by Captain Jean-Luc Picard in 'Star Trek,' "make it so" was implied and would be carried out.

A contingency plan based on this theme was created in the expectation the TSB would soon notify the RCMP that a criminal scenario was in Dr. Brown's report. From experience, I knew Lathem could never do anything unless he consulted with someone he trusted or unless it was already pre-planned. Because of his desire for promotion, he would never dare do anything contrary to or without the authorization and support of senior management. Could anyone possibly question the existence or nature of such a plan for Dr. Brown's report, particularly since anyone could easily work backward from its results to see what they arranged?

Anyone doubting this should remember the controversy over the RCMP's pension and insurance plans, and MP Boris Wrzesnewskyj being quoted by the CBC with comments about Commissioner Zaccardelli. Then add in the RCMP's involvement in the torture in Syria post 9-11 of Maher Arar and the three other Canadians who recently came to light. Zackerdelli was the RCMP's Commissioner during those incidents. It seems to show a pattern of total control and corrupt practices with no respect for Canadian law or human decency.

Once Dr. Brown's report was received, Gerden phoned Lathem to arrange a meeting for the morning of the 1st of December, 2000. During the call, besides mentioning the AES report, he complained about my recent actions in the hangar. In addition to my discussion with Cahill, he had tried to have Garstang obtain my assurance that I would not report on anything else I saw or learned while in the hangar. That attempt had failed when I had warned John not to be a go-between for Gerden while he tried to commit another criminal obstruction. This complaint provided Lathem an opportunity to assign Purchase to dig up more dirt by way of Cooper and Kerr. Once he reported on my alleged actions, or, in other words, made a complaint, Lathem then met with Kerr and Cooper to coax more out of them. These alleged complaints all served as his apparent reasons for the second ambush meeting and the pretext for the official written order to hand over the notes. There never was any legitimate purpose for that official order other than to try to learn what I knew about the AES report.

As for the morning meeting, Lathem needed a backup, so he brought along Tanner. It would be interesting to learn just what was Tanner's full role in all of this and did he attend the Ottawa meeting with Lathem? As for Neil Fraser, he could not return from New Brunswick in time for the morning session and, of course, his security clearance was not high enough because he had not yet been commissioned as an officer.

Gerden, Vance, Lathem, and Tanner, and possibly Jim Foot met in Gerden's hangar office to fine-tune and agree upon the Ottawa plan. The TSB would retain the file, and there could be no leakage of the truth whatsoever. They agreed that Dr. Brown would be persuaded to alter his report by using subtle means if possible that would include the use of his CANMET supervisor. Testing would continue to find a legitimate source. However, the report had to change by eliminating the criminal scenario. Meanwhile, every effort would be made to convey a non-criminal source for the criminal elements in the beads. There was no hurry because the longer it took, the more likely people would forget there ever had been a magnesium problem. Out of sight, out of mind! As for turning over the AES report to the RCMP, it would not happen officially since this was being called a preliminary draft report and a second report was necessary. That would be the excuse to be used. Both Foot and Sidla used this term on several occasions. Whatever term they might use, the goal was to cleanse the next report of any reference to a criminal scenario, thus eliminating any need to hand the file over to the RCMP.

Discussions included the problem Lathem had with his stubborn physical evidence investigator who had been speaking about the magnesium problem with other agencies. Obviously, that had to stop immediately. There were other concerns about who else I spoke with and what I already knew about the report. Speaking with others had to stop. They had to ascertain how much I already knew about the AES report and other findings. I needed to be isolated from all new reports, especially all future AES results. So I could not influence others, information meetings were forbidden. These guidelines had all been decided back on the 15th of November in Ottawa. That was why I was not allowed to attend the burn committee meeting two weeks later on the 28th of November, 2000. Just imagine if I had attended and mentioned AES. With the US agencies and others present, the TSB would have lost control of this extremely sensitive issue. That was why in the second ambush meeting of December 1st, 2000, both Lathem and Neil Fraser questioned the need for my attendance in Ottawa to go over trip notes with Garstang and Fogg. There was too much risk that I knew the contents of Dr. Brown's report and would tell Fogg.

Whatever else they might have discussed, their definite requirement was to know what information had passed between Dr. Brown and me and the extent of my knowledge of the AES report. Since the end of the file was coming for the RCMP, it was an opportune time to collect my notes and review them. Lathem had to be sure he had them all, and his official order to turn over the notes ensured it.

That written order helped to prove this whole scenario because why else would he go to the trouble of having such a document prepared and then arranging such a pretext for its delivery. The second meeting in my office was a sham even if the first was no better. The written reprimand for merely leaving the meeting proved it. A week or so earlier, Lathem had asked and was told the notes were available but only about eighty-five percent complete. He was told they would be up-to-date by the 15th. His was a ridiculous question. What I needed to complete were the various photo data tables and exhibit description tables. I had a very specific way of entering exhibit numbers and details, and I wanted to ensure it was correctly done so they could be accurately searched for information about any exhibit. Remember they were contemporaneous notes for an active ongoing investigation, so each day there was new material to be added. However, he seemed not to care about that. He had to find out what and how much I knew of the AES report.

What Lathem chose to call controversial areas in the notes easily lent themselves as an excuse to demand their alteration, but only after continuing the pretense. His 'change-the-notes' meeting was merely more theatrics. He already knew through Purchase and Gorman that those contentious areas existed. Once he learned I did not have a copy of Dr. Brown's report, but that I did have enough to suspect a criminal scenario, the next goal was to discredit all of my potential evidence. By having me alter my notes, my future testimony would be immediately discredited.

This matter would never go to Criminal Court because they had planned soon after the crash to not have a criminal scenario. The last thing to be allowed was for me to be able to give evidence in a Civil Court case. My honest testimony would blow the lid off the file. Anyone could imagine what would happen if, during discovery, a lawyer asked me if there had been any indication of criminal involvement as the cause of the fire. My honest response would have been yes, there was ample evidence to indicate a criminal incendiary device. In response to a question asking what had been done about it, I would again have to answer honestly. Nothing was done to investigate this matter properly as the RCMP's Office of the Commissioner had decreed there were insufficient funds available to conduct a criminal investigation. The file simply remained as a TSB safety file. Once these new details came out, just how bold does one think the headlines in the media would be? Peter Mansbridge would have his breaking item for the CBC's 10 o'clock evening news. 'No money to investigate 229 murders!' I had to be shut down immediately.

Since now was the best time to start, at 1:15 pm the plan was put into action. Throw in Cooper, Kerr, and Garstang to ensure they, too, were threatened. Doing so gave the added level of embarrassment, humiliation, and intimidation. Above all, there was a need to ensure compliance. When Jim Foot mentioned that the AES report was out, it opened the door to see what response I would give. They just waited with bated breath. I did not say anything, even though I suspected a criminal scenario. I only suspected it and did not know for sure how Dr. Brown had worded his report. Under the circumstances, it was best to say nothing and perhaps Foot would elaborate. My style was not to bite onto such things but merely let them go their course to see what happened, especially in a meeting such as this. I had learned long ago never to let my adversaries know how much or how little I knew of something or what I was thinking, and above all, try to keep smiling. Merely commenting or asking a question would have given away how much I did not know.

Once the first ambush meeting was over, Lathem and Neil Fraser followed me across the hangar to my Identification office to have another round in the ring. It was only two on one this time, and there were no outside witnesses, but the room was tiny. Neil Fraser's notes made it appear Lathem was upset but not furious and only for a few minutes. However, Lathem was indeed furious, and he was not reserved in his manner. He went on to lie about Kerr and Cooper having complained to him of my actions, his snake maneuvers. He then produced the order to turn over the notes, all of them. He wanted to know what information or reports I had received from Dr. Brown as he was acutely aware I recorded everything in those notes.

"Oh yes, he was the Ident guy who kept **such good notes**."

With the intimidation factor set in motion, Lathem was ready to continue when suddenly I got up and left the room saying I had had enough. That was the end of that fiasco. Since the order had already been delivered, all he could do was to wait and see. Providing the adverse reprimand several days later was just plain good planning for any upcoming assessment. A negative assessment would reinforce that my performance was substandard and thereby serve to discredit me if I lodged a complaint. He did not include any of his alleged wrongdoings because they were fraudulent and he could never substantiate them in a grievance without disclosing the facts of the investigation. However, walking out on a commissioned officer was considered as insubordination, and there was no defense. So inadvertently I had played into his hands. Perhaps, because Fraser was there, he had hoped for a violent reaction as that would have sealed my fate.

What evidence was there the report was not turned over to Lathem and Tanner during the meeting, but they knew of its conclusions? After all, they were in the hangar, there was a meeting, and the AES report most certainly was discussed.

It would be the 19th of June, 2001, before I was told by Lee Fraser the reports had been officially turned over to the Force six weeks earlier and Gorman was looking into the matter. However, Gorman was no longer an investigator for the file, no longer in the file's command structure, and he had no idea what materials had been tested or even what was involved in AES. He did not even go to speak with Dr. Brown. Not ever! In addition to Fraser's admission, I received an email from the Ottawa Lab Chemist who had been on the sorting line, Wendy Norman. Wendy mentioned she had been to an important meeting in early May 2001, with Fraser and Gorman. No details were supplied as she had likely been told not to disclose the contents of the report.

Then I had John Garstang's comment on the 28th of June, 2001, that he recently pressured Gerden to turn over the AES results to the RCMP, obviously due to the potential criminal-related content he believed needed to be investigated by the police.

To confirm the date of the turnover, I have received correspondence through access to information that provided an official turnover date of the 3rd of May, 2001, for the first and second AES reports. That was the official turnover date. I also have Lee Fraser's handwritten and typed notes of a telephone call from Gerden that initiated this turnover meeting.

Fraser's notes indicate that on the 20th of March, 2001, at 3:20 pm, Gerden discussed with him what can only be the second report. The very first two points of the notes he wrote were:
"- Not changed appreciably since the last info but it is not going away
- It has taken on a life of its own"

Fraser was obviously discussing the magnesium issue with Gerden, but he provided no initial notation for the first report's conclusions. The word sabotage would surely have appeared in his notes if he had not already learned about it from Lathem. So the two lines imply previous knowledge of the first report and the magnesium issue. After these two lines, he only noted Gerden had received a report from CANMET. It was quite apparent Fraser already knew about the first report courtesy of Lathem.

It would be another month and a half, on May 3rd, 2001, before Fraser's group would meet with Gerden and his people to discuss the issue. Only then did the official turnover of the two reports take place, signed for by Fraser. Nobody seemed to be in a hurry, and why should they as they already knew of the contents and there was no intention to do anything!

As for Lathem's order, on the 15th of December, 2000, a copy of everything was turned over and it all went off to Fraser and

Gorman in Ottawa with a cover memo that the notes were too technical for Lathem to review. Having Identification members read Identification notes due to their technical contents sounded like an excellent excuse to anyone who did not know any better. However, those Identification members had no more idea of what was being described in those notes than did anyone else not associated with the file. Using them was a cover, and the bonus was they might find other things to be used against me. The notes had already been searched for any emails or entries related to Dr. Brown and his reports. Because they were in Word's .doc format, a simple word search procedure could have been performed by anyone, even Lathem.

There was something exceptionally revealing that Lathem said during our discussion on the 19th of December, 2000. That was when Lathem presented me with the reprimand form 1004 for leaving the meeting of the 1st of December, 2000. He mentioned there would be a face-to-face meeting with Lee Fraser over file issues instead of having me write a hangar report similar to that written for the morgue. However, Lee Fraser's memo providing the results of the reading of the notes and advising of the face-to-face meeting would not be drafted until the 22nd, but not of December 2000. The date on it would be the 22nd of January, 2001, or more than a month later. Even more revealing was that Lathem did not write his memo to Fraser and send off my notes to Ottawa until the 20th of December, 2000, the day after he mentioned the upcoming face-to-face meeting. So is it not telling that Fraser was the first to mention it in writing even though Lathem already knew of it a month before? That future meeting should not have been Lathem's idea because, as he wrote in his memo, the notes were too technical for him to read. It should have been Fraser's due to the unacceptable entries the group-of-eleven had found in those notes. I know this because I have received a copy of both memos. Why would Lathem know of the upcoming meeting unless it was all part of their plan?

That plan had to have been discussed over the phone by Fraser and Lathem shortly after the morning meeting of the 1st of December, 2000. That was when Lathem and Tanner had been unofficially informed by Gerden of the first AES report's conclusions. The phone conversation between Fraser and Lathem not only included details of the report, but it surely included a discussion by both about what they were going to do with me and my notes. After all, both had been at the meeting with the Commissioner in mid-November, and it had been decided then that any potential court witnesses had to be discredited by whatever means available.

Anyone might suggest the meeting on the 20th of February, 2001, had been preplanned for the discussion of file methods and techniques as Lathem had indicated. However, the notes of the 'change-the-notes' meeting reveal what was discussed. Not one word of investigative methods and procedures was ever mentioned. No, this upcoming meeting that Lathem described on the 19th was solely centred on changing the notes, discrediting me, and removing me from the file, nothing else. They had it all planned long before Fraser ever mentioned the meeting in writing.

So now we come to the change-the-notes meeting. I have received Lee Fraser's notes of his meeting held the day before, the 19th of February, 2001, with Lathem and Gorman. Some of the by now well-known phrases appeared in those notes.

"The investigation is parked because no evidence of criminal activity or human intervention as cause of crash.
If anything comes to light, we will go at it in a full blown investigation
....
As of last conversation – nothing of criminal intent. If something comes to light TSB will notify RCMP right away."

These words were all Lathem's and Duncan's script from previous meetings. Now Fraser used them in his notes. He went on in the notes to indicate the file would be finished as of the end of February 2001 and after that, any requests for Identification Services would be handled by the RCMP Identification Section in Ottawa.

Something needs to be realized about the change-the-notes pre-meeting on the 19th of February, 2001. Fraser wrote those notes! The next day, he provided the demand that I alter my notes, something that was a criminal offence. So, could anyone trust what he put in his notes? Next, during the meeting on the 20th of February, 2001, both Lathem and Fraser expressed their concern over access to information and the release of my unedited notes. Again, can anyone not imagine that notes for any of these meetings were written by the two Frasers, Lathem, and Gorman with this concern in mind?

What's more, those notes implied no knowledge of the first AES report. This was more than two-and-a-half months after the ambush meeting. How foolish did they think we all were? Their notes most certainly would have been contrived to reflect only what they wanted to be shown upon release to the public. After all, if it ever came time for a Court case and the truth of the AES findings became public knowledge, they would not want anything on paper to indicate a criminal act or a conspiracy. Instead, they would want written material to discredit me. Keep in mind that my copy of the change-the-notes paper, my smoking gun, was just a photocopy. It could easily have been fabricated by me, and that would have been their claim. It was not until Lathem turned over a copy in the grievance process that there was corroborating evidence of the change-the-notes demand. By that time, several years later, it was well known all civil proceedings had been concluded and, therefore, there would be no risk of any public disclosure of the truth. I was out of the Force, and Lathem's boss was MacLaughlan. We have seen what he did for the matter by the three questions he posed to the Internal Investigation Section.

As for what he wrote in his notes, if he were ever challenged on this issue, Fraser would have to explain why they had not started a criminal investigation. After all, he wrote:

"If anything comes to light, we will go at it in a full blown investigation."

Something else is revealing. Notice the dates on the two assessments provided by Lathem and Gorman after the change-the-notes meeting on the 20th of February, 2001. Lathem's interim assessment was dated the 19th of February, 2001, the same day as this pre-meeting, and Gorman's was dated the 20th of February, 2001. It stands to reason the meeting on the 19th between Fraser, Lathem, and Gorman also included a discussion of what was to be written in the assessments and the reprimand. Why would it not be done that way considering everything else underhanded they had done or were about to do? Since discussions about and preparation of the two assessments never appeared in Fraser's notes, what else was discussed and never recorded?

Something that surely influenced this meeting was that Fraser and I had been good friends since 1977. While in New Brunswick, I had gained a reputation. I had taken on a detachment commander for wrongdoings that resulted in two of his members eventually being fired. Later, I stood up to an incompetent Coroner at a potential homicide scene. Doing so, I defied the Chief Coroner and the Criminal Operations Officer in Fredericton. It didn't matter that the same local Coroner was later fired for his incompetence. Fraser knew these things and would have understood neither he nor Lathem could ever approach me with the truth to try to have me back away from the file. After all, Lathem, along with Gorman, had already told me to cease my investigation, and they had failed. Gerden had even tried through John to curtail my reporting and had failed. Fraser would have known the only way for anyone to keep me quiet was to come at me with a full broadside to finish me permanently, and this they did on the 20th.

Something else had occurred that possibly influenced them. I had reason to suspect that an Inspector from Ottawa came into the hangar in mid-May 2000 to sound me out with regards to the file. He described his position as being from 'Best Practices' and connected in some way to the Privy Council. By his over-friendly approach, his knowledge of my brothers' and my backgrounds, and the questions he asked about the file with his responses that encouraged a more open conversation, I suspect he was there to see if I could be bought off. After all, I was the main witness in any Court case. If that were his purpose, he obviously left with the correct opinion of me because I was never offered any incentive to drop the file or to look the other way.

By February of 2001, the plan was in full force. Lathem's written demand was presented along with nothing less than a full verbal requirement that it be obeyed. The plan also included removing me from the hangar, but they realized doing so would hurt the TSB's investigation. My questioning of the legality of the document along with their actions met with a reply that it was indeed legal, that they had checked with Scott in Halifax HQ. That was certainly a lie because that member would never have given such an approval. What is more, they could never have risked seeking advice from someone outside of their circle. They instead had received authorization from the Commissioner's office, but Lathem could never have said that, so he had to come up with a lie. Lathem not only had the backing of Fraser, but of those in Ottawa far above him.

The meeting of the 19th of February, 2001, set the stage for the change-the-notes meeting on the following day so the demand could be signed and the notes edited. I did not even have to make the changes myself as Lathem could easily have had someone else do that and then insert the edited notes into the file. For all I know, there were two versions of my notes, one edited by Lathem and the other unedited and supplied by me at the end of the file.

Once the paper was signed, their thinking surely was if the matter ever went to Civil Court, an edited version of the notes along with this signed paper should be sufficient to force me to follow their restricted guidelines of what evidence could and could not be given. To do otherwise and reveal the truth, I would certainly face criminal charges of obstruction of justice by altering the notes. These four witnesses in the room surely had planned a story so I would be implicated. The threat would be that they would ensure I went to jail if the scheme was ever revealed. What is more, if properly edited, I might never be called to provide evidence.

As for the Winnipeg promotion and his written comments that I was not promotable, Lathem could hardly recommend me for a promotion on those forms and then try to discredit me later if I ever took the witness stand as a new Staff Sergeant and Division Forensic Identification Supervisor. What Lathem did not count on was that I would go to the Division Rep and then to the Internal Investigation Section. That put me in the lead with two independent witnesses for my claim of wrongdoing and of what my intention was in signing the paper. In any event, the file never went to a Civil Court, and the whole thing stayed quiet until the initial grievance process revealed the matter. A few phone calls and MacLaughlan's well-planned three questions to the Internal Investigation Section investigator put that problem to rest until it eventually came to the attention of the Ethics Advisor.

As for the TSB, the media conference of early December 2000 with Bouchard and Gerden at the podium provided numerous announcements regarding, among other things, the flammables in the aircraft. Missing from those announcements and unknown to anyone outside of the Gerden-Lathem-Tanner loop was any mention of a criminal cause for the fire. There was not a hint, and even I had no idea of what was planned. The file was to be worked as usual to seek more safety conclusions and possibly a cause of the fire, accidental of course.

Next, pressure was applied to Dr. Brown to change his report. What better way to do so than through his supervisor? Dr.

Brown indicated this to me in his email of February 20th, 2001. So then what were the conclusions of the second report, dated February 2001 or just before the change-the-notes meeting?

"CONCLUSIONS

. . . .

Eight (8) arc melts from seven (7) exhibits have near-surface chemical profiles that suggest they are possible ignition sources of an on-board fire, i.e., eight electrical shorts on seven separate wires of four different gauges would have to occur in a relatively clean atmosphere (prior to a mature fire). This AES protocol, developed for classical arc beads, may be providing false positive readings (i.e., arc causing fire) in some or all exhibits due to unknown analytical factors.

However, the AES protocol used herein appears to be reliable for the arc melts not exhibiting obvious post-arc heating symptoms suggesting a multiple shorting event involving many wire gauges likely occurred nearly simultaneously and prior to a fire.

Also, the aircraft components examined to date by AES do not adequately explain the source(s) of magnesium found in many of the exhibits' arc melt chemical depth profiles. The surface and near-surface chemistry of copper arc melts found on electrical wires shorted to aircraft skin and frame Al-alloys would be expected to have an aluminum-magnesium correlation and a high Al/Mg atomic ratio if they were the primary source of magnesium. Many AES depth profiles reveal high and sometimes discontinuous magnesium contents through considerable depth with no detectable aluminum however. Seawater (S = 35‰) contains about 1300 µg/g dissolved magnesium and is thus a very legitimate source candidate. However in the author's opinion this element anomaly exists in key exhibit arc melts which display no chemistry, structure and/or morphology features readily assigned to post-crash phenomena.

. . . ."

While the report was indeed toned down considerably and there was no use of the terms "sabotage" or "magnesium ribbon wrapped around wires", there was indeed the fact that magnesium was present and a legitimate onboard source could not be found. Nor could the source be attributed to seawater or post-crash effects. So it was better but still unacceptable for the TSB. There was still a magnesium problem that again implied a criminal scenario.

More testing to find a non-criminal source had been conducted with Jim Foot controlling what was supplied. His actions did not go unnoticed, as indicated by Larry Fogg's comment on the 26th of January, 2001, that no one may ever know the truth of the test results. Without any monitoring, Foot could create whatever results he required. He could then force Dr. Brown to comply. That was the reason for the earlier complaint about me sending exhibits to Dr. Brown independently of Foot. He could not control what I was supplying.

Sidla seemed not to get it right, and at the third FAA burn test, he indicated a seawater source as the culprit for the elements. To ensure no questions were asked, there was no mention in the TSB report of magnesium, and AES was downplayed to less than one-half page by basically stating it did not provide consistent results that could be applied to the investigation.

As a point of interest, one might wonder what was gained by members of the TSB. Gerden and Sidla both retired a short time after the file finished. Gerden undoubtedly received his bonus for a job well done if he was eligible for such remuneration. Gus, as indicated earlier, was replaced by the scientist from CANMET, Dr. Brown's former supervisor. However, all the TSB members attached to the file, at considerable expense to the taxpayer, worked long hours, and many continued to do so right up until the issuing of the final report. The usual routine for more than four years was a ten-hour day, seven days a week. Stop and think about the financial cost to the Canadian taxpayer for that effort as compared to the benefits gained from the faulty investigation. This issue could result in lengthy arguments with points scored on both sides, but when talking safety, their investigation did not deter 9-11 and what happened thereafter.

Another item of interest was that Jim Foot and John Garstang were in the running for the TSB's Ottawa Lab Manager's position. John, out of favour with his management, retired while Jim received the promotion. I have said enough already that provides my thoughts on this issue.

Meanwhile, back in the domain of the RCMP and the role of Lathem and Fraser in the change-the-notes meeting, there was a question that begged to be answered. Did they have any knowledge of the contents of the second report before the change-the-notes meeting? It certainly would be even more damning for them if they had known of it, if that were possible. Nevertheless, they were successful in isolating me from AES and Dr. Brown. As Gerden told the CBC, I was "out of the loop" and above all, I could no longer influence the course of the file.

By now the reader likely has thought this was too much overkill to simply keep a file in the domain of the TSB instead of conducting a criminal investigation. Too much to have happened this way. However, one must keep in mind this should have been a major international murder investigation that could have influenced world events had the truth been revealed, had the culprit been identified and linked to a foreign country or terrorist group. One might even think the underlying reason for these dishonest dealings was that the foreign country was instead a friend and ally. Whatever the reason, and whatever may be thought about these underhanded decisions from the Commissioner's office, there is still more to be revealed.

Through access to information, the way Dr. Brown's reports were handled by the RCMP can be seen. Keep in mind that Dr. Brown's first report was received by the TSB in November of 2000 and the second report was prepared early in February 2001, just under four months later. The change-the-notes demand occurred on the 20th of February, 2001, and the Gerden/Fraser telephone conversation took place on the 20th of March, 2001.

The first RCMP document of importance after that was dated the 11th of May, 2001, from Gorman and Fraser to the RCMP Crime Lab in Ottawa. It stated:

> "2001 May 03: I chaired a meeting to discuss findings that were documented in a report prepared by Dr. James BROWN of CANMET. Colleagues at this meeting were: from the Transportation Safety Board (TSB) - Vic Gerden, Jim Foote (sic), and Gus Sidla; the Central Forensic Laboratory - Wendy Norman and Dave Ballantyne; and the Forensic Identification Services – Brian Yamashita and Vic Gorman."

The memo was written and signed by Gorman for Fraser, and it seems he still did not have Foot's name spelled correctly. Gorman seemed not to fuss with trivial matters such as correct names and especially ranks. In correspondence supplied for the assessment grievance, he seemed not to know Sgt. Andy Kerr was, in fact, a Constable.

The memo went on to describe Dr. Brown's AES contribution to the file and what his findings were as listed in the first report. Fraser's signature was on a second document, an associated TSB memo acknowledging receipt of the two AES reports on May 3rd, 2001. So this was the written confirmation the RCMP did indeed receive a copy of those first two AES reports, but not in an official manner until more than six months, or half a year, after the first report was issued by Dr. Brown, and only after Garstang pressed the issue with Gerden.

The memo went on in part:

"I am requesting that the Central Forensic Laboratory review Dr. Brown's reports. Wendy Norman and Dave Ballantyne advised that they would assist in this matter if supported by the Forensic Laboratory.

I have copies of Dr. Brown's draft reports and literature which was received from the TSB. These reports and articles are available if this request is supported.

(Signed) Vic Gorman for Lee Fraser."

Gorman forgot to say please! What was going on? This matter was a possible homicide, and he was writing with language like "if this request is supported."

Brian Yamashita, who worked out of the Ottawa Headquarters Identification Research Unit as their principal scientist, was at this meeting. Brian with his Ph.D. was very knowledgeable in his field, but he knew nothing of Dr. Brown's areas of expertise. His notes reveal how the emphasis had changed from magnesium, aluminum, and iron to simply magnesium. Brian's notes included the following comments.

"- Brown claimed that the amount of magnesium and the depth at which it was found (7000 A) are not consistent with burning of nearby materials containing alloys of magnesium, or of magnesium from seawater (I believe he has no expertise in this area)

- In one draft of his report, he speculated that an incendiary device may have been present on the aircraft. (Again, I believe he does not have the expertise to make such a claim)."

Brian was expressing an opinion without knowledge of what Dr. Brown had for credentials or experience, so Brian was the person without the expertise. What's more, it seemed Foot and Sidla had failed to mention either the seawater wire tests or the Seattle tests. Brian was very well thought of within the RCMP Identification Services, and his opinions went a long way. When he expressed these views, he influenced everyone else in the meeting.

"- TSB personnel have spoken to Dr. Brown about his speculation, and he has modified his conclusion in a subsequent draft of his report. If an incendiary device had been present on the Swissair flight, then the crash becomes a criminal act, but no other indications of foul play have been discovered."

Brian had no knowledge of what was found or that there were other indicators. So he based his opinion on the biased and not necessarily truthful statements of those present in the meeting. He may have called Dr. Brown's opinion "speculation", but he was getting his information from "the speculation board." How reliable was that?

"- According to Wendy Norman, the use of Auger in fire investigations is quite controversial. . . . . In initial blind tests with wire supplied by TSB, Dr. Brown was fairly successful in identifying the conditions used to produce the samples. However, in later tests with wire from fires, Auger spectroscopy was correct in only 50% of the cases."

No disrespect is intended here to Wendy Norman because she was excellent at what she did, but she did not do AES. She had a BSc with Honours in Chemistry, but she did not have a Ph.D. in Geology and did not know the AES process. What's more, they were comparing apples to oranges. The blind tests Brian mentioned dealt with the Anderson theory and attempts to determine which one of the short-circuits may have started the fire through an interpretation of the AES data of the beads' contents. It was a theory that remained unproven and was solely intended to find the initiating wire. Auger Electron Spectroscopy was the tool used, and it was a proven method to determine the contents of whatever was being examined. Dr. Brown had a problem with some of the wires because they were covered in carbon from the smoke of the test fire. He certainly could not be faulted for that.

What the RCMP was now being asked to consider was if the undeniable presence of magnesium, aluminum, and iron in the beads indicated a criminal matter. Sieverts' law described the process by which those elements arrived in the molten copper, and that law was sound and accurate science with no interpretation required. The Anderson theory played no part in this request.

Brian went on with this.

"- All present seemed to agree that the finding of magnesium does not have to be challenged. However, Dr. Brown's interpretation regarding the source, and the significance of the concentration and depth, may be incorrect. These conclusions are not based on any extensive testing of wires, especially under the extreme conditions associated with the Swissair crash."

The first line was true in that the findings could not be challenged. The rest was something completely out of Brian's field of expertise and experience, and the last line was not true. The amount of testing undertaken by Dr. Brown was extensive. That was the reason for the Seattle and the seawater wire tests. Add to that, Dr. Brown had twenty years' experience examining a wide variety of materials with AES equipment. Those at this meeting seemed not to have been fully informed of these tests, although later correspondence makes it apparent the tests were at least mentioned, but in what detail was not revealed.

Nevertheless, the unexplained presence of aluminum, iron, and magnesium indicated some form of high temperature accelerant, something Yamashita, Norman, and Ballantyne should have been aware of as it was their job to know such things. Brian failed to provide the obvious answer in that Dr. Brown should have been consulted for explanations. If more testing was required, then do it. Then obtain a second qualified opinion to verify or reject his findings.

However, what was there to verify? Dr. Brown had found traces of magnesium, aluminum, and iron from an unknown source. They were elements found in an incendiary device, a fire bomb, a high temperature accelerant. Together, those elements were the fingerprint left behind by the tools of the crime of arson, or in this case, murder. Brian and the others had accepted the AES readings of those elements, but they had failed to link those elements to arson. Did this occur because they were not qualified? Considering they were forensic chemists, the other more likely reason was they were adversely influenced, especially since it was a link any qualified forensic chemist should see. But it was something that would warrant a criminal investigation, and Fraser did not want that to happen. So instead of getting on with it, they dropped the ball.

That should have been the end of the meeting. Give the file back to the hangar investigators to do their work. Consult with Dr. Brown, perform further tests as needed, and then find someone qualified to give a second opinion. Whatever senior management and the politicians thought, get on with a criminal investigation. Instead, the meeting went on for hours.

It was a meeting involving members of the RCMP who were present to discuss the potential of a criminal device even though they had no technical knowledge whatsoever of the subject matter or the events. At this get-together was another group, the TSB, who by law could not investigate anything of a criminal nature. Because of the rules governing the TSB's method of investigation and the fact that they stood to lose all prestige and credibility, the file could not be deemed anything other than a non-criminal accidental fire. They were setting the table and providing the information, undoubtedly biased. That information was molded by them so the RCMP members, with no knowledge of the materials, methods, or circumstances, could decide upon criminality. What's more, the two RCMP members who were co-hosting the meeting had already committed themselves to fully supporting the TSB and to shirking their responsibilities as sworn police officers by having committed what I believe to have been at least several serious criminal acts. Additionally, they had failed to make either of the two choices available. They had their physical evidence investigator with a thorough knowledge of the players, the methods, and the materials. Or they could go directly to Dr. Brown, the expert in the method and materials involved. They refused to utilize either source.

Closer examination shows this was all part of the strategy. Gerden, Foot, Fraser and Gorman organized the meeting so the outcome was controlled. Wendy Norman and Dave Ballantyne were civilian members of the RCMP working as Forensic Crime Lab Scientists. Brian Yamashita was a scientific advisor in daily contact with Lee Fraser in his office. None were actual file investigators, and they were not regular members or investigating police officers as designated under the RCMP Act. They were what was called civilian members with no actual powers as a police officer. So it was not their job nor were they allowed to pick up the phone and call Dr. Brown or anyone else. That was why Wendy Norman would not tell me what the meeting was about when she mentioned it to me in June 2001.

My presence at the meeting would have enabled an explanation for many of the questioned areas. They could not allow that because to introduce such information into this session would have defeated its overall purpose.

An observer might think Fraser had put into the meeting three seemingly independent scientists who apparently had limited prior knowledge of the facts. However, Brian would have been previously influenced because he worked in the same office as did Fraser and Gorman, he was consulted by me in September of 1999, and he visited Dr. Brown at CANMET at that time for a two-hour tour of AES and other methods. During the visit, Brian told me he could not offer me any advice on the matter because he knew nothing about AES or incendiary devices. As for the two lab members, they were just minutes away in the adjoining Lab building right next to Lee Fraser's building. I had consulted them in October of 1999 when the matter of the questioned elements and incendiary devices had first been discussed. Also, Wendy had spent months on the sorting line in the hangar. So, five people with ulterior motives and ambitions controlled the information being provided at this meeting. The two individuals who could create a level playing field were not invited. By doing so, those five influenced the outcome so that the management of both agencies obtained the results they wanted. Just wait and see what happened!

There was something else about the meeting that has bothered me. It should never have taken place in Ottawa. Superintendent Lee Fraser as the Director of the RCMP's Forensic Identification Services and Vic Gorman as the Staff Sergeant in charge of creating the Canadian DNA Database should never have undertaken this meeting. They were in strictly administrative positions in Headquarters, Ottawa and were no longer involved in the file in any way. They had no knowledge of the investigation, the processes involved, nor the tests that had been performed. So why were they here at this meeting when it should have been me? The only answer I could ever provide was they did not want me to attend the meeting for fear of what I might learn and say. The meeting vindicated the position I had taken throughout my investigation, and my presence would have been an admission by them that I was right all along. Plus, my input would have forced the meeting in the opposite direction because of what I knew about the other evidence. Just imagine! Without the two reports, I was already conducting a criminal investigation. To be presented with written suspicion of sabotage by Dr. Brown in this manner, it would have been impossible for them to stop my work. Fraser, Lathem, and Tanner knew this. However, they were confident I did not know of the two reports' conclusions. That had been the reason why they had demanded and searched my notes and then interrogated me during the 'change-the-notes' meeting. They had wanted me removed from the file to ensure I never saw any of the reports. I believe criminal corruption was too mild a term for their actions.

Wendy Norman and Dave Ballantyne, having been exposed to the naysayers from the TSB and the RCMP with all the rhetoric they could muster, would now attempt to review the draft reports. So what happened? Ballantyne, in his handwritten notes, wrote:

"Problem is not with the analysis but with the statements in the interpretation."

This line seemed to sum it up for them. The data printouts for magnesium, iron, and aluminum were real and present. They could not alter those facts. As indicated by Yamashita, it was the interpretation as to how those elements came to be in the wire that was their problem. Changing that interpretation made the whole matter go away. However, they ran the risk of reinforcing that interpretation if they were to seek a knowledgeable independent expert.

Ballantyne also wrote:

"- Blanks prepared by placing in sea water – but not subjected to same environment"

Likely Jim Foot suggested the crash wires were in contact with magnesium debris while on the seafloor, his favourite source for the magnesium. He conveniently forgot there were only four magnesium objects the wires could have contacted, and they were tiny rudder pedals the pilots pressed with their feet to control the rudder. Then it seemed he failed to mention that some of the seawater test wires were subjected to direct contact with one of those magnesium rudder pedals while in the seawater. Because of Foot's apparent lack of scientific knowledge, he likely never understood the real reason for the seawater tests and that they could have been performed in any depth of salt water. Galvanic current, the underlying scientific reason for those tests, takes place even in metal ships on the water's surface, or in aircraft as they are exposed to rain or especially salt water spray. These details likely never came out as there was no mention of the process in any of the notes. No one at the meeting was present for the seawater tests, but the one TSB member who knew and understood the whole process was strangely not present.

John Garstang could have set the record straight on the whole matter, but it would have likely cost him his job by doing so. TSB and RCMP management knew better than to invite him for the discussions.

The notes indicated the meeting lasted between 10 am and 12:30 pm. That surely gave Gerden, Foot, and Sidla ample time to provide their spin on the whole area of AES and its results. I have heard it all in previous meetings. The science was unreliable. The depths were so shallow. The amounts were so small. It was merely a pinprick in the surface of the bead. Those statements were just some of the rhetoric put forth by Foot. No one was there to counter those comments with the truth. After all, they had too much to lose if it went to a criminal investigation!

The next date in the list of supplied materials was the 14th of May, 2001. It was on an internal transit slip from the Lab supervisor to Wendy Norman and Dave Ballantyne. Of the whole lot in the Ottawa puzzle palace, Denis Nelson seemed to be the first to make any sense.

"The attached memorandum has been received from Supt. Fraser and is a request for your assistance in reviewing a laboratory report.
On the face of it, I am not sure what is required nor what we can do as a laboratory, in reading the report. Is this an interpretation of what has been written, in which case they should probably go back to the author of the report, or will we get involved in doing additional analysis?
Your advice please.
(Signed) Den."

Under this was a handwritten note from Wendy Norman to Dave Ballantyne, dated the 17th of May, 2001.

"<u>Dave</u> would you please compose a reply to Denis outlining what they want done & what you estimate the time involved is likely to be. I'm still not convinced we should do anything more than refer them to an outside expert (perhaps one on the opposite side of the fence from Dr. Brown)."

That last comment was rather an inappropriate one for Wendy to make considering she was supposed to provide impartial expert opinion evidence in the judicial process as an unbiased and independent Court witness. To find someone "on the opposite side of the fence," did she mean they would have to interview potential experts and rule out those who agreed with Dr. Brown? That may have been a long process. After all, the CBC only went to one, and Fritz only went to two. They all three had the same opinion of the readings as did Dr. Brown. However, Wendy was against the process back in 1999 when I first discussed it with her, and this showed her bias was still present in 2001. I had met with Norman, Ballantyne, and the Lab member in charge, Joe Buckle, on the 1st of March, 2000, for a conference call with Gorman and Lathem to discuss AES. All the Crime Lab members at that time had a very negative opinion of this, for them, new process, and this showed nothing had changed.

Of interest, Gorman had spent several years working with these members in Ottawa while training for his blood spatter position. According to Gorman, he and Joe were excellent friends. So Gorman's opinion would undoubtedly have had a strong influence on them.

Another point of interest was that Wendy Norman, Dave Ballantyne, and Brian Yamashita should have known about HTAA or high temperature accelerant arson. That was the name given to the use of magnesium and aluminum powders in arson fires to achieve excessively high temperature burns with small amounts of accelerant that left no residue. Because of the experience of the US BATF and the Seattle Fire Department, the subject already had been the topic of training seminars in the Vancouver area, and Yamashita would have been involved. Norman and Ballantyne, as Crime Lab chemists, were responsible for explosive and arson exhibit analysis from scenes across this country. They, too, should have known of HTAA. While nothing appeared in the notes, the meeting on the 3rd of May lasted long enough for a complete discussion of the topic, and both Fraser and Gorman should have been fully informed. If that did not occur, then were not these three negligent in their duties?

On the 24th of May, Dave Ballantyne replied, and he seemed to sum up the whole situation accurately. He wrote in part as follows:

"The issue here appears to be the conclusions given by Dr. Brown as a result of the auger analysis he performed on melted wire beads. Although the analysis was done for TSB investigation. The conclusions/opinions of Dr. Brown may require the RCMP to do further investigation from their standpoint. This further investigation includes trying to determine if the elevated concentrations of Mg found by Dr. Brown are significant and if so, what are the possible causes for this, in addition to what Dr. Brown suggests.

We do not have expertise in auger analysis. If we were to look at Dr. Brown's report, it would be done from the stand point of identifying other independent experts who might be qualified to review the analytical data and provide comment on the interpretation. We may also be able to assist in formulating the type of questions to ask of these independent experts as well as Dr. Brown, who may not have a background in forensic science or in airplane related investigations.

At this time we do not anticipate the need for us to do any analyses. Given the current demands on both Wendy and I, a limit of two days maximum should be adhered to on this particular request if we choose to proceed. We await TSB's list of reference material which they offered at the meeting."

Again, some common sense! Why were these guys not running the investigation? As for the reference material, did not Gorman, in his initial request, indicate that he possessed the reference material along with the reports? Why was it not given then to the Crime Lab members?

To put this in perspective, keep in mind this all took place in May of 2001. The change-the-notes meeting had been three months earlier, and I had not yet gone to the FAA burn tests in Atlantic City. At this time, I still had no idea this turnover had taken place.

The next correspondence was a memo from Ballantyne to Gorman dated nearly nine months later. I might be wrong, but by the dates involved, did not this potential mass homicide take a back seat somewhere along the way? Was this not just a method of passing the time until a suitable AES report could be provided?

Ballantyne wrote:

"I have reviewed the two draft reports produced by Dr. Brown and the attached literature. I reiterate that although I am familiar with the Auger Analysis, I do not consider myself qualified to give you an expert detailed scientific critique of the results. Based on this review, my experience in elemental analysis of exhibit materials and further conversations with Gus Sidla of the Transportation Safety Board (TSB), I can offer some general comments and advice on direction you may choose to take.

The literature references included do not provide sufficient information for comment regarding magnesium levels in copper wire melts. They deal more predominantly with carbon, oxygen, nitrogen and a few other common elements found in building materials. It is quite possible there are few if any references that will specifically include studies of magnesium levels as this is not a common major element found in typical building materials. Gus Sidla has indicated that additional studies have been completed by Dr. Brown since the first two draft reports were prepared and that he is in the final stages of producing a new report with revised conclusions based on the new findings. There are other potential experts cited in the literature who could be consulted with respect to evaluating the levels of magnesium detected, but it would be advantageous to review the findings in the latest report before proceeding."

There are a couple of things about this memo that must be considered. Ballantyne was the RCMP's best in-house choice for evaluating Dr. Brown's findings, yet he backed away by saying he had no expertise. Ballantyne was not a Ph.D., he had no AES experience, nor did he deal with physical evidence at this level that was mere atoms in size. Ballantyne worked with complete molecules that were usually compounds, more than one step up.

Even so, they were reluctant to suggest the obvious. The elements in question had to have come from some unknown source, probably something that did not belong on the plane, and they should seek out the proper experts. That would never happen because they had now waited long enough. The pressure had been applied to Dr. Brown for a final and acceptable third report.

This ended the contribution of the members of the Forensic Crime Lab of the RCMP. One might think this removed the onus from Lee Fraser and Vic Gorman. However, remember that nearly a year had passed between the receipt date of the first and second reports and then the final report. The obvious, as suggested by Denis Nelson, was never done. Maybe it was because it was merely a walk down the hall from Gorman's and Fraser's offices to the Crime Lab, but it was a trip of several kilometres across Ottawa to Dr. Brown's CANMET offices. Perhaps Lee as a Superintendent was not eligible for a chauffeured RCMP car. One might even think he was too proud to take a taxi or the bus and too cheap to drive his car. Whatever the reason was, neither Gorman nor Fraser ever contacted Dr. Brown or me. Then again, they already knew what I would say. So why was the obvious never done? Why was it so easy for the CBC and Fritz Muri to obtain similar independent opinions as those of Dr. Brown, opinions that seemed to verify a criminal scenario? Of course, back on the 19th of June of 2001 in the Fredericton Headquarters building stairwell, Lee Fraser's response told it all. Lee was asked what would happen when Dr. Brown's findings were verified. His look gave away his thoughts that this would never happen, but he said they would cross that bridge when it occurred. It would seem they did not even start out on the right road.

Something else was provided by the RCMP in response to this same access to information request that supplied this material. It had nothing to do with AES or with the Crime Lab connection, but because of its obvious link to a non-criminal cause for the fire damage, it was probably included in the belief it could be an influence.

It appears that after speaking with Garstang on the 14th of January, 2002, in Ottawa (four days before I vacated the hangar in Halifax), Gorman made an Ident report of that conversation. John spoke to him about "oxygen canisters and lines" and "their potential for causing the fire." It was first thought he was describing the generators above each seat that provided the oxygen by way of the drop-down facemask to each passenger in a sudden decompression. He was not!

"The oxygen canisters have a stem attached and on the end of the stem is a blue plastic cap. The stem is surrounded by installation (sic) in the ceiling and the blue cap is at the end of the stem in the cockpit area. He talked about a temperature change of the stem in the ceiling and the exposed blue cap in the cockpit?

He had conducted a number of tests with oxygen at 800 degree F under pressure of 70 psi for 2-3 minutes. The oxygen would leak near the plastic cap. He conducted further test at 1000 degrees F for 2-3 mins and the cap would pop off. John was not sure if this would act like a blow torch if heat was associated."

Instead, John was talking about the stainless-steel oxygen line running across the back of the cockpit ceiling. At about centre of the bulkhead, there was a T-joint with a short stem that ended in a blue aluminum cap. It was embedded in the Mylar insulation, not installation, and there was only one oxygen bottle, not multiple canisters. The line fed the four flight deck crew face masks. Gorman's report went on to describe the potential for the escaping oxygen to transfer around the overhead area due to the switching off and on of the 'oxygen recirculation fans', but there was no such thing. The fan system recirculated the cabin air, not just oxygen.

The point was that once again Gorman seems not have had a clue as to what John was talking about, even though it had all been previously reported by me. John likely said the aluminum cap plasticized due to the heat or became soft at the threads. As for the blow torch effect, this had been ruled out by Larry Fogg and Don Enns due to the lack of burn damage to the cockpit seats and other nearby areas. If it occurred as either a blowout or a slower leak, this oxygen line leak was likely the last major incident because it would have had a direct and detrimental effect on the pilots. Without oxygen, they would have been forced to breathe the lethal cabin atmosphere. On doing so, they would have become immediately incapacitated. Without the autopilot that had been disabled much earlier due to the fire, the plane would have flown into the sea within moments. There was no proof of what had happened to the cap because neither it nor the short piece of tubing were ever found in the debris. If it happened, it would have occurred during the last unrecorded six minutes and likely within the last half-minute of flight. The oxygen leak would have had nothing to do with "their potential for causing the fire" as the presence of oxygen does not result in a fire. Instead, the oxygen that leaked would have been consumed in the intense fire as an oxidizer long before it could ever reach the recirculation fans. John likely explained this to Gorman who, it seems, never understood any of it.

Gorman put this forward with the simple statement at the end that "It should be noted this is a theory." That would be fair if he were accurate in his recounting of the theory. However, once again, he was not. What he did was to throw out a red herring as the reason for the overhead fire damage that someone like Fraser or Lathem, who knew nothing about the fire, could then grasp.

Another similar document was an earlier email message dated the 1st of August, 2001, that was received in the same access to information package. It originated from Cst. Keith Stothart and was sent to Gorman and contained the following:

"Andy requested that I contact you to obtain a copy of a report pertaining to some testing being conducted on the electrical wiring by a civilian contractor. He would like me to follow up on the matter, however I'm a little vague on the details."

Gorman replied that it was the two AES reports from Dr. Brown and that Ballantyne did not expect the review to be completed until September 2001. He was given the task in May 2001, allowed two days to work on it, and it was not completed before mid-February 2002.

The purpose of disclosing this is to show two things. First, there is the link to the media lines put forward by the Force due to the CBC's program.

"A: The RCMP completed an extensive and professional investigation. The evidence was reviewed before a determination on the cause of the crash was reached. . . . .
A: The role of the IDENT officer was to gather all evidence at a scene that may be relevant to the investigation. The body of evidence was provided to an investigative team and a scientific team for review. . . . ."

Stothart was a key part of that "investigative team" and he had been working on the file from the start. His job was to maintain the file by collecting the documents and electronic data, and by organizing it into a functional entity. He had already received my notes and memos from the AES testing, yet it seems he had no knowledge of that testing, Dr. Brown, the reports, or what it all meant. Yet he had gone to the New York meeting and discussed AES with the Americans. He later criticized me for going on the air flow test flight. Only now it was revealed he seemed just to have put the papers in a box without understanding any of it. Yet he would be considered a key player in the RCMP's one and only Swissair "investigative team". Instead, he was just one of Lathem's three 'backroom boys'. He could have stood up for himself and made a difference, but he and the other two chose not to do so. That left Lee Fraser and Gorman with their Ottawa crew as the RCMP's Swissair "scientific team". Impressive, were they not?

The second point was that if an actual copy of Dr. Brown's reports had already been received, Lathem would have known about them even if Stothart did not. However, it was Lathem who instigated this request, and it implied that no copies were on file. Stothart did not even know what tests or who had done the work. It was most likely neither of the two other members of the "investigative team", London and Purchase, knew anything of significance about AES either. So this simple message confirmed the first turnover of the actual AES reports to the RCMP occurred on the 3rd of May, 2001, six months after the first report was issued. Those reports stayed in Ottawa with Fraser and Gorman for another three months. A copy was not immediately sent off to Halifax where the file and "investigative team" were located, where the reports belonged. This confirms Gerden never supplied a copy of the first report back on the 1st of December, 2000.

Now, the other side of the coin is that one would expect if Lathem did not know the reports' findings, Fraser would immediately send him a copy. Surely that would be standard practice. That the file was going to the Major Crime Unit and would be handled out of that office was what Lathem had previously boasted so loudly. So why were the reports not sent earlier? Because Lathem already knew what was in the reports back on December 1st, 2000, and February 2001, soon after each was released. At that time, he had no intention of doing anything about them. Even more important, he did not want to risk the possibility that any of his investigators, especially his Ident investigator, would find out the true details in the reports. That might have happened had they been in the Halifax file. By the time those reports arrived in Halifax, the 'investigative team" was disbanded and no longer working on Swissair. There would then be no fear that anyone might read them. When the reports finally arrived, likely they were filed away by Lathem's secretary without Stothart ever seeing the envelope's contents. After all, it seems Stothart had failed to review any of the earlier material. So why would he review these reports?

So there was something to consider from all of this. If Lathem and Fraser want to argue they knew nothing of those two AES reports before that date, that made Gerden guilty of obstruction by not informing the RCMP. Because Gerden will likely say he did notify Lathem and Tanner back on the 1st of December, 2000, it tends to make them, along with Lee Fraser and Vic Gorman, negligent in their duties and culpable of some serious criminal offences.

Now does that not make a person feel warm and fuzzy all over? It certainly cannot make anyone confident everything was done to conduct an "extensive and professional investigation" as the media lines suggested.

As for Ballantyne's final reply dated the 12th of February, 2002, his report was paraphrased in a memo by Gorman dated the 6th of March, 2002, that went to Stothart for the Major Crime Unit's file in Halifax. His review had taken nearly twelve months from Gerden's first telephone request. Who was it that said big wheels turn slowly?

"CM Ballantyne was not able to provide an expert scientific critique and has advised that Gus Sidla of the Transportation Safety Board (TSB) advised him that Dr. Brown is in the final stages of producing a new report. Supt. L. Fraser, OIC Forensic Identification Services wrote to Mr. Vic Gerden, TSB on 2002-01-20, requesting a copy of Dr. Brown's final report. A copy of that report has not been received to date."

The reader knows how that third and final report was influenced. This was Lee Fraser's idea of "If anything comes to light, we will go at it in a full blown investigation" as written in his notes on the 19th of February, 2001. Lathem had made the very same statement in several earlier meetings. It sure was some investigation, eh! To quote Lee Fraser – "Shameful".

CHAPTER 11 – HOW FAR DOES IT GO?

Many people might find it hard to believe members of these two Federal Government agencies could have acted in this manner. Perhaps that was why writing this book was so difficult and took so long. There was a constant search for a legitimate excuse for all of this, and even though it had happened to me, there was an initial denial that it was real. More to the point, there was a self-doubt, a feeling I might have been mistaken, that somehow something had been missed or I was now overreacting to what I had uncovered. I found it hard to believe I had been so blindsided and taken advantage of by my supervisors, people I and others trusted.

However, if anyone doubts this recounting of these events, or if they argue that putting everything together creates circumstantial evidence, remember this book was not intended as a Court trial, and no one has yet been charged. The factual details presented here did occur, and most were recorded in contemporaneous and accurate notes. Information to reconstruct the remainder was gleaned from the documents collected during the investigation, or supplied by the RCMP and the TSB through access to information. One can easily view the website for this book to see copies of many of those documents, notes, AES readouts, videos, and Dr. Brown's reports. If there ever is a Court case or an Inquiry, sources can then be subpoenaed to provide their evidence. Keep in mind circumstantial evidence is admissible in the Courts of this country. Until then, joining the many dots of information has created a seemingly incriminating sequence of events that has allowed what happened between those known points to be easily deduced. However, only when all the evidence is presented can there be a verdict, and there is still much information hidden away in the file boxes of material held by the RCMP and the TSB.

If perchance I have been mistaken and if everything done by the management of the RCMP and the TSB was legitimate and proper, there are questions to be answered. Why was I not told of the results of the first AES report on the morning of the 1st of December, 2000, or for that matter, at any time after that date? Why were test results and reports as well as other key pieces of information concealed from me as if it all was a secret I as the main and only forensic physical evidence investigator had no right to know? Why was I made to believe I had done something terribly wrong by conducting my criminal investigation? Why were Karl and I told to change our notes and, in the case of Dr. Brown, coerced to change his official report? Why has the Commissioner of the RCMP placed in jeopardy every court case in this country in which an RCMP member might appear simply by his delegates affirming that police notes can be restricted and altered by the investigator's supervisor?

There was a legal obligation on the part of my managers to inform me of the various documents as they came to light. Ironically, they used the term 'team-player', but they barred me from their team with the intent to obstruct justice. As anyone can see, they worked very hard to do that, too hard for them not to have been hiding something. Neither Lathem, Fraser, nor any of the Commissioners involved would ever be able to give a valid answer that would account for this apparent series of lies, abuse, and intimidation, as well as the lack of decency and respect they handed out to me and, by association, the victims and their families. Everything indicates they had no legitimate excuse or sound reason for their actions. If they ever do try to present an explanation, let that be done in Court under oath. Otherwise, beware they are quite possibly providing deception and lies.

Some may have trusted the TSB's Vic Gerden. To the public, he appeared as a very mild-mannered and respectable person. In my experiences with him, such trust was misplaced. Vic Gerden either lied or was incompetent in his official capacity when he claimed not to know of the contents of the first AES report when he spoke to me on the 5th of December, 2000. I spent nearly four years working beside the TSB members with Gerden as their Lead Investigator. He was not incompetent nor did he abandon his required duties. However, I found him not to be an investigator. He appeared to me as an autocrat and micromanager who demanded total control of the file and the way the investigation was handled. The TSB investigators would inform Vic of every minute detail, including each report as it arrived. He then compartmentalized all of it on a need to know basis. Any decision, no matter how small, was his to make.

Gerden was faithful to the values and principles of the TSB to such an extent that he appears to have stepped beyond his legal bounds. His background as a senior military officer had conditioned him to require total onsite command and control and to provide complete loyalty to his superiors. He knew the management team of the RCMP would do nothing to impede his power. Gerden, with Lathem subservient to him, gave the appearance that he looked down on all of us in the RCMP as being minor players without authority, that we knew nothing about aircraft or flying, and therefore we could never understand the intricacies of a major crash investigation. The MOU between the RCMP and the TSB helped create and reinforce that environment.

Then perhaps the question should be whether or not Gerden acted legally. As has been shown here, he knew about the AES findings from the very beginning in September of 1999. On the 7th of October, 1999, he had a conference call with Dr. Brown and John Garstang to discuss AES, and Dr. Brown confirmed his initial findings with him, including the potential for an incendiary device. I had a meeting with Gerden and Gorman on the 30th of November, 1999, during which we discussed the continuation of the AES process. When Gerden asked if it was good money being spent after bad, he was told the readings were real, and the rules were that the scientific process, once started, had to be followed and completed no matter what the findings were or where they led. Later on the 16th of May, 2000, Gerden and his TSB crew met with us to discuss what would happen to the beads once AES was finished. Between those dates, there were at least two official meetings and several other exchanges during which AES, along with the magnesium, aluminum, and iron problem, were discussed with Gerden and his team. I kept pounding away at the issue every time I met him. Even in Long Beach, California, on January 25th, 2000, when we were down for the air flow test flight, I discussed the seawater wire test with him over breakfast and explained what the plan was and why it was necessary.

So yes, he certainly knew of the AES findings and their implications before the delivery of the first report by Dr. Brown. He was aware the readings of those suspicious elements never faltered and no legitimate source was ever found. Jim Foot and Gus Sidla, as the two TSB members running the AES testing, kept him informed and would have told him immediately if a legitimate onboard source had been located. They were so eager to find that source and write off the AES tests that they submitted exhibits of a questionable nature, possibly designed to derail the tests. If so, it was likely done on Gerden's authority.

There was a question of whether the TSB would follow through with one of their normal processes of systematically grinding each bead to nothing while allowing the microscopic examination of its internal structure. Meetings were held during which I unequivocally told Gerden they could not do it until the incendiary device problem was settled.

So waiting for Dr. Brown's report before warning other agencies of the potentially dire consequences of the AES results was not a viable excuse. Gerden knew what the test's implications were, and there was no denying it. When the first report was released, it was his obligation to know immediately what was in it.

What about after the TSB received the first AES report? It was delivered to them at the end of November 2000, the week before the Fire Committee meeting. I had my conversation with Cahill on the 28th and John came to me on the 30th to ask about the exhibits to Dr. Brown. At that time, Jim Foot had the report in his possession and had not yet signed it over for filing in the TSB's system. Then during the ambush meeting on the 1st of December, 2000, Jim Foot casually stated he had received the report "last week." He knew its contents before the 28th, and he would not have kept that information secret from Gerden.

Foot provided his presentation to the Fire Committee, but never once did he mention AES. Since I was not allowed to attend the meeting, how did I know? The answer came from Pat Cahill with her comment about not hearing anything recently of the AES test results and asking me why nothing had been said in the meeting about the high magnesium readings. She then went on to confront the TSB after she asked me if I had ever been told to keep quiet about the matter. That was why Gerden and Lathem were so upset with me during the ambush meeting on the 1st of December, 2000, three days later. The secret had nearly come out. It seems Gerden must have lied to Cahill by saying it was no longer a problem because she never said another word to me about it. If Cahill had been told the truth, surely she would have reported it to her supervisors, and the American FBI would then have been involved in an ongoing criminal investigation. As we have seen, that never happened. Gerden had set the controls for what information was to be given out at that meeting. While those limits would have met no protest from Foot, it would have been Gerden who directed that AES and its results were restricted and not to be mentioned.

During his December 5th, 2000, conversation with me, Gerden made the comment that they "want only the facts and numbers, no speculation." The obvious observation would be if he did not know the report's contents, how did he know it contained "speculation"?

What about the November 15th, 2000, meeting in Ottawa? Lathem discussed AES with the Commissioner. Zackerdelli could just as easily have read a written report if it had not been a major interagency decision-making meeting. However, it was interagency, and it was indeed major. Decisions were required to determine how the TSB and the RCMP were going to handle the file once Dr. Brown's criminal scenario was issued. These decisions had to be made in concert with each other because legally the file should have been turned over to the RCMP for a mandatory criminal investigation. When Dr. Brown's report was released, there existed more than adequate reasonable and probable grounds to suspect the capital crime of murder had occurred on that plane. So the TSB had to have the permission of the RCMP before they could continue working the file as their own. Obviously, an agreement was struck because the TSB maintained control and the RCMP curtailed my criminal investigation, notwithstanding that such an undertaking was illegal. Gerden as the Lead Investigator undoubtedly was there along with his TSB boss. Can there be any doubt that it was agreed what information would be given to the other investigative authorities including the Swiss and the Americans?

So the implications of Gerden's part in the illegal decision to keep secret the AES results must now be considered. Knowing that reasonable grounds existed to suspect a criminal device had been planted on Vaud, Gerden likely gave his directions to Foot that no information about the AES results would be provided at the Fire Committee meeting. Present at that meeting were the FAA and the NTSB. These two American agencies were instrumental in aircraft and public safety in the USA as well as internationally. By not telling these agencies about the AES results and the implications of those readings, he in effect failed to provide a warning of possible terrorist activities. The 28th of November, 2000, was the date of the meeting. The 11th of September, 2001, was nearly nine and one-half months later, or two hundred and eighty-six days of lost time to prepare defensive measures that might have helped thwart the attack that killed almost three thousand Americans, Canadians, and other nationalities, and that led to at least two wars. The TSB, by not allowing the truth to be told, in effect lied to the American Federal authorities and the people of the USA. It did not matter if the American authorities would heed that warning. As the best of neighbors and the closest of allies, there was a legal and moral obligation to tell them. Does anyone trust him or the TSB now, or for the same reasons, the Commissioner of the RCMP?

As for Zaccardelli, the public record speaks for itself. Read the report called "A Matter of Trust" of December 14th, 2007, that is available on the Web. The CBC News report of June 15th, 2007, gives the following comment attributed to investigator David Brown who wrote the report.

"He described the actions of RCMP management as a 'fundamental breach of trust' with the force."

Zaccardelli had gone through basic training in Regina several troops behind me in 1970. He eventually moved to Ottawa to become a Deputy Commissioner in 1998 and in charge of Headquarters Division. When Swissair 111 crashed, the file immediately came under his control due to international implications and budgetary requirements. It was likely that Commissioner Phil Murray, with his background in human resources and the non-investigative areas of the Force, would have relied on his Headquarters Commanding Officer for the required decisions. Zaccardelli moved over to the organized crime and policy area in 1999 until on the 2nd of September, 2000, he became the Commissioner and again able to control the file.

Thus Lathem's 15th of November, 2000 meeting in Ottawa and the Sieverts' rule request. Zaccardelli needed to be updated. Lathem was the man to do it, and decisions had to be made. Remember that the first AES testing was not until September of 1999 and Zaccardelli, no longer involved in the file, had no reason to keep up to date on file matters. Also, keep in mind Duncan had shut down the RCMP's task force in June 2000 upon orders from Ottawa. So someone highly placed in Ottawa maintained control and influenced Deputy Commissioner Duncan to change his mind about the file in the spring of 2000. That could only have been the

Commissioner, likely with input from then Deputy Commissioner Zaccardelli.

As for more recent RCMP senior management, to again stand behind the Conlin report would mean they condoned the obstruction of justice by altering an investigator's notes. In September of 2011, Commissioner Elliott needed to explain why his predecessors and their subordinates acted as they did. Instead, there was a concerted effort to lie to and mislead the media along with the Canadian and International public. These activities seem to have become the way of the Commissioner's office for many years now. The public needs to question just how much truth ever comes out of that office. If Elliott had provided an honest explanation when given the opportunity after the CBC program, it would have indicated knowledge of a prior criminal offence. He would have been asked why had no one been charged? Any defence offered now and any future lack of legitimate action by the Force's most senior management implicates them in a series of very serious Criminal Code offences. The same standard applies to the TSB. By defending or failing to take action against their predecessors, they might be exposing themselves to charges of being an accessory after the fact of a previous criminal act. It would be a continuation of the obstruction of justice offences. In more common terms, it is ingrained corruption.

As for the question of why Gerden waited so long to turn over the AES reports to the RCMP, the reason was that no one was in a hurry! They were waiting for Dr. Brown's edited report to eliminate the magnesium question. It is likely that the first two reports were turned over in May, 2001, only because Garstang learned of their contents and forced the issue with Gerden.

Getting back to Zaccardelli, why would he engage in such an apparently illegal undertaking? Remember there was the MOU in place that stated the TSB would be the lead agency with assistance supplied by the RCMP. Duncan's words during the 3rd of May 2000 meeting for the closing of the hangar was that by day three he had been advised any criminal investigation would involve the FBI. However, the TSB could not conduct a safety file with sole jurisdiction as provided by the MOU and there be a criminal investigation involving the RCMP and the FBI. So no criminal investigation was ever started, and passenger profiling was ceased by day three.

As soon as the requirement for victim identification was completed, the TSB was left to run the file, and the cost for the RCMP came from the TSB's emergency budget allocations. Duncan fudged the rules of the agreement when the initial AES results of September 1999 were received. He reacted normally and gave instructions that I would be involved in all testing. Those initial AES results along with everything else were sufficient to form reasonable and probable grounds to suspect a crime had occurred. More high-level meetings were then held, and the result was Lathem's "folly and reckless" meeting of November 23rd, 1999. Having followed Ottawa's orders from the start, his words during the meeting were that the RCMP would

"stay the present course until there is **irrefutable evidence of a criminal act.**"

In April of 2000, the TSB refused to pay for the RCMP's backroom investigators, and the Force had insufficient finances to keep them on strength in the hangar, at least that was the excuse. The TSB could no longer be seen to be paying for criminal investigators, and the Force could not maintain their presence while claiming not to be involved in a criminal investigation. Kerr, Cooper, and I were seconded to the TSB solely as assistance under the MOU, and our expenses and salary were covered out of the TSB's special budget.

What happened to create Duncan's apparent change in direction? Lathem and Duncan certainly did not take it upon themselves to go against their legal requirement to investigate the matter. Instead, they acted on orders that had come from Ottawa. To set the stage for the closure, seven months after the first AES results, on April 20, 2000, Lathem supplied his post-New York trip report to Duncan.

"Based on the lack of any physical evidence to date and upon these discussions, I am satisfied an incendiary device did not play a part in the downing of this aircraft."

Anyone could guess what might have happened if instead of shutting down the file they started a full criminal homicide investigation. Public confidence would have been shattered, and it would have been a disaster for both agencies. A criminal investigation would have been based on material they had known about months earlier. Investigators now would have to do all the work that should have been done initially including passenger profiling and cargo verification. The public and especially the victims' relatives would have demanded to know what had been going on all this time and why it had taken so long to come to this decision. The FBI would have to be involved. However, to go back to ask them to pick up the pieces after the fiasco that was the New York trip would be embarrassing, to say the least, for both Canada and the USA. After all, the US authorities had missed the initial crime because of lax airport security when the device had been planted on the plane. Senior heads would roll to appease the critics. Boeing and the airlines would refuse to change the insulation blankets. Why should they do it when the fire was a criminal act and not an accident? Improved security would have been their demand. That would have drastically increased airport security costs, but it would eliminate their high cost of changing the insulation. In the end, when all the dust had settled and the finger pointing had ended, the RCMP and FBI would have had an open homicide investigation with no suspects to charge and convict.

Perhaps it is giving Lathem too much credit, but it seems he was in a predicament. Lathem was at the bottom rung of the ladder of command, and he was being told to orchestrate the closing of the RCMP's task force in the hangar. However, he had to have been aware of two things. First, there were sufficient grounds to suspect the file was a criminal matter. Second, if the plans went amuck and the public learned the truth, the person who was instructing him was now so near the top of that ladder that Lathem would take the fall alone. Duncan, already promoted, would escape because he had leverage on the Commissioner and his underling, Zackerdelli. Lathem was hoping for his further promotion, but it never came about because D/Commr. Duncan, transferred to Regina, soon became too ill to work. Lathem was on his own and dealing with the sharks in Ottawa. One would expect that once he had committed himself, he had to do everything he possibly could to keep the plan intact. He would have to "walk the centre of the road" and ignore the truth around him. However, Lathem was unsuccessful in controlling me, and Gerden must have complained to Zackerdelli when he became the Commissioner. Lee Fraser, because I was Ident, was called upon, and there would be no promotion for Lathem. We have seen how Fraser handled his Ident investigator.

One might ask why all the tests were conducted if it was a pre-planned outcome. Two people that were central to the investigation were Boeing's Larry Fogg and Swissair's Othmar Hummel. Both were deeply embedded in the TSB's investigation and knew what was happening on the hangar floor and, to a point, in some of the tests. However, they knew nothing about and could never learn of the behind-the-scenes intrigue because they represented the interests of the plane's manufacturer and the airline companies. Completion of the TSB's safety investigation, especially with the controlled and restricted release of information, ensured the airline companies would make the material changes that had been ordered by the FAA. In effect, the whole investigation was a sham designed and controlled to bring about the outcome the TSB management wanted with the laurels going to the TSB's management. Gerden's boss, Ken Johnson, was about to retire, and I was told he wanted to leave with a glory file to his credit.

What was required to make the RCMP follow the plan? First, the RCMP's Commissioner was a Deputy Minister of the Government of Canada. At that time, he was responsible to the Solicitor General who was a member of the Prime Minister's cabinet. That made the Commissioner answerable to the Prime Minister and the PMO, the Prime Minister's Office. He also had budgetary controls imposed by his Minister and the Treasury Board.

Mr. Bouchard was likewise a political underling, but his boss was the President of the Queen's Privy Council of Canada. That is a body of elite political appointees who advise the Prime Minister and the PMO on many aspects of Government policy. Now Mr. Bouchard, very politically savvy with abundant experience, could never directly influence the Commissioner of the RCMP. Nevertheless, there's more than one way to fry fish. Soon after the crash, one can easily suspect the Commissioner was advised by someone with authority that he must allow the TSB to run the Swissair matter as a safety investigation with the Force only supplying technical assistance as laid out in the 1993 Memorandum of Understanding. What pressure and words were used are open to speculation, but the Force was to forgo any criminal investigation. It is even possible the initial pressure on the Canadian Government originated from the British Government. All one needs to do is research the name Richard Tomlinson, formally of MI6. Whether guilty or not, any criminal investigation would have pointed in their direction as one of several potential suspects.

Keep in mind it was common knowledge in the RCMP that the Air India file was not going well. Zaccardelli was involved in that file. Most likely he gladly gave up another similar file especially since no potential suspects were waiting to be arrested. Any such arrangements would never be known by anyone in the RCMP, other than Murray and Zaccardelli along with a select few on a need to know basis. Duncan would have been told once he was promoted to the rank of Deputy Commissioner. That accounts for his change of attitude by the time of his 3rd of May, 2000, hanger meeting when he announced the parking date of the RCMP's file. No one else needed to know the reason because it was simply an order coming from the Commissioner. Anyone who asked would be told it was for financial reasons and a lack of evidence, the same story Gorman and Lathem frequently tried to force upon me.

This may seem like a logical way to have operated, especially for senior bureaucrats who knew nothing about investigating a sudden death. What's more, with the MOU in place, there was likely a feeling among senior RCMP management that they were obliged to follow through with the agreement. Perhaps there was a sense of relief they would not have to undertake such an expensive and ongoing investigation. However, that was not the way to investigate a sudden death by an unknown cause. It was standard operating procedures for every sudden death to be treated as a murder until it was proven otherwise. That way all evidence was located and preserved without it being destroyed before ever being found. What's more, the very principle of senior bureaucrats determining how a file was handled went against all the rules of policing in a democratic country. President what's-his-name in some third world country might have been able to dictate the outcome of his pseudo-investigations, but that was not supposed to happen in this country. It is called the rule of law in a democracy.

The idea of budgetary restraints being the pressure applied to Murray to make him follow this route has considerable merit. International treaties dictate that the country in which the plane crashes covers the costs of the investigation. The Treasury Board and Paul Martin likely curtailed funds so badly, there could be only one investigative agency instead of two. The RCMP's budget had no surplus to allow for this added expenditure. After all, part way through this file's investigation, Murray closed the RCMP's training facility in Depot, Regina for a six-month period. The explanation was it was a cost-cutting measure due to a lack of finances.

However, it was not the legal nor the moral right of the Commissioner or any part of his team of advisors to restrict this or any investigation, especially once the evidence of a multiple murder came to light. These actions constituted a fundamental and flagrant interference with the due process of law.

What additional grounds were there to think it happened this way? There was Lee Fraser's comment made two weeks after the start of the morgue that the file would never go to a criminal investigation as the TSB had deemed it to be accidental in nature. Another interesting comment was made several times by Lathem when he quietly asked if I had any idea what would happen if the public learned that passenger jets were being attacked by terrorists. Then, of course, there was Deputy Commissioner Duncan's statement during the closing of the hangar for the RCMP task force:

"...even if an incendiary device is found, we will not be able to identify it to an individual at this late a date, so there is no use conducting such an investigation."

When has the RCMP ever backed away from a homicide investigation? I would have hoped never, but today I know they have in at least one instance! Murray, Zaccardelli, and their advisors did not have a clue as to what was required to investigate this matter. Like Conlin, they likely received most of their crime scene training by watching Hollywood movies. In fact, many of those in Forensic Identification Services had little or no experience with arsons, and fewer still had a knowledge of major plane crash investigations. Over the years, it had become apparent that there seemed to be no desire in senior management circles to have the expertise within the Force, and that is especially so today. Tanner's comment to me was that with my knowledge and expertise, I should be working for the TSB, not the RCMP.

With looming financial constraints and the lack of investigative knowledge, one can easily see that senior Force management, even with FBI involvement, did not want to become constrained by a never-ending and expensive file while having no manpower or adequate finances. Surely the words were said to let the TSB have the investigation. The Commissioner of the RCMP and his advisors succumbed to the political pressures that continue to this day. The 1993 Memorandum of Understanding became the instrument of action for the Force. The TSB would conduct their safety investigation, and the RCMP would merely provide the required technical assistance. There would be no criminal investigation. If something criminal surfaced, unless it could result in an immediate arrest and an ensured conviction, the problem would somehow disappear even if it meant discrediting investigators. What helped them was the prevalent attitude that to take down a passenger aircraft in flight and to murder hundreds of innocent people was something so rare as to nearly never happen, especially in Canada, eh! Added to that was the flawed belief the guilty party would automatically lay claim to downing the plane as though they were untouchable by authorities. Because this was the real world, such things do happen, especially if more elaborate criminal plans are afoot, or if it was a sanctioned action by a foreign government agency.

So why did the other RCMP investigators follow Lathem? First, none of them except Christiansen saw and understood the physical evidence. Even Gorman spent most of his time elsewhere and never developed an understanding of the fire and the materials involved. However, Gorman was seeking his officer's commission. In our first meeting about my criminal investigation of the fire, he stated he had to support his officer even though he agreed with the reasons for my actions. To go against Lathem in any manner meant losing any chance for an officer's commission. That was more important to him than doing the right thing.

As for the other investigators in Lathem's back-office group, one was totally out of touch with the physical evidence as one of her main tasks was to copy hundreds of video tapes.

Karl Christiansen was there because of his fire investigative background. Even though he saw only a portion of the physical evidence, it along with his other investigative results were sufficient for him to develop a suspicion and soon identify subjects of interest such as Al Qaeda if the file ever proved to be of a criminal origin. He had been privy to many conversations with other partner investigators as well as having learned of the potential for a criminal cause, and the explicit details of the fire damage. Soon after, he was removed from the hangar because he refused to follow Lathem's restrictive rules for the investigation. He had uncovered too many details Lathem wanted left untouched. Karl had reasonable and probable grounds to suspect a criminal cause for the fire, so Lathem's actions were a criminal obstruction. If Karl had altered his notes, he would then have been discredited in the same manner as Lathem later tried with me. I suspect Karl's notes were soon altered by Lathem after he ordered him out of the hangar. We might never know because the database containing those notes apparently no longer functions. Is that not convenient for the RCMP's management?

One further reason for Karl's removal from the hangar, and the demand to have no further contact with me or anything to do with the file, was that Lathem was likely afraid of Karl's discussions with the US BATF. Karl had arranged for their arson investigators to attend in Halifax on a training exercise, and Lathem had successfully blocked it. However, it seems Lathem could not risk that in further discussions with those BATF fire engineers, Karl might disclose to them the details of the magnesium, aluminium, and iron issue. They then would have seen the similarity with their unsolved HTA arson fires across the USA and made the link. The BATF and the FBI would have been in Halifax the next day. Lathem, Fraser, and Gorman had by then travelled across this country and the USA giving presentations on Swissair, and surely one of the trio would have learned of HTA, or high temperature accelerant during discussions with participants. However, it is also possible one of them had already learned of it through discussions with members of the Force's Crime Lab.

Of the other three backroom investigators, all were seeking their promotion, and their experiences with physical evidence and fire investigations were minimal. Only London had been on an MD-11, and that was for only a moment. Occasionally they viewed items on the hangar floor while going from their office through the hangar to the washroom or the lunchroom.

As for Brian London, he told me he never knew what my work was while I was on the hangar floor, work entailing the examination and photographing of many hundreds of thousands of pieces of debris. He also indicated he had never dealt with a fire of any type. From the Corporal's position in the hangar, he soon moved to a Detachment Sergeant's position and then to Staffing where he designed a new form for data. Because of it, he was transferred to Ottawa to receive his commission as an Inspector. He later retired as a Superintendent. Remember the dust balls and that he had written the New York trip memos for Lathem that eventually closed the RCMP's investigation. One must not think his commission was compensation for special work performed on the Swissair file.

It might be noted that only in very exceptional circumstances can a Constable or Corporal be commissioned. Usually the member must attain the rank of Sergeant before consideration.

Nepotism is a major problem in the Force's promotion system. To be promoted, a Constable, Corporal, or Sergeant needed to pass a written exam. He or she then had to provide two verifiable examples of activities in each of eight categories that they had performed during the previous five years. After being verified by the supervisor of that period, they all had to be agreeable to the member's present line supervisor or officer. So, many members throughout their promotable career looked for examples to eventually put on their promotion form while trying not to create friction with their supervisors. In my case, Lathem gave his overall assessment that I was not promotable. If I had initially knuckled under and gone along with the wishes of Gorman and Lathem, I most likely would have retired with a full Staff Sergeant's pension.

To obtain an officer's commission, a senior NCO must be sponsored by a Commissioned Officer and pass a series of intense exams and interviews within a time period.

As for the others, all except Constables Kerr and Cooper had left the file before an incendiary device became an issue of significance. Kerr and Cooper were caught in the middle between Lathem's directives and my stubborn defiance. It was evident they were going to follow Lathem even though, after the ambush meeting, they came to question his actions and motives. By the end, they just wanted out because the atmosphere was unhealthy for any up-and-coming Constable. An Inspector wielded so much power that he could make or break a career. Lathem certainly wrecked the rest of mine.

No one else, even Stothart, had any significant knowledge of AES. Nevertheless, Stothart, Purchase, and London should have known right from wrong and how a sudden death is to be investigated. However, for them, obedience to the officer and a hope of a promotion were strong influences. As for Gorman, we know what he thought. The draw of power and prestige was great. So I was the only one left who was willing to cross swords with

Lathem, even if I knew I had no support and would lose. Maintain the right even if one loses by doing so.

Tanner was another with power and ambitions but who showed me limited investigative abilities. His discussions with me were abrasive and biased without even considering their legality. He said, "You have been sitting on your ass for the past three years and you are now going back to work." His comment on the 21st of November, 2001, was that he had allowed me to go on the first FAA trip "out of the kindness of his heart." When are expenses incurred in the RCMP for that reason? He had not been in control at that time as Lathem had authorized the trip. Tanner did not want to hear about the investigative details. Quite likely he knew more of the file's secrets than I did. Surely that was why there was so much hesitation about sending me on the FAA trips. How much did I know and would I talk to the FAA?

Their problem was the TSB needed me on those trips to record the burn tests and process the evidence. Garstang was tied up with Air India and, without his presence, they had no one who knew the attic area of the Swissair MD-11 aircraft as well as me. I had spent weeks in Zurich examining and photographing every inch of the overhead area. Even Dr. Lyon believed the ducts were stacked instead of being side by side. Don Enns and Gus Sidla had never been on a Swissair MD-11 aircraft, and neither had any of the FAA people at the Burn Unit. Nevertheless, Tanner feared I might talk to the FAA, and if the tests failed, there would be more evidence that the fire load was insufficient to melt aluminum. They did fail.

The TSB's fraudulent third burn was intended to eliminate any doubts the aircraft frame could be melted. All that was required was to put the test frame on display and ensure I was not around to correct the viewer's false interpretations of their observations. To accommodate that, Tanner issued an official RCMP written order for me to vacate the hangar, and then MacLaughlan severely restricted how much time I spent working on any new TSB requests.

Tanner showed himself to me as simply another bully who held back my trip overtime and expense claims, and then he wrote a memo to my new boss. In it he implied I had forged my annual leave card, I had "sometimes travelled abroad without informing the RCMP", and my overtime claims were ridiculously extreme. His abusive and harassing memo was very unprofessional and even immature, so much so it should have seen him disciplined.

As for the TSB members, those who attempted to derail AES and then who made demands of Dr. Brown to alter his report contravened Section 137 of the Criminal Code of Canada. Causing the creation of a false government report for an ongoing investigation that could result in Court was more than just a breach of trust, it was an illegal attempt to alter and discredit a potential Court witness's evidence, an action commonly called witness tampering. Dr. Brown was certain to be a witness in any pending Civil Court case. This section also applies to the attempts by Lathem and Fraser to falsify Christiansen's and my file notes.

The TSB felt a criminal cause would interfere with their safety recommendations. This reason for them was ostensibly an honorable trade-off, although it could never be a mitigating factor in their defence, as the investigation of a capital crime must always take precedence over a safety investigation. Their real motivation was that they required a major international air crash investigation that would allow them to regain their credibility after the Gander air crash fiasco. That incident caused the disbanding of the Canadian Aviation Safety Board.

In that investigation of the crash of Arrow Air Flight 1285 on the 12th of December, 1985, in Gander, NL, misleading statements and lies were put forward to the public to make them think the cause of the crash was improper de-icing of the aircraft. Many of the victims, all dead immediately upon impact, exhibited evidence of smoke inhalation, thus indicating an onboard fire prior to the crash. Possibly it was arson! That "physically tiny bit of evidence" was purposefully hidden and ignored until it was finally made public. Les Filotas in his book 'Improbable Cause' provided the true details of the whole event. Out of the ashes of Gander arose the Transportation Safety Board of Canada. They were the same people running the new agency with the same mentality except their legislation had changed. They no longer were competent or compellable to any Court of Criminal or Civil Law in Canada.

So the TSB have done it again, but this time they broke many sections of the Criminal Code of Canada, all done with the help of the RCMP.

The Swissair 111 crash was their first major international air crash investigation as a new agency, and if correctly handled, they would gain worldwide prestige within the aircraft accident investigative circles. That this was a unique crash played right into that requirement. While planes that crash usually do so close to the airport, they frequently burn up upon impact with the ground. Pointing to the IFEN system as the cause was a convenience that was helped by the opinions of armchair experts in the media.

However, no matter what benefits came out of the TSB's work, I believe members of the TSB and RCMP acted illegally during this investigation. As a police officer, I was acting lawfully with reasonable and probable grounds to suspect that the premeditated murder of two hundred and twenty-nine people had occurred within the legal jurisdiction of Canada. Being the onsite forensic physical evidence investigator, it was my duty to investigate as the evidence developed. For me to not do so would have been an obstruction of justice, the same offence Lathem, Fraser, Gorman, and Gerden committed by not allowing me to conduct a criminal investigation. As a member of the Royal Canadian Mounted Police in Canada, I did not need authorization from the Commissioner or a complaint from another party to conduct my required duties.

If asked at what point I began my criminal investigation, my answer would be on the morning of the 3rd of September, 1998, when starting out at the morgue. Corporal Bob Gaudet had started it the night before when, as the on-call Forensic Ident member, he flew out to the HMCS Preserver to oversee the collection of human remains and debris at the crash site. As a sudden-death occurrence, it was a homicide investigation until shown to be otherwise. The bodies have always been the prime exhibits for evidence examination. That was why there was an Ident member at every morgue table who controlled the pace and manner of each post mortem examination. Before the AES tests, there were unexplainable burn artifacts sufficient in number to cause a major concern. Then when Dr. Brown stated his suspicions in September 1999, I had no doubt I was conducting a criminal investigation of a possible multiple homicide.

In their defence, no definitive evidence of a potential criminal cause had come to light before September 1999, although many aspects of the fire damage demanded explanations that were not forthcoming. It might then be suggested that the initial decisions by the senior managers were based on risk management principles even though doing so should be contrary to standard operating procedures. Those decisions were not legally theirs to make. Administrators must never determine the course of an investigation although they may feel it is their managerial duty as they are accountable for the finances. That must not be the yardstick by which major investigations are conducted because the money managers are not accountable to a Court of Law. It must be the onsite investigators, those with the knowledge and expertise to conduct the investigation, the people who attend Court and provide the evidence, not the Commissioner or his underlings. The file must be handled as a criminal matter until the evidence indicates otherwise. The TSB can conduct their safety investigation in cooperation with the police, but they must not interfere.

After Dr. Brown's initial findings in September 1999 and considering the burn damage to the aircraft with its questionable fire-load, things should have changed. They did not! The story about a lack of finances was indefensible as were the remarks such as "lack of political interest" and "loss of gloss". Lathem's claims of heading off public concern about terrorist attacks were just empty words. This country was still struggling through Air India, Lockerbie was still an active investigation, Egypt Air 990 was by every indication a suicide pilot, and Flight 800 out of New York was still being investigated with initial indications the plane had been shot down by a missile. Warnings of a major multi-aircraft criminal occurrence had been provided years before. Ramzi Yousef had planned to bomb simultaneously a dozen airliners while they were in the air over the Pacific. The bureaucrats needed to remove their heads from the sand, or wherever else they may have had them, to see what was happening in the world.

Now we come to my 2007 complaint to the Commissioner and Conlin's answering report. Did she authorize the writing of it? What ethical police person would want to do so after learning about what had transpired in the file? Surely she must have found out what had happened, and signing that report would have made her an accomplice. Murray must have known about the concern for the high magnesium during September of 1999 because Duncan, as an up and coming Deputy Commissioner and a police officer, would have informed him as would be his duty. Murray and his shadow were in Shearwater twice, so he had his fingers in the file. He did not come down from the Headquarters puzzle palace in Ottawa simply for a feed of lobster. He would have been briefed on the file by Duncan who was the 'H' Division Criminal Operations Officer and, as such, the main contact person with Ottawa. Both Lathem and Gerden were likely at those meetings.

Conlin would have been required to brief Elliott on something this important as she surely would have uncovered the real story. Somewhere there was a file with this information, although it most certainly was labeled with the highest security rating, and Elliott might have had it destroyed since then. After receiving her instructions from Elliott, she may have balked at the continuation of the sham considering she was the Ethics Advisor and had worked closely for several years with the former Commissioner Inkster. He possibly was the last Commissioner of the RCMP to have had any semblance of honor and decency, and he is still held in respect by many retired members. If Conlin had done the ethical thing, Elliott would likely have had someone else take over the task after ordering her never to disclose the truth. If so, then Elliott continued the sham, and as we can see, someone other than Conlin signed the document.

There was one very important point to consider about the Conlin Report. The only fault anyone had with my notes was that they contained too many revealing details, not that they were inaccurate. Therefore, the question begging to be asked was why did they create a document with so many misrepresentations, distortions, and absolute lies. The answer was to cloud the truth because of what the Commissioner feared would be revealed. There was every indication his predecessors, Murray and Zaccardelli, had failed to carry out their duties as police officers by shutting down and covering up what should have been a major homicide investigation.

As for Dr. Brown's opinion and the idea his evidence would have to stand scrutiny by itself without other corroborating evidence, that was a common misconception by many. All one needs to do is listen to a Crown Counsel during his or her initial address to the jury when it is often said the evidence to be presented will build one block upon another to create the whole story of events.

It was sheer nonsense for anyone to state the AES evidence was fleeting and trivial. It showed their ignorance of the value of advanced science. To have created the complete case for sabotage, one needed to include the evidence hanging on the frame back in the hangar for any competent fire investigator to see. Added to that there was the evidence from the various burn tests conducted across the continent and the collective evidence of experts from around the world. AES and Dr. Brown did not have to stand alone to make the case. Neither the process nor the person should have been cast aside by fools ignorant of advanced modern science and motivated by greed. Indeed, Dr. Brown's expert Court testimony would have been most difficult to dispute, and Dr. Anderson in the USA and Irwin Sproule in Ottawa could easily have been used to corroborate it. Then add the associated testimony of Dr. Lyon of the FAA and Dr. Quintiere. There were also the two Universities in Europe if someone wanted to go that far afield for an opinion, or there was the professor from the University of Toronto if one merely wanted to stay close to home. Then there was the video evidence from the FAA fire tests that showed a major part of the story. They are in the website for this book.

While mentioning the FAA burn tests, there were a couple of things about the burn test series and exactly how they were conducted that was more than a bit troubling. While putting together the details for this book, I found it a near certainty that the main ducts on Vaud were wrapped in Metallized Tedlar instead of the Metallized Mylar used in the fire tests. Therefore, the amount of flammable material at normal fire temperatures on Vaud would have been much less than the one-thousand grams suggested by Dr. Lyon. The tests wrapping the three main ducts in the flammable Mylar instead of a non-flammable Tedlar were not a true representation of the fire load on HB-IWF. However, even with the wrong material, none of the tests except the last fraud test caused the melting of aluminum. This might all have been a moot point except that, yet again, it showed the lack of credibility of the TSB. Keep in mind that those tests were all micromanaged over the phone by Vic Gerden. John and Don had to keep him informed of every step, as I frequently saw John on the phone talking to Gerden during the tests.

There were other similar discrepancies between the burn tests and what equipment may have been on Vaud, but there's no need to go into them here. Of importance was that the material put in the FAA frame for the final burn weighed in at more than five kilograms or more than five times the one-kilogram Dr. Lyon had suggested. However, the photos revealed Vaud had much less than one kilogram of flammable Metallized Mylar in the area. So the real figure was at least six to eight times the amount in that final burn. It was loosely crumpled with abundant air, not flat with insulation between the layers.

Something else was of interest. When Dr. Lyon first suggested the final loose MPET burn test, the reaction of Don Enns and later John Garstang was that they did not like the idea at all and it would not be done. One must wonder why the change and how it occurred. Dr. Lyon, as the expert, believed the 1,000 grams of MPET would never melt aluminum. So, it is no surprise the TSB did not want to conduct an accurate test as it would prove the fire load without an accelerant could never have been the cause of the damage on Vaud. However, by the third trip, John and Don thought and acted differently. It seems they had been told to ensure aluminum melted during this final burn, and only one person could have ordered that.

So the final burn test was, in fact, a fraud. The real value of the trips came from another test series, Dr. Lyon's cone calorimeter tests. They showed that none of the legitimate materials on the plane burnt in an unusual manner to provide unexpected or excessive heat.

However, no matter what the TSB's reasons might have been to do what they did, if the file had been handled properly, would 9-11 and the subsequent two wars have occurred? I have thought about that every day since then, and it is the last thing on my mind every night.

Now in all fairness, allegations of wrongdoings have been made in this book, but they are simply that now, and no one has yet been charged or convicted. However, I believe an extensive amount of criminally based wrongdoings have been committed. Therefore, I feel there is a need for an independent police agency or other competent legal investigative body to conduct an independent and in-depth investigation into this whole matter. They need to locate and examine the evidence and, if justified, prove in a Canadian Court of Criminal Law that senior Government officials in the TSB and RCMP are guilty of Criminal Code of Canada offences. No person is above the law, not even senior members of the TSB or the Commissioner of the RCMP.

As can be seen, I have fought the various Commissioners of the RCMP. So what problems were faced by going against them? The RCMP Act sets out what was required of Force members.

"5.(1) The Governor in Council may appoint an officer, to be known as the Commissioner of the Royal Canadian Mounted Police, who, under the direction of the Minister, has the control and management of the Force and all matters connected therewith."

This section deals with an RCMP member's duty to investigate.

"18. It is the duty of members who are peace officers, subject to the orders of the Commissioner,

(a) to perform all duties that are assigned to peace officers in relation to the preservation of the peace, the prevention of crime and of offences against the laws of Canada and the laws in force in any province in which they may be employed, and the apprehension of criminals and offenders and others who may be lawfully taken into custody;"

The problem was there were the two areas saying "all matters connected therewith" and "subject to the orders of the Commissioner." The word lawful was not present to describe those orders of the Commissioner. So was a subordinate obligated to follow orders he believed to be unlawful? Was I being insubordinate and breaking the law by investigating? Just for the record, Duncan, Fraser, Lathem, and Tanner were the Commissioner's delegates and represented him, so when a commissioned officer provided an order, his or her authority came by way of, and they were acting on behalf of, the Commissioner.

As an answer, if another Federal or Provincial Act is in conflict, then the Criminal Code of Canada rules. Section 25.1(11) pertains to the special powers of certain public officials. It states, "Nothing in this section justifies (b) the wilful attempt in any manner to obstruct, pervert or defeat the course of justice;". Section 129 states that to obstruct or to interfere with a police officer while performing his duties is against the law. For the record, I was a peace or police officer.

The Nova Scotia Police Act authorizes members of the RCMP to perform the duties of a police officer within the Province of Nova Scotia. The Nova Scotia Fatalities Investigations Act provides the authority for every fatality to be investigated by the police force having jurisdiction within the area. While the acts in effect today have been amended, the requirement and powers of the police to investigate remained the same during 1998 to 2002.

Going back to the Criminal Code, Section 139 describes obstruction of justice as a crime. The term "to obstruct, pervert or defeat the course of justice" is central to the charge, and the penalty is ten years' imprisonment. It also covers any attempt to keep a witness from giving evidence through corrupt means. The term "the course of justice" has no hidden meaning. If a police officer suspects a crime has been committed, it must be investigated.

A review of Sections 131 and 132 of the Criminal Code shows that they describe and provide a penalty of fourteen years in jail for lying to a Judge in Court, and it is called perjury!

There was no such thing as an investigation where a police officer was merely gathering evidence in a sudden death file without conducting a criminal investigation. I've done well over a thousand, and all were done as a criminal investigation until proven to be otherwise. While there may have been a Memorandum of Understanding between the two agencies for this file, it was simply an agreement and did not form any part of the Criminal Code. What is more, it certainly did not prohibit my primary function as a police officer, to collect evidence, including information by a method Conlin's memo called "acting as a police officer."

Shortly after the CBC program aired, Elliott was replaced by Bob Paulson who claimed to want to change the style and methods of the old management team. During one of his initial interviews, he stated he had flown a jet upside down as a former RCAF pilot. The problem was the Force needed to be flown straight and level after some severe managerial shakeups, and time seems to have shown he did not have the right stuff for the job. Even so, ever the optimist, there was hope, and a memo was sent requesting a reopening of the file.

Within a month, there was a very short reply from the Professional Integrity Officer, or PIO, speaking, of course, for the new Commissioner. The Ethics Advisor's position had a new name, so it seemed. His second paragraph, three words longer than the first, simply stated:

> "It is our perspective that there has been sufficient investigation of the issues you have raised. Please note there is no intention to revisit these matters."

After reading the memo, it was felt the PIO, Joseph Hineke, needed to be told about perspective. A memo was drafted asking why he was unable to see what prominent law-abiding citizens such as a Defence Counsel like Mr. Joel Pink, a documentary investigator like Mr. Linden MacIntyre, an author and journalist like Mr. Paul Palango and others, including a Crown Counsel, could all easily see. Several of the new Commissioner's quotes were included in the memo.

"Being trusted by Canadians is the most effective tool we possess. Without this trust, we simply cannot do our jobs."

"I have frequently spoken on the importance of ethical behaviour by RCMP employees."

His memo was taken apart word by word until there was a five-page memo in response. Unfortunately, doing that was the only satisfaction this effort would provide. I still had not put all the pieces together to realize Swissair was destined to be an accident from the very beginning, no matter what evidence had been found. It took time to put those clues together.

About six weeks later, a registered letter was received from the Acting PIO. Craig MacMillan had responded by saying Conlin had looked into the matter and I had already been told nothing further would be done. He agreed with those views, and there would be nothing further. Since the letter had come by way of registered mail, it was taken as a warning and a threat to back off and not bother them. That said a lot for honesty, trust, ethics, and professionalism within the RCMP HQ building.

Paulson, sitting on his scarlet throne once occupied by Elliott, appears to have the attitude everything amiss in the Force is the victim's fault and not that of an ingrained and inept system. That system promotes incompetence and nepotism with the Commissioner at the helm and ultimately responsible. Paulson, as a very senior officer within that system in 2011, likely would have viewed the CBC program and felt my complaint was trivial. Perhaps the Commissioner, along with senior managers in the TSB, should be reminded of some basic criminal law. Section 23. (1) of the Criminal Code of Canada deals with a person being an accessory after the fact. Knowing someone has committed a crime, it is illegal to assist that person so he might escape conviction and punishment. The RCMP's Commissioner must not forget that denial of these criminal acts after now being presented publicly with this amount of evidence could surely be considered a continuation of the crimes of obstruction of justice. It should be remembered copies of these documents including my notes are on file within the RCMP's and

TSB's system, and their existence was known to Conlin and her lawyer, or reasonably should have been.

What many in the senior levels of the RCMP management seemed to have missed or refused to acknowledge was that under the Criminal Code, as the on-site investigating police officer acting within the legal bounds of my duty, I had the legal authority to determine the criminality of this file while they had none. The Canadian Criminal Court system does not recognize rank or position, merely qualifications to offer an opinion. Up and down my chain of command, no one above me had any qualifications whatsoever and no legal authority to act as they did.

As for the TSB, they would have refused to appear in any court case because under their Act they are neither compellable nor competent. Just as well for them because the only TSB member who could ever have been declared an expert in this aircraft fire was John Garstang. Jim Foot had barely sufficient qualifications to say that wires had short-circuited, and he definitely could not offer an opinion as to when that occurred or how. It all makes me wonder how the MOU ever was accepted by the RCMP. If another crash is somehow determined to have been criminal in nature, how would that evidence ever be admitted into Court?

Dr. Brown, with his qualifications, would have been recognized and accepted as an expert in his field by any Court, even today, and his opinion would be heard and accepted.

No one had any right to interfere in any way with any police officer who was acting within the legal authority of the Criminal Code of Canada, no matter what the TSB's Act may say about their safety investigations and parallel RCMP investigations. Their Act takes second place to the Criminal Code of Canada, and the investigating police officers have the superior authority to conduct their legal investigation without interference from them. That was why Lathem refused to conduct a criminal investigation and tried to stop mine. There would then be no conflict with the TSB and thus he could keep the FBI out of the hangar.

Any similar crash investigation should be a cooperative affair. However, throughout their investigation, the police officers must realize why they are on site. The police must look for evidence of a criminal act first and foremost, even if it takes several years to find. While offering technical assistance to the TSB assists the safety investigation, its main purpose must be to further the criminal investigation. The TSB must not determine what information they parcel out to the police. Their investigation must be totally transparent and done in cooperation with and as an assistance to the police. To do otherwise is a complete dereliction of duty by the police and obstruction of justice by both.

One must realize that had I not been involved in all the testing procedures and photographic requirements undertaken by the TSB, the only people to see those results would have been the TSB members themselves. Since they cannot investigate such incidents as a criminal matter, the results would never have been viewed from that perspective. A criminal investigator would never have examined the lack of a fire load, that certain materials failed to burn or only burnt slowly, and even that the AES test results revealed evidence of a possible incendiary device. The present methods of investigating and the legislation governing the TSB must change.

The TSB have argued their independence allows them to obtain information from a guilty operator without incurring millions of dollars in expenses. This view of justice is short-sighted, naive and it fails to look at the broad picture. There is no deterrent value in their actions.

Two questions were initially asked of the reader, but there are other issues to be answered.

Even though the wreckage has been sold for salvage, the test results are all on file, and every important piece of debris has been photographed. Dr. Brown's opinion of sabotage needs to be officially verified or refuted by capable and knowledgeable peers. It is strongly suspected his opinion will be verified. If so, will the American authorities conduct a criminal investigation?

Next, there needs to be a Canadian inquiry to determine exactly why the RCMP and the TSB acted in the manner as they did. That may open a whole nest of snakes, but so be it. We are in a free country where the public has the right to know. The Liberal Government claims to be totally transparent, so their actions must speak louder than the words of the previous Government. However, I question whether any Police Force in this country can be free of the influence of the RCMP and its Commissioner, whoever it might be. Perhaps the investigators must be from outside this country, but not the USA or Great Britain.

Several other things need to be done. The TSB's legislation allowing a non-police agency to oversee and run an investigation that from the initial moment must be a death investigation needs to be amended. If it still operates after this, the TSB must take the passenger seat for their review of safety matters without interfering in any police investigation. The US authorities have a working system that allows the police to maintain their jurisdiction while conducting the investigation with the NTSB. The reason for this is America is acutely aware they have enemies in this world while Canada seems not yet to have realized this.

However it is achieved, something must be done to change this illegal system with its faulty Memorandum of Understanding. This present system unlawfully supersedes the power of the Judiciary and the Police in potential criminal incidents, including sudden death investigations.

Also, there must be a broad look at the methods of promotion within the RCMP. The present system is unacceptable. This review should be wide open to proposals for the promotion system for both NCOs and commissioned officers.

As should be obvious by this recounting of events, there must be a review of the complaint system within the Force. The present system is completely unacceptable and it must be scrapped for an outside complaint review system with no connections to RCMP management.

These are only some of the things an independent inquiry should investigate.

Commissioner Paulson and his senior advisors, as they have recently shown, seem to think that simply throwing money at the victims of the Force's inept and sometime corrupt human resource management system and offering a tearful apology will suffice. Paulson, as the Commissioner and a Deputy Minister of the Crown, is getting paid more than enough to act out anything the Department of Justice lawyers tell him to do. However, putting on a tear-filled and emotional show for the public will not fool those members who have been the recipients of the wrongdoings by other members. It is not, as he says, the 'hand of God' that must descend upon these criminals in red serge. Instead, the gavel of a Criminal Court Judge is required.

The Commissioner needs to realize that the problems within the RCMP, both past and present, are not the fault of the Constable and NCO who work the street every day. They have been created by poor and incompetent leadership and the flawed policies put in place by past and present commissioned officers, too many of whom know little if anything about policing and law enforcement, or proper human resource management. The most senior create these inept policies or rubber stamp those passed down from the politicians above them. Then the lower-ranked commissioned officers ensure everyone follows them, even if they are impractical or, in some instances, illegal. Those in this chain of command give the appearance of being managerial because they have followed the doctrine as set out from above. All the while, the constables and NCOs on the street are left to work with the shoddy environment, equipment, and methods, as well as the lack of credible leadership.

Enough from my soapbox!

As a side note, it is interesting how the small things, a "tiny bit of evidence" can be the key to the big picture. What was noteworthy about the morning meeting of the 1st of December, 2000, was the way I found out about it. The next day, Commissionaire Wayne Wells asked me who this secretive super-sleuth trench-coat guy was who the previous morning had snuck into the hangar by the back door. He showed me his name in the sign-in book and said he had not wanted to sign in. So I noted the name and wondered what his connection was, but eventually I set it aside as I was unable to piece together why he had been there that particular morning. When the clues were finally organized for the writing of this book, my notation of Wayne's super-sleuth trench-coated Inspector was the thing that started the ball rolling to put the true behind-the-scenes story together. Had the Inspector not been so secretive and such an arrogant jerk, he might have gone unnoticed. Wayne is still an excellent friend.

At one point in the change-the-notes meeting, Lee Fraser made the comment that I could not be trusted. He was right, at least not by him and his kind! Fraser could not trust me to follow along with their plan because, if I had known or even had a hint of what they were doing, they would have been in handcuffs so fast their heads would have been spinning for a week.

Those RCMP and TSB members involved in and responsible for this injustice, without any doubt, have let down the membership of the Force and their agency, and especially the citizens of Canada. They are a disgrace and have tainted the hard work done by so many others on this and other files across the country. They must be prosecuted. Where does it all end? It goes right to the top and into the Commissioner's office, the Chairman's office, and perhaps beyond that.

Just how far does the rot go?

About the Author

I joined the RCMP at the age of nineteen after growing up on a large beef and sheep farm in the Eastern Townships of Quebec. On completion of six months of basic training in Depot, Regina, I spent the next four-and-a-half years performing general detachment duties on the Northwest Coast of British Columbia.

In the fall of 1975, I trained to become a member of the RCMP's Forensic Identification Section, or what is commonly called a crime scene investigator, and was assigned to the Prince Rupert Identification Section. Over the next twenty-seven years, I worked in Bathurst, N.B., Iqaluit, N.W.T. (now Nunavut), Yellowknife, N.W.T., New Minas, N.S., Halifax, N.S., and finally the Swissair Task Force, all the while performing forensic identification duties. Those duties involved attending crime scenes to locate, preserve, identify, and present in court all types of physical evidence. Courts in five provinces and two territories have accepted my opinion evidence.

On September 3rd, 1998, I was assigned to the temporary morgue for the Swissair Flight 111 disaster. My duties were to oversee the fingerprint identification of the victims, a process that identified forty individuals. I also maintained the logistics for the RCMP members in the morgue and the aircraft reconstruction hangar, and the quality control of the forensic identification processes undertaken in the morgue.

After sixty days, the temporary morgue closed with the identification of all 229 passengers. I then worked in the aircraft reconstruction hangar, being seconded to the Transportation Safety Board of Canada to provide technical assistance in photography, physical match processing, exhibit control, forensic analysis of exhibits, lab report evaluations, fire evidence analysis, comparison, and evaluation, and other tasks. This work lasted until mid-January of 2002. I then continued part-time to perform exhibit control and photographic tasks for the TSB until mid-December 2002.

In September of 2002, I retired from the RCMP as a Sergeant with 32 years of service, 27 of which had been as a forensic crime scene investigator. During that period, I had processed more than one hundred murder scenes, more than a thousand sudden death scenes by accidental, natural, and self-inflicted means, and thousands of lesser crimes, including hundreds of fire scenes.

After retiring from the Force, I performed several different jobs until I fully retired this past year. During that time, I worked on the Swissair matter on a continuous basis by undertaking various actions against the RCMP with limited success as noted in 'Twice As Far'. This included a documentary with the CBC's The Fifth Estate called 'Swissair 111, The Untold Story' in September of 2011. Since then, I have written this book that discloses my Swissair experiences.

Made in the USA
Middletown, DE
28 September 2020